A Starter Garden

Other books by Cheryl Merser

Honorable Intentions:
The Manners of Courtship in the 80s

Grown Ups:
A Generation in Search of Adulthood

How to Sell Cookies . . . etc.

A Starter Garden

The Guide for the Horticulturally Hapless

Cheryl Merser

with illustrations by Simon Dorrell

HarperPerennial

A Division Of HarperCollins*Publishers*

HarperCollins books may be purchased for educational, business, or sales promotional use. For information please write: Special Markets Department, HarperCollins Publishers, Inc., 10 East 53rd Street, New York, NY 10022.

FIRST EDITION

Designed by C. Linda Dingler
Illustrations copyright © 1994 by Simon Dorrell

Library of Congress Cataloging-in-Publication Data

Merser, Cheryl.
    A starter garden : the guide for the horticulturally hapless /
Cheryl Merser. — 1st ed.
      p. cm.
    Includes index.
    ISBN 0-06-096933-4 (pbk.)
    1. Landscape gardening. 2. Gardening. I. Title.
SB473.M44 1994
635.9—dc20   92-54852

---

94 95 96 97 98 ❖/RRD 10 9 8 7 6 5 4 3 2 1

For Joan Cooney and Pete Peterson

"Either some very dear person or some very dear place seems necessary to relieve life's daily grey, and to show that it is grey. If possible, one should have both."

—E. M. Forster, *Howard's End*

Contents

$\mathcal{I}$ntroduction

$\sim$

I always listen in amazement when friends who are far more passionate gardeners than I am sit around and argue about, say, whether
Colchicum, the so-called autumn crocuses, are of the same family as
lilies or irises. These corms are in the lily family, as it turns out,
whereas real crocuses, the spring-blooming ones, are, strictly speaking, in the iris clan. Supposedly, you can discern this for yourself
because one genus or the other has a superior ovary, and the other one
has a tube for a stem, not a stalk. So the autumn crocus is not even a
crocus at all! On top of which, for all the fuss, it's not even that pretty.

What I want to learn instead, about colchicum or any other plant,
are the more urgent issues: If I plant it, what are the odds that it will
grow? Is it a better idea to plant it in the sun or in the shade? If it
does grow, will it be worth the trouble? Is it going to get very big?
When is it likely to come up? What color will it be? Is there any
chance it'll come back again next year? What will happen if my dogs
eat it, or trample it? Does the plant have a downside? That kind of
thing. It's too bad about the one with the inferior ovary, but that's not
really my problem.

I don't understand what's happened to these friends of mine.
They're people I've known, most of them, for years, and they didn't
used to be this way. In the past, we'd talk for hours, and just as heatedly, about the issues of the day—mostly sex, drugs and rock and roll.
We'd have long lunches in cafés, and spend evenings dancing in
nightclubs. In those days we argued about novels, not garden books.

But now, divert them from the subject of colchicum, and they'll switch without a pause to mulch: cocoa husks, ground-up cedar, peat, shiny little Japanese pebbles or buckwheat hulls.

Older, more settled and under the misguided impression that gardening is restful and nightclubs are for the young, my friends, along with thousands of other new converts all over the country, have been transformed from normal, fun-loving people into avid gardeners: different genus, different species. And to judge by the number of new nurseries that have sprung up (and the nightclubs that have closed down) in my area alone, to say nothing of the increasing numbers of gardening-supply catalogs clogging my mailbox, gardening is gaining.

In fact, gardening has ceased to be a hobby you can take up or not and has become instead a matter of get-with-the-program peer pressure, a politically, ecologically and socially correct way to pass the time. Just as we all once took up exercise, bought food processors and claimed to like high fiber more than doughnuts, few of us will be independent enough to withstand this horticulture trend entirely.

There have been horticultural fads before; a few years ago, the in thing to do was to buy houseplants and talk to them. These days, we don't talk to plants; we plead with them. This more recent wave requires a larger commitment: If you have a house, now you'll want to have, at minimum, a little perennial bed in the corner. If you have an apartment with a terrace, you'll soon find yourself learning about container plantings. If you have a window, you'll install a window box. One tentative turn of the trowel and you've declared yourself. You're a gardener.

And you'll see why gardening can be so satisfying now, and why it feels more compelling than simply the next fad to have come along. Perhaps we're mourning the earth we've done so much to wreck and trying to make repairs, each in our own way. It may be that gardening is the most primal antidote we know to the noise and uncertainty that bombard us so relentlessly in other realms of our lives. Possibly it's that gardening is our most soothing way to look toward the future: There's no way to start a garden without imagining the ways in which you can make it better, lusher, more complex next year.

I have no argument with any of this. It's true that there's nothing more wondrous than watching a tiny plant push its way up through the soil, reaching for the sun. I love finding plants that feel at home with me, helping them flourish, watching them come back each year, fuller than ever before. I love walking through all the colors, textures and fragrances of even the smallest garden, such as my own garden, only two years old, still in its very early stages. As gardeners promise, there *is* something pure about gardening, something decent and spiritual and eternal about nurturing a living thing meant, with care and luck, to keep flowering long after we're all gone. . . .

Fine. Gardening is terrific.

But why does it have to be an academic discipline combining Latin, geometry and calculus, subjects I thought I'd put to rest years ago? Labor intensive and sometimes discouraging, yes, I can accept that. Slower results than I'd like, okay. Sure, you have to learn some new stuff; that's fair. But does gardening really have to be so punishingly intimidating and arcane? That depends on whether you want to be a gardener or a fanatic. Me, I just want a garden.

Like the fanatics, I take pleasure in working outdoors—but only up to a point. Where fanatics are up at dawn to fend off birds who might steal their newly planted sweet peas, at dawn I'm asleep. Fanatics are often up at midnight, too, prowling the garden in their bathrobes with flashlights, ambushing slugs, truly vile creatures that give a new resonance to the word sluggish; some people put out saucers of beer to thwart them. At midnight I prefer to be asleep. High noon finds fanatics deadheading (which means pruning or pinching back blossoms as they fade, which often extends a plant's blooming season). Come high noon, I prefer to be at the beach, thinking ahead to lunch. My Latin is halting, I can never remember what the pH factor is all about, and I always forget till it's too late to put up those ingenious round metal grids, the support hoops, that keep the peonies from toppling over. (If I did think of it, though, I'd remember to put petroleum jelly on the joints where the legs screw into the grid, to prevent against rust and make it easier to take the thing apart in the fall.)

In short, and this is not false modesty, I'll never be a great gardener.

On the other hand, as a result of some trial, more error, occasional spurts of real energy, a fair amount of armchair studying, and a genuine desire to have my yard look like a garden, I'm working toward becoming a pretty good gardener. Good enough anyway not to bother with colchicum, which is just too hard to get excited about, particularly that late in the season, and good enough so that I'm not embarrassed anymore if my friends happen to drop by before dark.

My hunch is that pretty good is good enough for you as well, or you'd have picked up the third edition of *Hortus,* an unreadable encyclopedia, instead of this less-threatening, albeit less-ambitious volume. Besides, you've got to start somewhere, and if you want to later on, you can always go beyond pretty good and graduate to a harder book.

Meantime, those of us who feel garden shy have a number of traits in common.

Setting aside the psychological lapse that enables us to aim for a garden in the upper-middle range instead of the top, we have jobs, interests and lives outside the garden, which take up a lot of time and energy that could otherwise be spent tilling and weeding and sculpting the borders to perfection. Some might call us lazy or haphazard; I prefer multifaceted.

We're secret snobs. We're sophisticated enough, we've been around enough, not to want a garden that only looks okay. We don't want just a pot or two of geraniums, a bed of impatiens and boring straight rows of hosta. We've seen the photographs in magazines and garden books, where spectacular *drifts* of flowers overflow into other drifts. We want drifts, too. We want a real garden, with a few touches and surprises that more serious gardeners might even exclaim over.

We also don't have endless amounts of money. If we did, we'd surely know enough to hire excellent gardeners. What is more, we don't want simply to order a garden and have it delivered, like Chinese takeout. We want to find our own way into the garden.

The need for instant gratification is important to us; we're not of the plant-now/enjoy-later school. Plants, shrubs or vines that promise to bloom in their third or fourth year, once the roots are established, are generally not for us. As most women past the age of thirty know, no one will ever admire your roots, however well established. We realize that a garden will take some years to settle in fully, really feel abundant and look as if it's always belonged there, but we want as much show as we can get as soon as possible.

We are, in other words, fairly sophisticated garden snobs with hardly any money who want a garden we can be proud of right now.

It is a fact of gardening that some plants are easier, prettier and less troublesome to grow than others, and it's also a fact that it's surprisingly hard to figure out which plants fit into this category.

The catalogs, which after all (and fairly enough) are in business to *sell* you plants, not teach you about them, will, for the most part, highlight the virtues and not the drawbacks of their merchandise. Seed packets—some of which, even at this late date, don't offer so much as a *picture* of the plants on the front—will give you as little useful information as their distributors can get away with. In the nurseries, where perfect plants are lined up right on the verge of blooming, anything seems possible. And most garden books themselves are written by high achievers who disapprove of cheating and shortcuts, and who would prefer to cultivate a rare, challenging, and worrisome (though spectacular) specimen plant to growing a more easygoing but perfectly agreeable plant that you don't have to think too much about. It's hard to get access to enough unembellished information to get you started.

This book starts from the premise that the reader knows very little or maybe nothing about gardening and wants to learn how to start an ornamental garden and get it in good working order, fast. The strategies suggested amount to less work, camouflaged to look like more. The plants recommended are as nearly foolproof to grow and carefree to tend as possible, and the principles involved will always weigh heavily in favor of taking the easy way out. This book, in other words, is a primer for the horticulturally impaired.

I used to get discouraged when I met gardeners who had vivid memories of plants they'd known and loved, and gardens they wanted to re-create, since childhood; I always thought I'd never catch up. My only distinct early garden memory is of a huge horticultural clock on a steep bank somewhere in Massachusetts, with the hands made out of what must have been marigolds or zinnias, which I thought was amazing at the time but which now I'm sure I'd think was hideous. The only other plants I knew in childhood, from hanging out more at shopping malls than outdoors, were plastic and dusty, *P. dusticus.* As a corporate brat, I moved around from city to city, suburb to suburb, where the houses were new and the families were young, with not much time to garden. Besides, they never planned to stay long. I don't think you can have much of a love of gardening till you acquire a longing for permanence. Early middle-age, on average, some of the experts say. So it doesn't matter when you start; gardening is a dance you can definitely enter in the middle.

I also got discouraged, when I first took up gardening, by the *weight* of the information available. I couldn't figure out what I needed to know, and what I could skip: all those weeds and pests! All that distasteful talk about manure and compost! Divide this plant all the time, *never* divide that one! Prune in spring, or prune in fall, or prune as necessary (but how do you tell when it's necessary?)! Cut back just before the plant seeds itself, or—no!—just after! I saw minefields everywhere. I truly couldn't keep the instructions straight, which made me think I'd never get the garden straight.

The truths about gardening (think of them as the *Cliff Notes* to that larger body of knowledge) are in fact much simpler: The more you do it, the better you'll get. You don't need to learn everything before you start; you'll learn more, without having to struggle so hard, as you go along, even picking up some helpful Latin along the way, without having to memorize. It's harder to make mistakes, and easier to correct most of them, than you think. If you're attracted to gardening, you're probably suited to it. And you can achieve the bare bones of a pretty good garden in just a season or two.

As with most occupations, there are different ways to approach the garden.

The absolutely right way to start a garden, for instance, is to bulldoze your whole yard, then, according to a friend of mine, a brilliant (if obsessive) gardener, spend some time in it naked, in the middle of the night, wandering around looking for microclimates—those slightly warmer or slightly cooler pockets of air that hover over even a tiny tract of land. After that, you start measuring and marking with stakes and string the beds and borders, and enrich the soil with different things depending on what you're going to plant where, after installing a complicated and expensive underground sprinkling system that will meet the various needs of each of your microclimates.

Meanwhile, months ago you made careful lists of new and replacement plants you needed, and ordered them all from the catalogs, early enough to make sure you got what you wanted. You've also been germinating and grafting plants for weeks in your greenhouse or electrically heated cold frames, so that everything will be ready at the right moment, gauging by the last frost date plus a few extra days to be on the safe side, to plant outside in an orderly blooming sequence. You are armed and ready for spring.

Perhaps a less desirable, but still reasonably effective, way to start a garden is to notice one day that the weather is sunny and fine and to think that it might be fun to plant a few things and see what happens. And then a few more.

From these small beginnings, pretty good gardens can grow.

1

The Gardener's Sensibility

Attitude

∾

My first garden was a sweeping shady place, all rounded edges and different colors of green, which I took care of for some years, until it became another casualty when my relationship with the man who owned it fell apart. Leaving a man is one thing, I found out; leaving a garden can really break your heart. A lot of what went on in that romance is fuzzy to me now, but I still remember every inch of that garden.

The "bones" of this garden were already in place when I took it over, so my tentative efforts—I knew *nothing* when I started—only made it more or less lush, depending on how well or poorly I chose what to plant; less lush in the beginning, more so later.

There, with my sharp new clippers, pristine gloves and high hopes, I must have made every single mistake that a neophyte gardener could possibly make, and then some.

My first season, for example, I decided to tackle a scrubby woodland area way out back. A gardener friend suggested that I plant a kind of mountain laurel, one of the *Kalmia* species, among the taller trees that were already growing there, so as to draw together all the disparate elements of the area.

Sounded fine to me. I looked up mountain laurel in one of the best nursery catalogs, saw lovely mounded shrubs (they'd grow six feet high, the catalog said) flowering in icy pink, and I could easily envision them draped through my new domain. Surprised by how affordable they seemed, I ordered a dozen, hoping that wouldn't be too many, and wondered vaguely whether the UPS truck could manage them all in one load.

Not a problem, as it turned out; the UPS driver could have managed them all in one *hand*. The box containing all twelve "shrubs" was smaller than a shoe box, and the shrubs themselves were spindly twigs with a dried up leaf or two on each. No icy pink flowers in sight. Using a teaspoon, I dug tiny holes amid the myrtle that trailed through the woodland and carefully planted my shrubettes. Six feet high? Not in my lifetime. I never saw my plants again.

In that same catalog, I'd noticed a perennial, called *Tradescantia*, that resembled a purple perennial we already had growing in great numbers, whose name I didn't know at the time, but whose disadvantages I was already well aware of.

The summer before, when I was still circling the garden, afraid to touch, I'd seen how these plants work: first come slim, delicate pointy leaves, sometimes faintly edged in red, followed by fat tube-like stems, which themselves were followed by nice enough but not great flowers in late spring, which bloom for a couple of weeks. After the bloom, the stems literally topple over, like gunned-down soldiers, so that you have to cut the plant back to the ground, leaving the ghosts of the fat stems, which remain in place for the longest time, wedged into the ground in such an aggressive way that you can't really plant anything around them to cover the stem remains.

This new plant, though, this tradescantia, promised to bloom, the catalog copy said enthusiastically, from June till about September. My plan, which I thought brilliant, was to install this desirable purple tradescantia, which also answers to the common name Spiderwort, around my less desirable topple-prone plants, so that their continuous bloom would hide my leftover stem bits.

When my tradescantia arrived, delivered in another shoe box along with the mountain laurel shrubettes, I planted it around my existing plants, pleased that the pretty leaves matched so well. The blooms, when they appeared, matched, too, a little *too* well, I thought;

it was soon apparent that I had ordered tradescantia to hide my tradescantia. When the blooms, both old and new, petered out, long before September or even July, all the plants—the old and the new—toppled over in unison.

Gardening 101: By definition, and enthusiastic catalog copy or nursery descriptions notwithstanding, *no* perennials bloom all season long. False advertising may be too strong a charge, but in my experience, the blooming season for most perennials is always less, sometimes much less, than that promised by the otherwise trustworthy people from whom I buy my plants. Maybe gardeners are just excitable types, but it's best to err on the side of caution: Always shave off a few weeks from the promised blooming schedule and you won't be disappointed.

I later read somewhere that after the nuclear "accident" at Three Mile Island some years ago, the purple blooms of the tradescantia planted nearby turned pink after exposure to the radioactivity. If I were to come across purple tradescantia now (not to be confused with another variety that's *meant* to be pink), I'd keep it as a radioactivity gauge, but move it to an obscure corner of the garden (doesn't need full sun), where it could topple in relative privacy. But I didn't know then that you can move most perennials around as easily (and carefully) as you can rearrange furniture, or knickknacks in a cupboard. I also didn't know then that it wasn't violating a sacred principle to get rid of plants you don't like much and give them to someone else who does.

And I didn't understand then how to translate the garden I had in my mind accurately into a garden in the soil.

Disappointed by my venture into mail-order gardening, I decided to splurge at a nursery, and bought, among other things, a big healthy forget-me-not in a pot maybe ten inches high. The plant I imagined in place would be a fifteen-inch-high jumble of those tiny, wonderfully clear and, as promised, unforgettable blue flowers. What you see, I said smugly to myself, is what you get. But when I dug my plant into the ground, in the place I'd picked behind some white bleeding hearts, I saw that I'd miscalculated again. You couldn't see the forget-me-not behind the bleeding hearts. You'd never remember it forever, let alone give it a second thought. It wasn't fifteen inches high at all; in my planning, I had neglected to subtract the ten or so inches of pot.

Gardening 102: Everything you order or pick out yourself, with the possible exception of tradescantia, will look smaller than you think once you've planted it, at least the first year.

As consumers—and, sentiment aside, gardening is surely a consumer activity—we're used to a world where things are supposed to work. You buy a toaster, and from then on, till it finally expires years later, you *have* a toaster and all the toast you want. There are warrantees to protect you, repair shops to fix problems as they crop up, 800 numbers to call for help. It's satisfying to know that once you have a toaster, you can pretty much count on toast.

There are no such guarantees when it comes to gardening. When you take up gardening, you have to rethink the way you look at the world, change your expectations, revise your assumptions, calculate the odds a little differently. If you try to copy your garden too closely from a garden you admired in a book, for instance, you'll never get it right. By all means, choose some of the same plants, model your garden after a *form* that appeals to you, follow a sensibility. But a garden isn't a toaster. With too fixed an idea of the way it should "work," you'll lose sight of the way it *is* working, all by itself, under your generous tutelage.

To put it another way, I've learned to allow the garden a life of its own. I can't obscure or transform tradescantia; it is what it is. If I have it in the garden, I have to let it be itself and think *around* it. It's said that good parents teach their children to use their independence wisely; in the same way, good gardeners allow their gardens a measure of freedom, a fair hearing in the decision-making process.

Just because you paid good money for a perennial doesn't mean it's going to bloom the way you want for its allotted two- or three- or four-week run each season. It also doesn't mean that it's going to quintuple in size where you decide to plant it, or even return next year at all. Bizarrely enough, it may come back, but in a different place. There are, of course, plenty of things you can do to guide nature or help it along, but gardening also is a matter of giving plants the room to follow their own courses, develop their own characters.

Perfectionists, I've observed, with their love of orderliness, uniformity and neat, straight lines, sometimes have a hard time adjusting to the garden, which has rhythms of its own. Perfectionists usually fight with their gardens, and their gardens usually win.

Not to confuse myself with a perfectionist, but last year, for example, I dug three small lavender plants into the front of the border I'm cultivating in my garden now, knowing they'd look pretty if they were to grow in bushy and thick. I planted the lavender a foot apart, in the same soil and, so far as I could tell, the same sun; they were, after all, only *one foot* apart. The one at the far end grew easily six inches its first season; the other two, though they remain perfectly healthy, didn't seem to grow at all.

So what do you do? A perfectionist would go quite mad, wanting all the plants to line up in the same way, same height, same fullness. Perhaps he or she would snip away the larger plant to match the smaller ones, until they all got so small as to be invisible. A more casual gardener, on the other hand, will be happy letting nature take its course: I just moved the big lavender to the middle of the three and forgot about them, and now the subtle tapering effect, which continued into this past year, looks fine, like a little lavender hedge.

It's easier on the gardener and still effective to adopt a laissez-faire attitude, recognizing that perfection in the garden actually looks a little weird. The natural world is a jangly, asymmetrical place, and a garden with too much order imposed on it looks stilted, constrained and unnatural, unless it's obviously a very formal garden in a very formal setting, in which case it can be a spectacular triumph over the randomness of nature. But if one happens not to live in the palace at Versailles, the garden should look as if it's always been there, slightly rumpled and lived in, appearing, for all your work, as though it happened by itself. If the plants meander a little beyond their apportioned space, and tumble around some, so much the better.

Plant now, in other words, with a plan that leaves plenty of leeway for the garden to grow.

And it will.

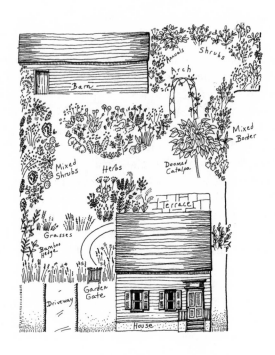

$\mathscr{A}$ims

We live—my husband, Michael, and I—in an old saltbox in a village
out toward the eastern end of Long Island. The house, perched not too
far from the street, looks brave and upright from the front; the front
door and two windows to the side are all you can see straight on. The
whole plot is small—between a quarter and a third of an acre.
Thankfully, certain parts of it (those covered by the house itself, the
dilapidated barn in the back, the driveway and the front walk) require
no horticultural effort or imagination at all. It's the rest of the land that
needs filling up; apparently not one of the previous owners, even
though the house was built in 1810, took much interest in gardening.
And a quarter of an acre can seem as endless as the Sahara when
you're trying to turn it into a garden. Witness my lessons in Gardening
101—remember the mountain laurel shrubettes? Plants don't take up
too much room before they settle in.

   At first the land seemed as unpromising as the house, which
needed major renovations—like heat. The front yard was stark naked,

with no plantings to set off the house or shield it from the street, but the backyard was what needed more immediate attention. The falling-down barn out back had been rented to a young man whose enthusiasm for fixing cars clearly exceeded his talent for it. Rusty engines and car doors rested all over the yard on freestanding tree stumps, and the dirt had been tamped down so rigorously that the earth was as unyielding as concrete, even after a rain, and permanently black in spots from what appeared to be oil deposits. There were weeds pushing their way through the rolled-down windows of the shell of a vintage Mustang. In despair, the neighbors on one side had put up a stock fence partway down one side of the yard. On the other side, there was a scraggly peek-a-boo privet hedge that didn't offer much privacy to either the neighbor or us.

Along the back side of the house was an ugly white stone rectangular "terrace" and, beyond that, our one mature tree, an old catalpa, covered in (and, as it turned out, being strangled to death by) ivy, surrounded by an uneven, knee-high cinder-block wall (which was also contributing to its demise).

Our driveway presented another problem. Facing the house, the driveway came up the left side till the tar sort of crumbled away beyond the back door; deeply embedded tire tracks continued halfway back through the yard.

Exhausted and dispirited, I did nothing in the garden the first summer, except to note that much of the soil that wasn't already tamped down was pretty sandy in spots (we're not too far from the bay) and also to note that sooner rather than later, something horticultural would have to be done: As the house began to feel cozier and more welcoming, the land around it began to look more pathetic and splotchy. Putting in a garden, or at the very least some lawn, no longer seemed to be a choice.

That first lazy summer wasn't a total waste, however. Just as cautious architects recommend living in a house and seeing how it *feels* before making any major architectural changes, it also makes sense to live in a yard a while before you make it a garden, to consider some fundamental structural decisions, study the light—and to buy yourself some time; this could be your last respite.

WHERE SHOULD MY GARDEN GROW?

The most graceful gardens seem all of a piece with the houses they envelop; by following the traffic flow into, out of and around the house, a garden becomes an extension of a house's living space. Thus, rather than creating a garden that people will have to go out of their way to find, you'll want to know where you naturally find yourself hanging out before you decide where to create your garden. This may be an easy decision for some. If you have a terrace, or a pool, or glass doors leading outside, you may want to accentuate these indoor-outdoor connections first thing. On the other hand, you may want to start a garden to devise a privacy shield from neighbors or the street. But make the garden come to you.

I know one family, for instance, with a house—the wonderfully rambling, shingly kind that used to be called, euphemistically, a "cottage"—set way back from a road that's not much traveled. The first thing you see, driving up, is a wide front porch (where they have most of their meals when it's warm) with wicker sofas and chairs and tables, always covered in books and magazines and toys and projects: They seem really to *live* here in the summers. Out back there's a small terrace, mostly in the shade, where they've put the barbecue grill and, curiously, the garden, thinking, perhaps, that gardens *belong* in the back. But only the maître de grill, and whoever does the weeding, sees the garden, and no one seems to take much pleasure in it; out of sight, out of mind. If they dismantled this whole virtually invisible garden and moved it, plant by plant, to the front of the house, they'd have a garden that made better sense for the way they live.

Another couple I know bought a contemporary spec house with a pool, which the developer had landscaped to the hilt: shrubs and flowers on a berm all around the pool, with elaborate container plantings on the deck. In itself it's fine; the trouble is that there's no other landscaping in sight. From the starkly modern house, with its expansive glass windows, you see from afar this beflowered pool and garden, in effect with nothing but lawn in between you and Eden. There's no garden to *get* you to the garden, so to speak, no way for your eye to connect the dots, to lead you from here to there. Because the scale is grand, the leap from house to garden is too great for the eye or imagination to make. Even a few beds of flowering shrubs leading from house to pool could supply the missing links and offer horticultural bearings to those passing through.

To avoid a misplaced garden, there are some questions you need to ask and answer before you tuck in even your first plant:

∾Where will the perimeters of the garden be?

∾Which features of the yard need to be played up, and
which need to be obscured?

∾What are the outdoor-to-indoor areas that should help
delineate your garden?

∾Do you use the front door or the back?

∾Which windows do you find yourself looking out of from
inside and, if your eye were a stone skipping across
water, at which points across the yard would it stop to
rest?

∾Which area gets morning sun, which gets afternoon sun,
and which stays sunny or shady all day long?

∾Is there a slope or is the land level?

∾Are the boundaries of your land crisp edges (that might
need to be softened) or blurry (in which case they might
need to be more crisply defined)?

To say nothing of these important questions: Are you really up for this? And where is the money going to come from?

I myself couldn't answer many of these questions, because at our house there was no natural meeting place to which people gravitated outdoors, no clear-cut start-here place for my garden. What Michael and I had was basically a square with no inviting aspects. I noticed that whenever people went outside to explore the "grounds" during that bleak first summer, they simply decided against it and came back in.

The one question I could answer was, What bothers you most about the land? Easy. The driveway, with its tire ruts, was driving me crazy. Because there was no gate, anyone driving by could look up the driveway and see the entire side and yard as well as anyone who happened to be in it, which was disconcerting, because our street's fairly busy. I'd noticed that throughout the village, many people had nipped their driveways in half by putting up a gate. This not only gained them privacy but also gave their land, at least behind the houses, an enclosed and unified feeling. In my own yard, doing this would also give us an "extra" garden, right outside the back door. There it was: I wanted to start my garden with a garden gate.

This would provide a starting place, a Point A, for the garden, and would begin to create the sense of enclosing, and thereby unifying, the space—essential, whatever the final design would come to look like.

I knew that I wanted lots of perennials, which I had come to love in my first garden, and I also wanted to make a space for annuals, so I could have bright flowers to bring indoors all summer long. Add to that an herb garden—a functional one, because I like to cook—and comfortable places for us to sit outside.

But even all this wouldn't be enough. If I began my perennial garden bordering the fence-side of the house, and my herb garden outside the back door, for convenience, the rest of the property would look lopsided—no shrubs on the privet side, to balance the perennials, nothing at all in the little courtyard square off to the side of the barn.

The garden, I saw now, would have to be balanced all the way around, or a square, as it were. Otherwise, the eye would go to where there *is* something to see, and then, in puzzlement, to where there *isn't*. For it to feel lush and private and gardenlike, this ratty backyard space would have to be set off from the neighbors, enclosed in form and feeling, and framed and cushioned in shrubs and whatever else I could think of to frame and cushion it. (A lot of work!)

Suddenly, my little perennial and herb beds, big enough projects as they were, were dwarfed by the grander plans I began to dream up for my quarter acre—pergolas and groupings of shrubs, some water somewhere, tricks with mirrors. Thank God I hadn't been allotted forty acres and a mule! My small garden would be at its peak, I figured, for my two hundredth birthday.

That October, we finally got around to building the garden gate. Then we went inside to wait for spring.

Tools and Terms

Entering the world of tennis or golf, one has the strange sensation that the language, the customs, the costumes and the equipment you need to play the game add up to a whole new culture. Your first immersion into the gardening world will probably fill you, as it did me, with that same Alice-in-Wonderland, where-am-I sensation. But gardening is actually more like swimming than it is like golf or tennis. After you learn a few fundamental rules, it's up to you how deep you want to go, how seriously you want to train. Even so, we all start at the shallow end.

At a party recently, someone told me about a friend of hers, a clothing designer who, sensing a whole new arena for fashion, was thinking about launching a line of "designer" clothes for the gardener and didn't I think it was a great idea?

I'm sure I lied and said it was a fabulous idea, but in fact I think it's depressing. Gardening isn't about clothes, fashion or even necessarily about the gardener: It's about the *garden*. Go out and buy a stylish new set of clothes to wear while crawling around—literally—in the mud? My oldest, grubbiest clothes are fine, thank you, and the less equipment the better. There's enough to do, learn and spend money on in gardening that the sartorial aspect should be the last thing the gardener should have to worry about. Besides, I'd rather give any extra share of the budget over to plants.

A woman I know started her garden by calling an 800 number—to order a trug, one of those long, flat-bedded baskets that garden writers are often photographed carrying as they snip mounds of cutting flowers to bring indoors. She also bought waterproof clogs, overalls with tool pockets, knee pads, a Day-Glo visor, and a few dozen metal plant markers, on which you can etch the names of plants indelibly in pretty handwriting. I don't know what else she bought, but as yet, she reports sheepishly, there's no sign of anything growing anywhere near her, except for some mildew on this unused gear.

I have another friend, on the other hand, who has a spectacular garden and who creates the most beautiful indoor arrangements, which she seems to change almost daily. No trug for her. She has a stack of plastic buckets into which she—sensibly—puts a few inches of water as she walks around her garden collecting flowers for the house. The extra buckets are always out on loan to friends who fortuitously happen to stop by when she's gathering her bounty.

STARTER TOOLS

One of the great pleasures of gardening is how little equipment you need to make so much happen; your hands, in fact, will be the primary tools you'll need. The rest of the gardening hardware is timeless, not very different from the tools people gardened with centuries ago. It's satisfying that a spade is still a spade (though I've always thought a cordless, high-powered electric spade would be a useful and back-saving invention). The form-follows-function aesthetic really holds when it comes to gardening. The best gardeners I know use the fewest tools.

Where you can get into trouble is skimping on the *quality* of the tools you buy. The cheaper trowel may look the same as the more expensive one, but will bend back when you use it with any enthusiasm. In most cases, the hardware you buy should be top of the line; otherwise, you'll be buying it again next year. There are many good toolmakers around, and any good hardware store, agricultural supply company or nursery will offer a number of choices.

Tools should weigh more, not less, and feel centered, with a heft to them—kind of like buying a good kitchen knife.

If a handle is made of wood, make sure that it's really well varnished, because tools often get wet, particularly if you're the kind of gardener who forgets to put his or her toys away. You don't want the varnish to wear off, leaving your tools splintery. Check, too, to see that the parts are welded or riveted together solidly. You should be able to run your thumb from the metal part to the wood part without feeling much of a divide.

A gardener's starter kit would include the best trowel you can afford and a sturdy spade. In my opinion, a flat-edged spade is better for digging pot-shaped holes than one of the curved and slightly pointed shovels. This may just be my opinion, however, because I only have a spade; others swear that the curved shovel is better for scooping up dirt, an opinion that also makes a certain amount of sense. I'd also consider indispensable my small, child-size rake—with its adult-length handle—for clearing out (and spreading things around in) places that are hard to reach.

Buy hand clippers. You'll need them from day one. Choose scissors clippers on which both blades are sharp and matched (as opposed to the anvil models with a curved rim where the second blade would be); scissors clippers are better and easier for all-around use. Scissors clippers *squeeze* what they're clipping, if that makes sense, rather than seeming to *snap*. And choose bright orange. I had a great pair of clippers in blend-in-with-the-soil black not long ago that felt really light though solid in my hand and stayed sharp for the longest time; I still hope to find them one of these days out in the garden.

It's best if you can start with two pairs of clippers, because one pair will constantly be misplaced or need sharpening (which you can do yourself with a sharpening tool, or have the hardware store do better). I know there are people who are always oiling and sharpening their clippers, then wrapping them in chamois or oiled rags, which I'm sure is the right way to do it, but I'm too lazy. An easier but still responsible way to look after your tools is to fill a bucket halfway up with sand, dump in some oil left over from an oil change, then dip the tools in the bucket to clean them before storing in a dry place.

It may seem to you, if you don't at this point have anything visible to prune, that you don't need long-handled pruning loppers, but that may not be the case; they come in handy, too, for breaking up snarled roots and vines under the ground. As I wait for my shrubs to grow big enough to prune, I'm doing a good amount of pruning where you can't even see it.

Do wear gloves, although you may find yourself putting them on and taking them off many times throughout the day. Simple cotton or leather work gloves that fit, which you can usually buy even in the supermarket, will protect your hands nicely. The earth is always heaving up artifacts (like nails or, particularly around old houses, broken glass and pottery), and some plants are sharp and thorny. Be warned: Gardening will surely tear up your hands. (Gardening will also wear out your gloves. I have a friend who is constantly getting holes in the thumb of her left glove. She keeps buying new gloves and stockpiling the right hands.) I've been given Godzilla-size canvas-lined rubber gardening gloves and also enormous suede gardening gloves, both of which are so stiff that I can't bend my fingers in them; cotton works fine for me 90 percent of the time. Buy your gloves in easy-to-spot white, and don't worry if they get dirty. The missing glove to my soft brown pair that fit so well is probably also outside, somewhere near my black clippers. The mud-encrusted white ones are still easy to find.

SECOND-TIER TOOLS

As for second-tier tools, I couldn't say that a smaller spade is essential, because I don't have one at the moment, but I do sometimes think about how nice such a spade would be to have. A pitchfork also looks official, and it's the best way to turn compost, but you can wait to get it until after you start a compost pile. Our secondhand wheelbarrow had a flat tire, so we ended up giving it away, something I still regret every time I'm dragging a shrub or a bag of mulch around. Gardening is heavy work, and although it's an investment, it's a good idea to have a wheelbarrow from the start. If you have a bad back, a wheelbarrow is essential. A narrow trowel is another item some gardeners swear by, so I bought one not long ago, but because I haven't used it yet I couldn't call it essential. Though I've never once longed for a hoe, I couldn't manage without an edger. For carving clean lines around garden beds, or working out anger, an edger is deeply satisfying, and I'd definitely have to buy one if my neighbor hadn't forgotten that "mine" is really hers. She comes and borrows it when she needs it.

In short, don't overbuy when it comes to tools. Take those cylindrical bulb installers, for instance, which seem like such a good idea. You'll never need one—a trowel will work fine—and you'll never use it, except possibly as a cookie cutter. As for baskets, urns and fun accessories, yard sales are a good source. I recently found the most beautiful trug—an old one—for $5. But the necessary tools, the tools that will actually serve you best, aren't all that much improved over those that served your ancestors best.

STARTER TERMINOLOGY

"I guess I'm doing a border, or maybe it's a bed," a friend of mine said last summer, as he rototilled and fertilized a kidney-shaped area in his yard. "Which do you think?" This, in gardening terms one needs to know, is the equivalent to the child's question "Why is the sky blue?" There's every answer, and no answer, which is why gardening, like being a parent, is an art and not a science. A bed or a border? Depends. Books are surprisingly vague on the subject, and every serious gardener I queried had a different answer.

A pretty good answer is that in its purest sense, a border is a garden bed that's on the edge of something—a wall, fence, driveway, row of shrubs, whatever.

The English writer/gardener Gertrude Jekyll popularized the concept of a border in the last century, and implicit in her concept of border is *perennial* border, although Jekyll herself (pronounced JEE-kel) was known to include in the mix small trees, shrubs, a few annuals and bulbs. Her perennial borders (altogether she designed about four hundred, imagine!) were forty feet long, at least, and full of mostly perennials, with all different colors and textures of foliage and with a complicated blooming agenda—so that there were blooms here and there in a perfectly balanced way all through the season. She had studied to be an artist, and it was only when her vision began to fail that she turned to gardening, but color remained a preoccupation.

To attempt a thumbnail history of the art of gardening in what is essentially a paint-by-numbers gardening book like this one would be misguided and probably foolhardy, but the ornamental gardens we're aiming for here trace their inspiration straight to Jekyll (and her mentor, William Robinson). The sprawling, effusive borders that Jekyll designed were in direct rebellion against the horticultural artifice and formalism of the gardens that had preceded them—you've seen the pictures of geometrical, rigidly perfect gardens that abutted the houses and grounds of the very rich: worthy, certainly, if intimidating and not very practical for most of us.

These new gardeners, on the other hand, stressed plants that would seem to be growing "wild," naturally and hardily in their environment. Robinson and Jekyll believed that plants should not be confined and restrained, but encouraged to settle into their sites, and drift and grow more freely. The hand of the gardener, while still tending rigorously to the form and symmetry (and presumably weeding and drudgery) of the garden as a whole, wouldn't be so apparent. Not that these gardens were disorderly or makeshift affairs—anything but. Jekyll would work with an architect, notably Edwin Lutyens, and set her gardens against grand walls, terraces and other architectural counterpoints. The casual look never comes easy, especially in gardening.

A century later, give or take, the mixed border or—if it's not bordering anything—bed is the hybrid border concept that makes more sense for us to aspire to. The "mix" comes from adding to the requisite perennials a few shrubs (flowering ones, for softness and to keep to the floral text, or evergreens, to serve as architectural pillars and posts). Some annuals, too, are essential to the mix, more so in America than in England, because our hot summers can foreshorten the blooming seasons of many midsummer perennials. Annuals offer color during the perennials' off seasons, and fill up the empty spaces in the garden that will inevitably capture your attention more than the flourishing ones. You can have, in addition to your border (or borders, God forbid), all the beds you want—islands of shrubs; the rock, herb, rose or cutting garden; terraces; waterfalls; separate little groves of things, whatever it takes to enclose the garden and make it feel self-contained and secluded from the rest of the world.

My aim was still fairly elemental: to start by enclosing the garden with shrubs, to create a (mostly) perennial border along the fence-side as a centerpiece to the garden, and to find room for beds of annuals and herbs. To start a garden.

DECODING PLANT NAMES

What you'll put into the border are families, genera, species, cultivars and varieties. Plants can have as many names as a member of a royal family, and if you were to ask simply for a King Henry plant (but don't, because as far as I know there isn't one), you might get the Fifth when you really wanted the entirely different Eighth.

Let's say you were a plant having a reunion, with all your aunts and uncles and second cousins twice removed. You'd have it with your family, the umbrella term for all plants grouped together by some family trait—the leaves of the Iridiceae, to take one fairly distinguishable family, are all different but, at the same time, all recognizable as iris

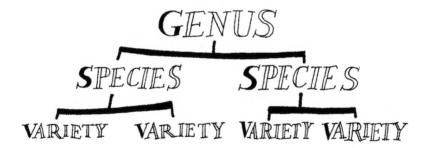

leaves. Sometimes the family traits are more apparent to a botanist or a showoff than to the casual observer, though, in the way a freckled redhead might sneak into a predominantly towheaded family, so you can't always rely on your eye alone to tell you the family name, which is fine, really, because you can garden for years without having to pay very much attention to family names.

Genus names, on the other hand, *are* important, and you'll find yourself learning these as time goes on. The genus is a plant's immediate family, closer bound than the extended family. (Or consider a parallel metaphor: In the General Motors family, Cadillac, Chevrolet and Buick would be among the GM genera.) While you still can't always be absolutely sure, many genera, once you have even a passing familiarity with their members, fairly shout their genus names—names like *Astilbe, Rosa, Hosta.* It's easiest, of course, if the genus name is also the name the plant most often goes by, like astilbe or hosta, but you can't count on that often enough.

Like family names, genus names are capitalized when used in a technical way, which is how, when you're reading about plants, you can tell you're reading about the genus. But not always; hosta or astilbe are usually written about in the less daunting lower case. (And botanists are always changing plant names, which can be even more confusing.)

Like family names—Taylor, Porter, Smith—every genus name tells a story: the *Iris* genus, for instance, was named for Iris, the rainbow goddess. Many genera were named after the men (never the women, alas, so far as I know) who "conquered" them: The *Hosta* were named for the physician to an emperor of Austria, Nicholas Host, who lived from 1761 to 1834; the Spanish author of the first book about horticulture in the New World, Nicholas Monardes, took as his namesake the *Monarda* genus. In the same way, Messrs. Fuchs, Forsyth and Tradescant claimed *Fushcia, Forsythia,* and *Tradescantia* as their horticultural heirs.

Next division down is the species, with all the genetic twists and turns, good and bad, that result from marriage and breeding; Henry V is one species, Henry VIII is another. If you don't know *something* about the species, the usually uncapitalized name that follows the genus (i.e., *Rosa rugosa*), you might get yourself into real trouble, because the clues for what you're getting come as often in the species name as in the genus name.

Gertrude Stein was wrong. Let the buyer beware: A rose isn't a rose isn't a rose. You can even get on the wrong track with irises, by planting, say, an *Iris foetidissima* in a delicate spot where you would have been better off with, say, a graceful *Iris sibirica.* The clue here comes in the species name: *foetidissima.* Their fragrance is apparently a little on the foul, as in fetid, side. These irises don't even flower in the usual sense. Instead they produce pods full of orange seeds that burst open, in a supposedly ornamental, and definitely uniris-like way (I've never seen—or smelled—one), in the fall. Fine for a woodland setting, perhaps, but hardly suitable for a genteel border display. The moral is that plants, like golf clubs, tennis gear and anything else for sale, warrant a little consumer study in advance.

As to cultivars and varieties, way down at the bottom of the family tree, some plants have cultivars and varieties and some plants don't have any. These are the variations even more fine-tuned, variations on an observable theme—a plant with a slightly different flower, leaf, height, color. Sometimes these variations occur naturally from plants breeding any way they happen to; these are *varieties.* At other times, they are created in the lab, like test-tube babies, after scientists have grafted or cross-pollinated or whatever they do to different species. These are *cultivars.* This is what Dolly Parton, Whoopi Goldberg and Queen Elizabeth have in common: All have rose cultivars named after them. (Or to go back to the GM metaphor, if that's easier. A Cadillac convertible—a variation on a recognizable Cadillac—would fit in here; same car, with the variations in the options.)

The distinctions among species, varieties, and cultivars aren't discussed much in casual conversation, either, and most beginners and even intermediates can easily get by with only a vague grasp of what the differences are, so long as you remember that plants with different names are different plants. I've raised it here not to be discouraging but to point out that you can't just go out and buy *Veronica,* any more than you can go out and just buy beef. There are different cuts of beef, and they matter. So do species, cultivars and varieties. You don't have to know everything that goes on in the lab, or in nature, but if you want your veronica to match, blend together or even be planted in the right place, you'll want to learn a little about its lineage.

With all this nomenclature to hold up, and given how hard to remember and hard to pronounce the genus and species names can be, many plants also have nicknames, or common names, which they sometimes go by. When I first took up gardening, someone advised me that if I were just to learn one name of a plant, forget about the common and learn the proper name. It's good advice, because there are mine fields even among common names. The *Lythrum* species, for instance, can go by the name of purple loosestrife (especially confusing because *L.* 'Morden's Pink' isn't even purple), while the yellow *Lysimachia nummularia,* different family, different genus, is also sometimes called loosestrife.

On the other hand, picking up the common names can teach you a wealth of lore about the plants. Study the flower of the *Dicentra* to see why they're called bleeding hearts; they're the most touching flowers I know. Consider the tulip: The name *tulip* comes from a Persian word for "turban," and doesn't a tulip look like a turban? And why are *Dianthus* species, whether speckled, white, red, or pink, called pinks? Because their edges look as if they were clipped with pinking shears. Or dogwood—why dogwood? One of the dogwood species, according to legend, used to provide a salve to cure dogs of mange.

If every plant has a story to tell, every garden is an anthology that is edited by the gardener, reflecting his or her strengths, weaknesses and bold gestures combined with, one hopes, a streak of sentimentality, even a touch of silliness. Yes, it's important to learn the plant names to avoid making mistakes. In the end, though, it's probably more important to learn their names because that's the best way to begin to connect with their souls.

A Field Trip to the Nursery

What surprised me most when I took up gardening was how knowing something, even a little, about plants can electrify your senses: You come to see, hear, smell, touch and taste the world in a whole new way. Seasons won't come and go so illegibly once they're marked by the plants that come in and out of flower at particular times each year. For years I cooked with herbs by rote before I began to grow them. Now their fragrance, taste and texture, as they're cut fresh from the garden, give them an almost ethereal dimension. Maybe those old wives' tales are right: Herbs are magic potions. In the same way, I don't know how I ever read a novel before I gardened. It seems to me now that so much fiction is enriched by things growing—the mention of a cluster of trillium by a stream, for instance, evokes a resonant image only when you know what trillium actually *looks* like and how it grows. For most of my life, such images were lost to me. I suddenly noticed, too, maybe for the first time, how much art and architecture draw their inspiration from the natural world.

And then there's the companionship. I look forward now each year to visiting my friends' gardens. There's something about these ritual tours, seeing how these gardens fill in more from year to year, that encourages confidences and closeness. Gardeners are a generous lot, and usually send visitors home with a memento; there's hardly a greater pleasure than tucking a clump of something from a friend's garden into one's own.

It's an arcane fraternity, gardening, with terms and tools and customs of its own, but mud on your jeans and some honest dirt under ruined fingernails are pretty much all you need to gain entry. That, and a genuine appreciation of and respect for all the love and work that goes into bringing plants to new life. The salient questions are where to begin and how to know what you need to know—not so much, really—before you begin.

As boring and uncreative as the answers sound, the place to start, before you plant a single thing, is with a garden tour of your own neighborhood. Just take a walk around the block and see which plants and shrubs you notice most often, how they're arranged and what blooms up and down the block from month to month. It doesn't even matter at this point if you know the names of the plants; just see what they look like, how they settle into the earth, how much space they take up once they're established. Pick up a leaf, if you can, from a shrub you like, or memorize a flower, to study later at the nursery. There are *reasons* why people plant certain things in certain places, and the primary reason is that they *grow* there. What grows for your neighbors will very likely grow well for you, too.

Like many fledgling gardeners, instead of studying the plants around me, I approached gardening the same way I would have approached a term paper in my school days. I turned to the books, the serious kind that would look impressive in a bibliography, by writers even I had heard of—Eleanor Perenyi, Vita Sackville-West, Russell Paige.

I found these books exciting if inscrutable, fairy tales about mysterious places. But the language washed over me, and I began dreaming about emulating all the wrong gardens, English gardens, mostly, which were probably already flourishing at the time of the Boston Tea Party. I fell in love with the sound of yew trees, for example, without knowing that virtually the only yews that grow between me and England are the shrubs; I should have been thinking instead about maples. For what I needed to know at the time, these were wish books.

It would have been more sensible, and useful, to have gone where the plants are—to a nursery.

THE NURSERY: A USER'S GUIDE

Though there are stunning exceptions, in most cases nurseries could use a few lessons in creative marketing. Most will unwittingly teach you everything about keeping plants apart and very little about how they should be put together. Unless you have true vision and a great deal of confidence, it's almost impossible to go blithely from the perennial department at the local nursery, to the shrub department, to the rose boutique, to the herbs and annuals, and put together a garden in your head, much less in the ground.

I was lucky to have worked at one of the exceptions not long ago; when I was thinking about writing this book, friends of mine who own it thought I should have some hands-on professional experience. As much arboretum as plant store, this particular nursery felt like a park—water garden over here, groves of trees over there; all of the offices and landscape design studios were surrounded by minigardens of their own. Railroad ties enclosed sample display beds—a June garden, a midsummer bed, a garden for late in the season. You could walk through acres of trees, some for sale, some planted many years before, prospering now and there for show. Customers' dogs would head straight to the manmade pond, diving through graceful ornamental grasses and a newly dug section, where plants especially suited to the seashore, only half a mile away, were taking hold.

There were ideas for gardeners everywhere. Under one shade tree (not flush with the tree, which would have looked prissy and out of proportion, but farther out) was a partial arc of bluish-leaved hosta, with a sort of petticoat around *that* of maidenhair ferns; fully in the shade, the lighter, delicate ferns seemed almost lit from underneath against those leaves of hosta. More than one customer of mine came in to buy the plants to copy this totally trouble-free display, which would take about a minute to settle into any garden, so long as you already had the tree. For an idea of how ostrich ferns jump around, all you had to do was look at the fence by the display of herbs, where five had been planted a few years ago; now there are dozens hopscotching along the fence. A climbing hydrangea grew against one wall, so visitors could study for themselves how to secure the branches with nails specially curved for the purpose. Japanese iris grew in a little cottage-size pond, their bulbous roots permanently submerged.

While some of the plants for sale were lined up in conventional perfect rows, others were clustered in their pots where they belonged in your garden or mine: shade plants were gathered under a big shade tree, herbs were set out alongside a sunny terrace, the inevitable impatiens were lined up in the dappled shade of a long pergola. *Presentation* was the word that kept coming up: The entire nursery was on display.

An early spring visit to the nursery will offer you an array of the staunchest plants, those that can survive cold nights, even a frost, in their pots. These are perennials, plants that come back year after year, along with shrubs and trees, and are the first plants to arrive. Growers like to ship plants just as they're coming into bloom, for showiest effect on display at the nursery. If you buy one in bloom this year, next year, without the help of a greenhouse, it will bloom in your garden a couple of weeks later. Fill up on too many of these early spring plants, as I saw many neophytes do (and have done myself), and your garden will be spring-heavy, and barren later on, after you've run out of steam. Better to leave some holes for now, and make further trips to the nursery as the season goes on, when later-blooming plants begin to arrive. Most nurseries receive shipments at least every week, and some have sales on the out-of-bloom plants that haven't sold. Plant them now and wait for them to bloom next year.

Some people would come in, look over the perennials and ask things like, "What do you have in blue?" If you want blue, fine, nothing wrong with blue; I'm partial to blue myself. But find out *more* about the perennials, blue or not, before you make your choice. When does it bloom, and for how long? What's the foliage like when it's *not* in bloom? Can you do anything—vigilant deadheading?—to extend the blooming season, as you can with, say, cornflowers (*Centaurea cyanus*), a quiet mounded perennial with electric blue flowers, centered in black? What are its spreading habits?

"These come back every year, right?" was another typical question asked about perennials, and the automatic answer is yes. A more truthful answer is yes, *but.* . . . Yes, but some perennials are iffier than others; yes, but the conditions have to be right; yes, but some may need special care; yes, by definition it will, but don't count on it— yes, in other words, in a perfect world. You can tell me all you want that monkshood (*Aconitum*) is a perennial, but not for me; aconitum and I just don't get along. If I want it, I have to plant it every year, as if it were an annual.

Some customers, of course, knew exactly what they wanted, and why, but I always worried about those who didn't, those who seemed timid about asking questions and left with their blue plants or monkshood and who, I suspected, would later be disappointed. One woman, I remember, kept exclaiming over the delicate Scottish bellflowers, *Campanula rotundifolia* (with, not surprisingly, tiny blue bell-like blossoms), already in bloom; they would be perfect for a gap at the center front of her mixed border that, she said, looked rather like a missing tooth. I tried to tell her that the foliage pretty much evaporates after they've bloomed (which would happen any second, in this case, as they were already blooming at full tilt), and she would still have the hole. The more I tried to dissuade her, the more obstinate she became. She left with her bellflowers. (Curiously, reverse psychology was a great selling strategy in the nursery. When one man asked whether deer would eat columbine, I said yes, and if deer were a problem, he might as well go home and forget about a flower garden. Instead, he bought six columbine.)

Appearances in the nursery can sometimes be deceiving. More than one customer used to comment on the *Achillea*, which in their pots would look particularly thirsty at midday while the other perennials nearby looked perky and fine. "Achilles heel to grow, I bet," one guy chuckled. (Yes, it was named after Achilles, who would give it to his soldiers during the Trojan War, to stop the flow of blood—and it does help clotting.) I too wondered how you could plant it among other plants if it wilted so fast. Not a problem, as it turned out. Well-drained soil is its most important requirement, more so even than fertile soil, so the growers had potted it in a sandy medium, knowing that it was better off wilting a little than getting waterlogged.

The annuals arrive a month or more after the perennials. Mostly tropical plants that can't survive a cold winter, they're too tender to be put out early, as they can be damaged by a late frost. By then, the nursery finally feels replete with the promise of summer. Annuals are plants, usually surprising inexpensive, that will last one season only, but brilliantly; some even reseed themselves, and go on year after year as reliably as perennials. A few years ago, annuals were a horticultural faux pas, considered unworthy among some serious gardeners—too vulgar, too gaudy, too easy to grow. And until a few years ago the annuals most widely available *were* pretty vulgar (although I happen to like a touch of vulgarity in a garden). Today, however, annuals are in favor. Now it's fashionable to be enthusiastic about annuals, and horticultural fashion aside, most gardens are unimaginable without a generous sprinkling of annuals. Even better, with more sophisticated gardeners around, growers are responding with more sophisticated annuals, way beyond marigolds and geraniums, and savvy gardeners scour the local nurseries to get the most exotic annuals first.

I used to get impatient with customers who spent a lot of time peering at the annuals, deciding if the stem of this purple salvia or that one was too crooked. Annuals are more rugged creatures than you'd think. If the salvia stem is crooked, just snip off the crooked part when you plant it and it'll grow back fine. If a few leaves look brown, pluck them off. Annuals aren't meant to be fussed over.

NURSERY VISION

These tiny plants in their tiny trays are hard to imagine full grown unless you know exactly what you want. "Four-feet high, purple flower" is what the tag says, which describes any number of plants, including my new, six-inch verbena. Would you accept a blind date with a person described only as six feet tall, brown hair? Nor should you accept such a vague outline in a plant, especially because you'll probably spend more time together with it than you would with a blind date.

What would help? A picture.

In all the time I worked at the nursery, only one customer asked if she could see a picture of what a certain plant would look like in bloom, and we were happy to show her one. For the neophyte gardener a photographic dictionary or encyclopedia to perennials and annuals is as essential as a trowel. Nurseries are a *resource* if you use them as such, and if you pick a good one, with a trained staff, you can practically get your whole garden designed for free, although my friends who work as garden designers will probably never speak to me again for saying so.

Because it was so lovely, people always assumed that the nursery where I worked was more expensive than the competition, which wasn't the case (I checked). As it happened, they specialized in designing and installing grand-scale gardens and by stocking beautiful garden furniture, big trees and the like. They were too smart, and too decent, to try to get away with overpricing the smaller plants. Because so much of their work was actually *doing* gardens, all the people on the staff—except for me, the friend of the owner—held certificates in landscape design or degrees in landscape architecture, or had years of experience behind them. This is why the prettiest nursery around was staffed by people who cared about plants, who *saw* them as plants, living things, not "product." And they were there to help.

If there's one thing I've learned about gardening, it's that hanging around nurseries can teach you a lot if you're not shy or embarrassed about asking. Try all the nurseries in the area, see which plants look the best, note that nurseries have surprisingly disparate selections, especially when it comes to annuals; for example, to date there's only one nursery near me—a tiny, family-owned greenhouse—that sells larkspur and white cosmos.

As if the nursery were a department-store dressing room, take the pots out of their neat little rows and if you want to plant them together, try them together. It won't take long to see which nursery has the most knowledgeable salespeople. Ask to see pictures, ask all the questions you want. I've been given some wonderful advice by fellow customers, who in general are eager to share what they know. One woman, a complete stranger with whom I struck up a chat, talked me into buying a Mandevilla, a small, tropical tree with sequential deep pink blooms; she had coaxed hers along, winters indoors and summers outside, for four years now. It's not a plant, it's an ornament. It looks heavenly climbing and sprawling around the back porch door, right up through the early frosts in the fall. See what plants other people are buying, too, and which plants are selling the fastest. If you like the look of a plant but aren't sure, go back and look at it two weeks later, when it's two weeks bigger. Become something of a garden pest yourself; immerse yourself in the world of gardening before you cultivate your own.

2
Planning the Garden

Turning a Yard into a Garden

☙

"The best way to start from scratch," someone had advised, "is to bring in a landscape architect to draw up one-, three- and five-year plans. Start small and build." There is never a way to argue with sensible advice like this, but I decided not to follow it. I was intimidated by the idea of a landscape architect or landscape designer or even a landscaper. I was afraid somehow that if I had a professional helping me, it'd really be his or her garden, not mine and that it would probably be too ambitious for me to handle on my own. Without checking, I'd also decided that professional help would probably be too expensive and too doctrinaire. Five-year plan? Didn't seem very spontaneous. It was springtime, and I was restless to get going.

I've since found out that many good nurseries offer all kinds of on-site services: They'll come to your house, talk over your aims with you, and maybe even make a few recommendations right there. (Gardeners have a hard time *not* giving away ideas.) Sometimes these preliminary visits are free; sometimes there's a nominal charge.

The cost of having plans drawn up varies widely, depending on the kind of professional you consult and how comprehensive you want the plans to be: Broad-stroke outlines are cheaper than detailed plant-by-plant plans. If I were starting now, I'd definitely consult a few design professionals, and given what gardening costs over the long haul, I might have saved myself some money, and gotten off to a more authoritative start, by actually having a rough design proposed for me—which can cost as little as a few hundred dollars—that I could have referred to or altered as the garden evolved. When it comes to gardening, the cost of impatience can be exorbitant. Even if I didn't follow through by having a formal plan drawn up, I'd at least be sure to forge a relationship with a designer familiar with my property—and thereby with a good nursery—first thing. Fortunately for me, by working at the nursery, I had managed to pick up much helpful advice and probably averted more than a few mistakes.

Like therapists, who can be qualified in different ways to treat patients, there are all kinds of experts who work with gardens. And as with therapists, it's not only the kind of degree that hangs on the wall that matters but also the bedside manner, the feel for your problems, and the *personality* of the professional and whether it clicks with yours. Check, too, to see whether the professional is also a plantsman, which means he or she knows as much about the plants themselves as about designing what are known as the "hard" elements—terraces, walls, pergolas and so on.

Top-of-the-line landscape architects are, in fact, architects of the land and have studied for up to five years and passed a series of rigorous exams. They know all about grading and erosion and can transform wastelands into gardens, on any scale. After one year of study, landscape designers, one tier down, are certified to design the groupings of shrubs and flowers (and paths and ponds and anything else) that make up a garden. This isn't always true, but I tend to think of designers as more hands-on than architects, and architects more as the choreographers of crews. Landscapers, a catch-all term, are people who have done landscaping, not necessarily licensed or certified, but some have many years of experience and a real feel for plants and design, just as important as a degree. It's a subjective business, gardening; the right professional (and do be sure to take a look at some of the gardens he or she has already created, which you can copy) can help smooth your way into the garden you had, however fuzzily, in your mind's eye all along.

Or you can be ornery like me, and choose to design the garden yourself.

ASSESSING WHAT YOU HAVE

Borrowed scenery is a phrase the Japanese use to describe a vista that is just out of reach of your own garden and yet an integral part of it: that tree smack over the borderline in the next yard; a far-off, gracefully sloping roofline you can see from your terrace; a soft hillside that crests with your neighbor's garden, just enough in view to become a part of *your* view, too, and thus your garden. If the outer edges are worthy, the garden should be created to enhance them. If on the other hand your peripheral vision is ordinary or worse, the garden's job is to obscure it.

When it comes time to design a garden, these horizons, everything the eye can take in, are its farthest outer boundaries, and must be considered along with the fixed, as well as the malleable, elements inside the space. A pretty bed of flowers on an otherwise unthought-out plot can be a nice accent, even if your outward perspective is that of the neighbor's clothesline. But an ornamental garden creates its own world from every inch of the space, starting with the outside and working its way in. You frame a garden before you start furnishing it with plants, the same way you frame a house before you start putting in sofas and lamps. Plan to obliterate the clothesline, in other words, before you pick where to put the petunias.

Not so daunting as it sounds.

Henry Mitchell, one of our great contemporary garden writers and surely the funniest, cites in an essay the five "commonest bad mistakes" made by gardeners, and the first, and presumably most dire, of them is this: "Failure to enclose the garden with shrub screens, hedges, walls, or fences, with the result that the scene never looks finished, no matter how well things are growing or how many things are in flower."* Enclosure again. In my case, if I were to do things right, my bed of herbs, or those perennials I wanted to plant, weren't the first

---

* Henry Mitchell, *One Man's Garden* (Boston: Houghton Mifflin, 1992), 28. Forewarned is forearmed. Mitchell's other "commonest bad mistakes" are (1) forgetting how big plants will actually grow and planting them too close together, (2) "ignoring the tremendous effect of small flowers massed" (we'll get to this), (3) planting so that something is in bloom during every miniseason of the year, and (4) seeking out plants that bloom the longest at the expense of those—like lilacs, for instance—whose moments of glory last only a horticultural minute, but a breathtaking one.

order of business. Instead, I should erect "walls," walls I could either build or plant.

In an ideal world, your borrowed scenery will already be a boundary of your garden—a tranquil water scene, the neat rows of a farmer's field or mature trees or hedges you can, for the purpose of defining your garden, claim and enjoy as your own. One garden writer describes how he planted two shrubs on his own property to frame his perspective of a beautiful, distant tree on someone else's, pulling the outside of his garden in. If you're not so lucky, your borrowed scenery might be an auto supply shop advertised by a neon sign.

At first, I thought I'd be happy to give my borrowed scenery back, until I began to see that what I had thought of at first as boundary eyesores could be, if I looked at them more optimistically, the skeletal outlines of my garden—the outer walls, the borrowed scenery. Not great, but offering the beginnings of a sense of enclosure, if not always of actual garden. The sense of garden could come from planting "walls" on the inside, in the form of shrubs (evergreen and/or flowering), trees and such variations on the theme as ornamental grasses.

On one side, there was that ragged privet hedge—privet being the common name (origin unknown, but I always think of it as having to do with privacy) of the hedging shrub that must screen more houses than any other shrub in America; the proper name, *Ligustrum vulgare*, suggests just how common it is. Growing high, thick and strong in surprisingly few years, it produces clusters of nicely fragrant little white flowers in summer. It's as useful as it is common. If I didn't have such a screen already, I might well have thought of planting one. Ours—or more accurately our neighbor's—hadn't been tended in years but, happily, this problem was fairly easily solved. A query early on to our neighbor, who was trying to sell the house, about whether we could prune the hedge ourselves, was greeted with an enthusiastic yes. Another year or two of severe pruning nearly all the way to the ground early in the spring will encourage the hedge to grow back better than ever before. On this one side at least, our as yet nonexistent garden was well on its way to having a horticultural wall: Our borrowed scenery was beginning to look better.

The stock fence takes up the other side of the property and, visible above the fence, there's a hint of what goes on next door on the other side: the roof of a small shed, the overhang of a couple of trees, and again, some privet—not a long hedge per se but several tall, mature shrubs that, from our side, look like the kind of electric hair-style you'd fire your hairdresser for giving you. As borrowed scenery, this wayward privet would look much crisper if it were trimmed, in a flat-top haircut or possibly a rounded shape, so that this privet free-for-all could become instead a "column" helping to offset whatever we'd end up planting in front of it, on our side of the fence—but that, too, could come much later. The fence itself would make up the second wall framing the garden. However ordinary it was, at least it was a fence, already in place (if a little tilted here and there) and thus a garden wall—easy enough to work with, and easy enough to hide.

I can't blame our broken-down barn on borrowed scenery, because it's all too clear to whom it belongs; as borrowed scenery for the neighbors behind us, however, it must be a terrible eyesore, except that they like to use its back wall for practicing their soccer kicks. Apart from the house, though, it's the biggest fixed element of the property, and the design would have to take note of it. At first the garden will have to go in more or less around the barn, in an attempt to camouflage its rickety angles. Later, maybe, if we ever get around to renovating the structure, we can adorn it with plantings so that it will add to the whole of the garden instead of detracting from it, the way it will for now. Lining the back of the yard as it does, the barn also helps enclose the space of our plot, becoming the back wall of the garden. A short strip of stock fence joins the barn to the longer fence on the side, neatly squaring off and enclosing the back quadrant, which looks a bit like an afterthought.

The gardener shouldn't be too hasty in deciding what's fixed, I discovered a little later on; nature may have other ideas, as it did with the old catalpa, another of my fixed elements. This tree would stick around only long enough to be included in the initial garden scheme, and to have a lot of pretty things that thrive in shady places planted under and around it, before succumbing to a devastating hurricane; we were at least relieved that it fell away from the house. Now the stump is all that remains as a fixed element, and the design must be modified again to accommodate or eradicate it.

We had other fixed elements: the garden gate, which turned out fine, and the not-very-attractive rectangular white-stone terrace lining the back of the house, which had to remain for now, we'd decided; there was no money to replace or redesign it. I drew all these elements in scale onto graph paper, the way you're supposed to, which took about five minutes and failed to turn up any pleasant surprises.

Then I made several photocopies of my sketch, and began testing gardens the risk-free way, in pencil.

MAIL-ORDER FANTASIES

Step one: Call 1-800-845-1124, the toll-free number for Wayside Gardens in Hodges, South Carolina, and ask them to send you their latest catalog.

Step two: Call 1-203-496-9600, the (not toll-free) number for White Flower Farm in Litchfield, Connecticut, and ask them to send you their latest catalog. While you're at it, you might also ask them why they don't have a toll-free number.

Despite their very different styles of presentation, Wayside Gardens (gushy) and White Flower Farm (studied-Yankee-quaint) are widely acknowledged to be the best of the American garden catalogs, selling mainly trees, shrubs and perennials, along with various other gardening paraphernalia. For gardeners at any level, these catalogs, with their hundreds of offerings, can serve not only as wish-books but also as textbooks, complete with color photographs of the plants full grown and at their glorious best. They'll tell you what USDA zone you're in, and thus which plants grow in your zone and which you can eliminate from your dreams and blueprints entirely. They also offer cultivation hints for growing specific plants, and occasionally they'll suggest plant "marriages"—that is, plants that look good juxtaposed with certain other plants. Best of all, they'll sell your name to other catalog companies, so that soon you'll have more plant and seed catalogs arriving in the mail than you'll know what to do with; the appearance of these catalogs each year is a celebrated ritual, an exercise in both self-indulgence and self-denial.

These catalogs will also help drive Mitchell's admonition home: Shrubs, they'll tell you over and over, are the *foundation* of the garden; or the *bones* or the *anchors* of the garden; or the plants of choice for hedging, screening, enclosing and starting the garden. This advice is nonnegotiable; ignore it at your peril. If you initially plant shrubs, and possibly a few trees, to suggest the outlines of the garden, you'll be several steps ahead of the game: You'll have flowers almost at once, often in the first year. Chosen carefully, a selection of flowering shrubs will provide a sequence of blooms outdoors throughout the season, and at the same time a sequence of blooms to cut for displays indoors.

Shrubs, most of them anyway, are low maintenance—maximum

effect for minimum effort. If you plant a few shrubs, you'll also have the issue of winter interest wrapped up. By definition, shrubs offer winter form and texture, and many will give you fall color as well.

If you have your heart set on a flower garden, shrubs won't preclude that plan in any way. To the contrary. You're not planting shrubs *instead* of perennials and annuals. Shrubs as a backdrop to a perennial bed or border magnify its effect. Spending a good percentage of your flower budget on shrubs will enhance the beauty and impact of your garden many times over.

Which shrubs? There are as many answers to that as there are gardens. Spread out the catalogs, along with any lavish picture books of gardens you can scrounge up, and bear in mind, too, those plants you've admired on your neighborhood garden tours and at the local nurseries. Picking out the shrubs you like will be a snap. Weeding out those you can't fit, or can't afford, will be considerably harder. And wield the garden in pencil first; it's easier on your back.

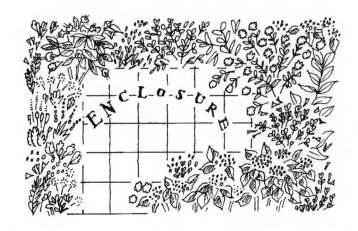

Building Garden Walls, 1: Hedges and Shrubs

A quick look at the dictionary recently answered a question that had been plaguing me for some time: What, I had wondered, is the difference between a "hedge" and a "hedgerow"? No difference at all, as it turns out; if anything, *hedgerow* is redundant (a hedge *is* a row) and one of those words that never made the passage successfully from England to America. As far as I can tell, the term *shrub screen,* a row or grouping of shrubs to set off and adorn a space, falls more or less into the hedge category, too, except that a shrub screen doesn't necessarily have to line up in a straight row, the way hedges seem to do. My dictionary has only a brief definition of *shrubbery:* "shrubs collectively." In a row? In a circular bed? Wrapping around a foundation? Too confusing. Best to leave hedgerows and shrubberies to the English. The rest of us should stick to hedges and shrubs and shrub screens to enclose our own gardens and worry more about plants than semantics.

Call it whatever you want, it was time to pick the shrubs to launch our garden.

So far, in the privet hedge, fence, barn and gate, all we had was the framework to the garden, and although handsome enough and definitely serviceable, privet is privet, and not likely to astound anyone with its cleverness. I began to picture how much lusher this flat backdrop would look with layers of shrubs or small trees filling in the space in front of it—flowering shrubs, perhaps, selected so that we'd have something in bloom throughout most of the season, and buttressed by a few evergreens to suggest the outlines of the space year round.

Knowing, too, that I wanted the (mostly) perennial border to emanate from the fence, I could see that there again, shrubs abutting the fence would be a more effective backdrop for groupings of perennials than the plain old fence. Shrubs on the privet side only would diminish flowers on the other side, making the shrub side look top heavy, but shrubs all around—with an emphasis on flowering shrubs on the fence side—would balance the scale, as well as adhering to Mitchell (and everyone else's) rule of enclosure.

Tempting as a "one of each" approach might be, you want to avoid having your garden appear like the jumble of a sale rack or so much clashing wallpaper. "A few of each of several" is closer to the right idea. Several of the same shrubs grouped together soothe and harmonize. And then, to avoid monotony and provide visual (and green or flowering) counterpoints, you can draw in as many other contrasting shrubs as room, budget and imagination allow.

Picture, for instance, a garden enclosed in evergreen weeping hemlocks—*Tsuga* is the genus and there are a number of varieties that weep (usually they're called Sargeant's weeping hemlocks), but just ask for weeping hemlock. These trees resemble pine or spruce Christmas trees, except that the needles are softer and the muted demeanor of the tree, which "weeps" down instead of perking upward, is slightly melancholy: I think their moodiness is wonderfully appealing. But a whole yardful of them would look gloomy, something the Addams family would plant with delight. A few weeping hemlocks, on the other hand, make an inviting soft statement or corner. Balance them by also planting, say, a cluster of hollies, the kind whose branches you also see at Christmas, with either pure green or variegated leaves (variegated means leaves with more than one color— green and white, or green and yellow), and the eye will cheer up before it has a chance to get depressed.

Another consideration is the form, or shape, of the shrubs, and how well they'll mingle together in the garden. Shrubs come in as many shapes as people do—tall, round, squat, square, pear-shaped, lean and conical. Some reach up, some droop down and some sprawl. Some are, in fact, trees, but are regarded as shrubs when used for screening or in any other shrublike way. Too many pear-shaped shrubs in formation will look like bowling pins at the end of an alley; a grouping of round shrubs only will look too frilly, like a scalloped ruffle. Breaking up a pear-shaped formation with a round shrub, or a round grouping with a square shrub, will add complexity to the whole.

Think also about the color and texture of the shrubs, both in bloom, if they're flowering shrubs, and not. There are dozens of shades of green—the dark greens of many evergreens; the silvery greens of such plants as the *Elaeagnus* (or silver berries, silverberries or oleaster), which sparkle in the wind; the bright crayon-colored green of the tiny-leaved boxwood, or *Buxus*. Just as too many bright colors coming into bloom at once can clash and dilute the impact of all of them, too many greens can clash as well. But choose several: silvery-green or variegated to brighten a dark corner, the bright greens to serve as a refrain, darker greens where you need solemnity and weight. As for shrub textures, they range from misty and soft to coarse and prickly. For example, many junipers (*Juniperus* is the genus)— the prickly, low-spreading shrubs you inevitably see landscaping the entrances to office complexes or the much higher, almost majestic-looking shrubs used to adorn the foundations of houses or mark entrances—would simply look coarse and wrong planted in front of a grouping of softly flowering shrubs. An arrangement of those same junipers, however, planted to delineate a sunny driveway, or to slink through a formation of rocks, would look totally right.

A more pragmatic shrub concern is the dreaded pH factor, a phrase so baffling it will make you want to give up gardening and take up golf. Thus far, for example, I've avoided any mention of the rhodo-dendron (or rhododen*drum*, as it's too often mispronounced), which I'm wary of because it's always uttered in the same breath as pH factor.

I know that pH matters, that it pertains to alkaline and acid levels (whatever they are) in the soil, and that some trees and shrubs— rhododendron, azalea, mountain laurel, blueberry and holly among them—need high acid levels in the soil to prosper. And I know that you're never supposed to use lime on these acid-loving plants, lime being the soil "sweetener" generally used to keep grass lawns happy. I have also pieced together that there are pH-checking kits (pH levels of 4.5 to 6.5 are about right for rhododendrons), and that some county extension services (whatever they are) will analyze your soil for free and tell you your pH level. Rather than dealing with all this, I had decided initially to avoid the pH issue, and rhododendrons, entirely.

Trouble was, hollies also fall into this acid-loving category, and I knew I wanted hollies, pH or not. I decided instead to conquer my pHobia up front, helped, in part, by the Little Azalea That Could.

I have never liked azaleas (which are, botanically, deciduous members of the *Rhododendron* genus) except in vast, parklike settings where they're allowed free rein to stretch and spread any way they want to. In those settings, and in bloom, they're breathtaking. However, seeing them snipped, shaped, and restrained in residential neighborhoods, I am always reminded of the terrible stories I've read about tropical birds having their wings clipped to better serve as house pets: a crime against nature.

My first spring in this house, before giving much consideration to a garden, I bought a potted azalea at the supermarket, forced into bloom for Easter. Amid the unpacked boxes, it would, I thought, provide a cheerful touch. After the blooms faded, I couldn't bear to throw it away, so I dug a small hole outside and stuck it in, in an entirely shaded corner out of the way, figuring that, out of sight, out of mind, it would vanish on its own. By the second spring, as I was getting ready to plant, I noticed that, sun and my pH negligence notwithstanding, the azalea was fully in bloom and twice the size. Believe me, I had done nothing to encourage this.

It could be that my pH happens to be just right for acid-loving plants, but I doubted it. Yes, I've seen rhododendrons and so on growing nearby—certainly the nurseries in the area carry row upon row of them—but I've also seen them growing in enough other places to make me think the pH paranoia is something of a consumer hoax, or at least an exaggerated threat. The preeminent English horticulturist Graham Stuart Thomas wrote this about rhododendrons in one of his books: "They are only satisfactory on lime-free soils, containing humus and of reasonable moisture. As a general rule the larger the leaves the more shelter they require." His calm tone is reassuring— not one hysterical mention of pH-checking kits. (Useful information, though, about the leaves/shelter ratio; bred for size, the big hybrids lose a little in fortitude. And no rhododendrons like sharp cold.)

As for humus (pronounced HEW-mus and meaning organic matter), it's easily provided. It's always added to the soil before planting shrubs, and it's no big deal; we'll get to it soon.

If you're longing to sketch pH-fussy plants into your plans, you might want to make the same compromise I did. Rather than tracking down my county extension service, I decided that when the time came to plant, I'd buy a bag of fertilizer specially formulated for acid-loving plants—a horticultural Pepto-Bismol but meant to *encourage* acid indigestion—and feed the plant accourding to directions; these fertilizers, which say right on the front that they're for azaleas, hollies, and so on, are available anywhere you can find regular fertilizers. If there aren't any rhododendrons (or azaleas or hollies) growing near you, you'll want to go to more trouble to find out why, by asking a gardening neighbor or someone at a nursery, and then deciding whether it's worth it to tamper with the soil or whether you'd be better off planting something else that's more suited to the soil you already have—an easier bet.

SHRUB SHOPPING

Tree and shrub shopping, I began the process of mixing and matching, laying out and layering shrubs together—on paper. More accurately, I was only mixing. Matching would have meant choosing one shrub to buy and plant in quantity to create a hedge. Because I already had a one-note hedge in the privet, this mix of shrubs would go in front of it.

It happened to be spring in my case, but you can just as easily tackle shrubs in the fall. The cool of early autumn is a splendid time to install shrubs, not least because often you'll find shrubs on sale late in the season. Even if the shrubs are losing their leaves, as flowering shrubs will, and are slightly ratty-looking, they'll be fine so long as the root ball remains strong and heavy in its pot. Shrubs should have a certain heft when you buy them, and it's more important that the root bear the shrub's weight than the growth on top.

I also began, finally, to understand the unassailable logic of those three- and five-year plans; short of winning the lottery, there was absolutely no way that I could have the garden I wanted in the first year.

Which didn't mean, however, that I couldn't *plan* the garden I wanted in the first year.

There's a barely discernible slope on the privet side of the yard, and I'd hoped to accentuate that slope by planting several "layers" of shrubs in front of the hedge, to make an ornamental screen with the privet as backdrop. If there are prefabricated kits for designing mixed shrub hedges, I've never come across them. There's no absolute right way or wrong way, but I've seen enough good ones by now to get the general idea: You design a shrub screen in the same way you plan a wardrobe.

The most basic items are those that'll carry you through most of the year which, in plant terms, usually mean evergreens, although the sculptural branches and stems of deciduous shrubs are also perfectly interesting to contemplate in winter (though not for hours at a time, as some gardeners would have you think). Building down from and around the evergreens, you add the seasonal touches, the shrubs that reach their flowering glory once a year. And as with planning a wardrobe, you'll also inevitably make some impulse buys, which will usually turn out to be mistakes. That's why it's better to plan on paper first, when you have your wits about you.

When planning the garden, keep in mind that most decent garden soil, well drained and not soggy, will do for most shrubs. As we'll see, the soil around them needs tending to (minimal tending at that) only about once or twice a year, plus weeding and watering. You can add seasonal potions and prunings as needed for those shrubs that lobby for special attention, but this is rarely a problem and you can figure it out as you go along, or check the Glossary here for more specifics (and also for how to pronounce the names of the plants). As for sun, the standard rule is that flowering shrubs need at least half a day of sun to flower their best, and most nonflowering shrubs in general need at least that much, too, although there are some that take well to shade.

I knew I wanted to mark the "entrance" to the shrub screen with arborvitae, those conical-shaped evergreens with weblike lacy green branches that somehow manage to look restrained and welcoming at the same time; often you'll see them planted as hedges, or used to mark an entryway. *Thuja* is the genus, and it offers several varieties in golden colors as well as the green I wanted, *T. occidentalis* 'Emerald', or some version thereof, which I could easily find at a nursery just by looking. They need full sun, and the spot I picked for them was sunny as could be. Three of these, small to start with but slightly graduated in size and arranged in a triangle, would invite you in from the side yard to the bigger square of the backyard proper, the center of the garden-to-be.

At the far end of this row of shrubs, marking a door to the barn, I sketched in three hollies, the Christmas kind. Because the yard is small, I wanted compact hollies that wouldn't eventually overwhelm the space; I also wanted something solid to frame the distant perspective of the garden from the house, both in summer and winter. Hollies would always give the eye a place to rest. And because I don't know even one of the four hundred species names, I couldn't tell you what kind I wanted; by studying the catalogs, I settled on 'China Boy' and 'China Girl' (the genus is *Ilex*) as plausible bets and with names that are easy enough to remember.

A few common yews, *Taxus baccata*, clipped squarely for a contrasting shape and spaced evenly throughout the space in between, would indicate "shrub screen" all year round; like the hollies and arborvitae, they'd stay green and anchor the area, as would the space into which, at each end, I drew two arcs of tiny boxwoods (*Buxus sempervirens*, to be precise—think of buxom, which they are when they're grown, though they grow slowly—but you can almost always, even in the company of serious gardeners, get away with calling a box a box).

None of these selections is staggeringly original, but originality wasn't my goal, at least not here. I wanted horticultural classics that would not take too much attention away from the flowering shrubs that I'd plant among them: They would be the main attraction. I also wanted plants I'd seen growing within a few blocks of my house, and all of these fit the bill. I knew they'd do fine with minimal fussing. Four lovely colors and textures of green; that seemed about right for this smallish area.

Now I could begin to draw in pencil the squiggly flowering shrubs.

First I drew in five *Hydrangea macrophylla* 'Nikko Blue' plants, staggered in front of where the slight slope ended, about eight feet into the yard from the privet hedge itself.

H. macrophylla 'Nikko Blue' is probably the most familiar of the many hydrangea species, the shrubs with big snowball blooms, from midsummer on, in that magical blue; I don't know who Nikko was. They abound where I live, and in other seaside places I've visited, on both coasts; they thrive in the salt air. Come to think of it, they also thrive far from any salt air. Point is, they thrive. (One tip: If your blooms aren't as blue as your neighbors', adding two tablespoons of something called aluminum sulfate per shrub in the fall will solve the problem for next year. Or you can live with the lesser blue, which won't hurt the plant. Never a problem, however, with a garden still on paper.)

I worried a little that these hydrangeas might be a cliché, but I decided to let that go. What I hoped was that with their perfectly rounded forms under the squared-off hedge and with other plants marking other levels in between, the staggered hydrangeas would look like waves tumbling into the garden, toward the fence on the other side. Eventually, once installed, they did in fact look like waves, sort of, albeit tiny waves lapping in at low tide. But they, like other hydrangeas, take hold incredibly fast.

Just behind, among the yews, I tucked in three flowering quince, red ones, which are stuck with the formidable name *Chaenomeles speciosa*. These bloom at about the same time you see the yellow forsythia blooming everywhere. They're much more exotic, though, with quirkily shaped branches, sort of Oriental in appearance, and small blossoms in the most delicate red, pink or white, depending on which variety you choose. Like forsythia, they're excellent for forcing indoors, which means nothing more than cutting the branches once the buds are formed, bringing them inside and "forcing" them to bloom early in water. Once mature, which only takes four or five years, they also produce a golden fruit (as in quince jelly) in the fall. Often they're trained to grow against walls, but I've also seen them kept small and grown among other shrubs. I wanted to try them here; they'd be the first shrubs to open up this section of the garden in the spring. Camellias, early blooming and much sturdier than they look (they look almost like tropical shrubs, with beautiful blossoms that you might wear in your hair, if you were the type), would also have looked nice, but they need a very sheltered spot, and I was afraid to try them here. (One word of caution: *Cydonia*, or sometimes *Pseudocydonia*, is an old genus name for quince that still turns up sometimes on nursery tags. And not all quinces produce berries suitable for making jellies.)

Behind the quince, at the top of the slight slope and spaced farther apart, I drew in five (and later reduced the count to three) *Cornus alba* 'Elegantissima'—*Cornus* is the dogwood genus—copying shamelessly from a friend who had one at the back of her perennial border, which had stopped me in my tracks: Beautiful. The leaves are pale gray-green with a white racing stripe around them, and I figured they'd light up all these other shrubs like a curtain in front of the privet wall. Its flowers aren't very pretty (the leaves are the main thing), but it produces berries in the autumn and, after the leaves fall, the stems are red all winter (as in winter interest). I have read that if you want these in a special shape and prune them accordingly, the new leaves on the new stems emerge at first in pure white (that's what the *alba* means), which is the result of a lack of chlorophyll but not dangerous to the plant. I thought that might look fine.

My shrub screen was beginning to look alarmingly full, and as I barely managed to squeeze in a couple of *Spiraea trilobata* 'Swan Lake' (compact shrubs to bloom profusely in white sometime after the quince and before the hydrangea), I realized I'd barely scratched the surface of flowering shrubs. Henry Mitchell's second "commonest bad mistake" came to mind: "Planting too closely. No gardener thinks time will pass and plants will grow. Even slow growers like box increase in bulk surprisingly, in surprisingly few years." I'd been guilty as charged, and more than once. Mitchell's advice, to concede the infant plants the space they'll need as adults, is both better for the plants (crowded shrubs even *look* unhappy) and easier on the gardener. Besides, my shrub screen defined only one side of the garden; I had three other sides to enclose. I could take my pencil elsewhere.

Building Garden Walls, 2:
(More) Shrubs and Grasses

❧

The shell of the vintage Mustang and the sundry car parts were finally removed, although we could still see their faint outlines in the crabgrass, like the chalk drawings the police use to demonstrate where they find dead bodies. The small corner off the barn, already fenced in, thus opened itself up to more horticultural possibilities: It could almost be a small garden on its own, slightly away from everything else yet still a part of the larger "garden." But Mitchell's first rule held here, too; this little quadrant had to be enclosed. More shrubs.

Having overcome my pHobia, I first penciled a single rhododendron into one corner of the square.

A single shrub or tree planted in a garden is known as a specimen. You'll often see it written that a tree or shrub is "suitable for use as a specimen," which means that it's strong enough to stand on its own and to make an excellent impression when planted solo. This doesn't mean you can't plant several, just that one, planted among other shrubs or set off by itself, will be showy enough to attract attention. A small rhododendron, I thought, could serve as a specimen in this far corner, readily viewed close-up as well. As to *which* rhododendron, I had no idea, but the American Rhododendron Society rates each plant according to hardiness, with those in the H-1 category being the hardest to destroy. I'd pick one of those and fine-tune the choice, depending on ultimate size and the color of bloom.

To call a rhododendron evergreen is slightly misleading, because although they remain green, the leaves curl up as if in pain during very cold weather. Some may think they're pretty all year long, but I suffer for (and with) them in midwinter, which is why I only wanted one, and a dwarf one at that. Still, just as the shrub screen needed anchoring, with weighted plants to hold the space between the deciduous shrubs (the ones that lose their leaves every autumn), this back corner needed anchoring as well. Without a little more evergreen in that back corner, the eye would have no place to rest throughout a good part of the year, except on one curled-up rhododendron and the skeletal branches of future deciduous shrubs neither in leaf nor in bloom.

To address this, along the fence, about three feet out, I sketched in three *Euonymus kiautschovicus* (sorry about that) 'Manhattan', just as easily found by asking for euonymus 'Manhattan'. These evergreen shrubs are named after the Big Apple because they flourish all through Central Park. They're impervious to pollution, they grow up to five or six feet in sun or shade, need no special care and they don't mind visits from dogs and, presumably, muggers. The reason I wanted them, though, is that they look incredibly *clean* all the time, even if it hasn't rained in a month. The leaves are shiny dark green, and shiny is a texture I wanted. What is more, these shrubs don't call attention to themselves, and I knew they could be a solid background plant if someday I felt ambitious enough to pull that bed forward and add to it. Left alone, their form is softly bottom-heavy, but you can also clip them to square them off, or plant them in a row to make a hedge; sometimes you can buy them pretrained to climb a trellis, wall, or fence.

There are many other varieties of euonymus in addition to 'Manhattan', and they're usually described without much excitement as "useful" in the garden, which I think is patently unfair. Yes, they're useful, but there's more to them than that. It takes many kinds of shrubs to cushion and enclose a space, to make it feel lush and rich and replete. Unassuming shrubs like those in this genus add color, texture, density and complexity; they're quiet, reliable performers whose presence makes the whole stage resonate—the essential chorus.

In the nurseries in my area, sometimes you can find several varieties of euonymus and sometimes not. Two that are usually available are *E. Fortunei* 'Variegatus' and *E. alatus,* commonly known as the burning bush, because the leaves turn a brilliant flame red in autumn; worth it, plus you can cut the autumn branches to bring indoors. The 'Variegatus' types (there are several subcategories of these, some with leaves that are yellowish, some with leaves that are grayish green) have small variegated leaves, grow up and out, and will also affix themselves to any wall or fence that happens to be behind them. In a nursery, you'd scarcely notice them. In the garden, you would. I tucked a couple behind my 'Manhattans', but showing through, up against the fence.

Staggered among the euonymus I drew several photinia, shrubs I'd seen for the first time just a few days before, when I was prowling a nursery: *Photinia benthamiana.* Though you'd never guess it, photinia is a distant member of the rose family. What drew me to the plant was its coppery leaves, growing not tightly together but loosely, so that every leaf seemed visible. They're evergreen, or evercopper, growing fast up to about fifteen feet, and they need sun. I could easily imagine them snug against the dark green of the euonymus.

Just in front, I drew a kerria (*Kerria japonica* 'Pleniflora'), a smaller shrub (also in the rose family, but neither of these requires the special care that many roses do) that flowers on the early side, and whose blooms always look as if they've been startled awake. The genus was named for a Kew gardener called Kerr, which sounds like the beginning of a limerick. There's something funny about this shrub, and vivacious, and whereas other shrubs are said to draw birds or butterflies when in bloom, this one attracts children. It may or may not go on blooming here and there throughout the summer; the stems stay green in the winter. 'Pleniflora' implies plenty of flowers, but all the kerrias, and there aren't very many of them, are easy and reliable, in sun or even a good deal of shade, and if this one wasn't available, I'd settle for another one that was.

Next, where the fence turned at a right angle, I sketched an arc of abelia, one of the prettiest shrubs I know and, again, one that doesn't generate the fanfare it should. *Abelia* is a small genus, with little variation among the few species. It's usually sold by the genus name only;

take what you can find. This shrub, which shows to better effect when you plant several together, is compact, about four feet maximum, and more or less evergreen ("ever pinkish green," really, with tiny leaves); most species produce tiny but lovely, trumpet-shaped flowers in one or another shade of pink late in the summer (one or two bloom early). It's quiet, and a plant that one comes to love more as time goes by.

At each end of the abelias, I sketched in one *Hydrangea paniculata* 'Grandiflora', known as the Peegee hydrangea, and in front of each of those, a couple of *Hydrangea arborescens* 'Annabelle'.

There were hydrangeas already penciled in on the other side of the garden, I know, but I thought a few more, and different ones, here and there would offer a "theme," or a sense of hydrangea refrain. Besides, the smaller Peegee blooms earlier than the 'Nikko Blue' and, because it never grows more than about four feet high, would suit this smaller space. The flowers are creamy colored, and fine for displaying indoors.

'Annabelle' blooms later, in August to September, and the blooms turn from creamy to pinkish; the lower branches are often clipped off to shape this shrub like a small tree. It's good for framing a gate, doorway or path or for marking the end of a row of shrubs. These are the blooms, too, that solve the problem of dried flowers for the winter. Cut them when they're scarcely past their peak, allowing plenty of stem. Then put them indoors in water. When the water evaporates, don't do anything else; just let them dry. Once they're dry, and this step is optional, spray them lightly with hair spray to hold the petals, and to make them easier to dust off (otherwise they get kind of cobwebby, at least in my house). Come the following summer, pile them in a bouquet in the fireplace, if you have one, and they'll look pretty all season, when it's not in use.

One more specimen was all I could squeeze into this back corner, even with the pencil newly sharpened, and probably more than would comfortably fit, but in it went anyway, for now: a fragrant viburnum, *Vibernum Carlesii*, a shrub which grows eventually to six or seven feet, blooms late in the spring and is, as advertised, sublimely fragrant. The buds are pink, and the flowers open to white. They're followed by berrylike fruits which, after that amazing scent, aren't going to change your life, but there you are.

No, on second thought, out came the fragrant viburnum, catapulted to just inside the garden gate. That fragrance, however seasonal, belongs closer to the house, I decided, and this way, I could enjoy it every time I went out or carried in the groceries, without making a special trip all the way to the back.

I had been sketching as if I had all the time in the world, when suddenly I noticed that not only had the house next door (privet side) been sold, but also that the new owners, a young couple who told us sweetly that they were planning a "few renovations," were erecting what looked like the Empire State Building right on the property line. The most drastic screening measures yet were called for: bamboo.

SCREENING WITH A VENGEANCE: BAMBOO

Bamboo is the king of ornamental grasses, one of the most efficient (too efficient, in the minds of some gardeners) ways to block out neighbors. The tall stems really do look like the tops of those window shades you bought premade for college dorm rooms, and the top foliage is evergreen. They grow tall, two stories high or more if you let them, although there are also dwarf varieties, and close together, so that they rustle meditatively, like quiet wind chimes without any clanging. Actually, the word *bamboo* is misleading, because several genera are included under the bamboo umbrella, but the one I had in mind is the most common, *Pseudosasa japonica,* which requires a sheltered spot and a fair amount of dampness.

There are no shortcuts to planting bamboo, however; it needs to be blockaded right from the start, because once bamboo takes off, spreading underground where you can't see it, there's no stopping it. If we were to plant it, we'd be okay on our side, I knew, because we'd be planting it where the driveway had been—the innermost part of the driveway, that is, that our new garden gate had cut off and that Michael, in a surprising burst of energy, had been able to break up with a sledgehammer and wedge. We'd covered it over with topsoil and grass seed, but left in the ground its deep concrete border. It was surely strong enough to contain the bamboo on our side.

I could see, though, that this as yet imaginary bamboo, thwarted on our side, would make fast headway directly into the new neighbors' foundation. Because they were clearly feeling guilty about taking away a good deal of our sun with their new, and very tall, house, I pounced on them with the bamboo plan, and they seemed just as pleased with it as I was. As part of their construction work, they had already dug out the earth around their foundation, and now unrolled into this moat-like dugout a twelve-inch sheet of metal, which would contain the bamboo on their side. Such are the negotiations, I hoped, that would make good neighbors.

By choosing bamboo to anchor this twelve-foot stretch of the property line, I had violated the sunny cottage-garden mood that the rest of the shrubs I had in my plans suggested. This might be a problem, but didn't have to be, if I could figure out in advance how to avert it. Bamboo imparts a mood that's cool, dark, quiet and serene—at its best a horticultural chapel. Planted here, at the entryway to the garden, the bamboo would serve as a foyer to the rest of the garden, a self-contained "room" with a self-contained mood. Ornamental grasses, a subject about which I knew nothing except that bamboo is usually placed in the same category, could set the space, and the mood, off from the rest of the garden.

ORNAMENTAL GRASSES

They're enjoying a burst of popularity now, the ornamental grasses, and they are a bold gesture, in the right place. Used in the back of a flower border, or as a shrub to help delineate the outlines of a garden, they show off the wind dramatically, keeping their form all year. They also grow thick, effectively blocking out any weeds underneath them. I've even heard that some people spray-paint them in bright colors in the fall, which apparently doesn't hurt them and might be whimsical against a snowy winter landscape, although it sounds like a lot of unnecessary trouble to me. They bloom—plume, rather—late in the season, and you can leave the plumes just as they are to dry over the winter (more natural and easier than spray-painting), before pruning in the spring.

One reason I'd never learned anything about them is that I've always associated them with the kinds of gardens I've never had—in big gardens at the seashore; in open, prairielike settings; near a pool or pond or in a garden, even a very small one, where you're trying to create a dense, jungle atmosphere. But most of them need considerable space, or so I'd always thought, to fit the scale of their surroundings.

Not for the first time, I was wrong. They're not all six feet high, and don't all bring to mind images of the great migration in Kenya. As demand for grasses has gone up, so has supply, and many of the grasses I see now in the catalogs and at the nurseries are softer and smaller scale, more in keeping with the way most of us plan to garden. There are also grasses variegated in greens and yellows, new varieties in blue and some grasses that tolerate a little shade.

Out came the fragrant viburnum from just inside the garden gate, and in went a *Miscanthus sinensis* 'Morning Light', with a couple of lower-growing *Hakonechloa macra* 'Aureola' in front of that, chosen from the catalogs spread out in front of me. A squiggle in front of *those* indicated that if I had enough room later on, I'd plant a row of grasses lower-growing still to edge this small bed. A few more 'Aureola' at a right angle to the bamboo, edged perhaps with hostas, which I saw in a picture, might be the right way to mark the far end of this foyer and open up to the "real" garden, but because these grasses were new to me, I wanted to proceed slowly and see how they worked. A straight line for now, with an opening in the middle to walk through; I'd fill in the rest of the "room" later.

. . . Fill in the rest of the room later: What was I thinking?

With any luck, I might be able to afford a *tenth* of these enclosing shrubs now, or next year, not to mention the time and work all this planting would take. Spring was moving along at its usual fast pace, and I wasn't planting; I was drawing squiggles. I had yet to plan my (mostly) perennial border, which had been the point of this entire exercise in the first place. With new resolve, I took my pencil, and my fragrant viburnum, to the border.

Border Checks, Border Balance

❧

New gardeners often make the mistake of thinking too small, reasoning that a flower border three feet wide will be easier to deal with than a border that meanders out farther, say six feet or more. I've also heard it said that you should be able to reach all the way to the back of the border while on your hands and knees. So long as you can squeeze in and out somehow, that's not necessarily true; in gardening, more (garden) can often mean less (work).

A small bed is a small-scale bed: If your flower bed or border is only three feet wide, you'll have to choose plants that contain themselves in an area that compact. If you're going to rely mostly on perennials to brighten a very small space, you'll have to time the sequence of blooms with split-second precision: Just when the Oriental poppies come into bloom and you think you can relax for a minute, boom, they're gone until next year, foliage and all, and you're looking at an empty border. In too small a space, perennials past their peak will often look scruffy, and there won't be room to divert the eye to the *next* plant coming into flower.

Perusing a bigger bed or border, the eye roams around more and tends to rest on the prettiest part. With reasonably careful planting, there is plenty of room for plants coming into and going out of bloom, room for plants to breathe and expand and room for the gardener to maneuver, weed, prune, hide. Even though gardens take several years (or forever) to fill in and look just right, a few dark patches of earth around new plants won't necessarily look bad, even at first; the *eye* will simply sweep across and unify them during the time it takes for nature to fill them in.

What is more, by planning a bigger bed/border, you can also integrate more shrubs into the overall scheme of flowering things. Flowers are, of course, necessary to a flower border, but even more important is creating a stage to show the flowers to their best advantage.

If your border is set flush against the wall of a house, say, or, like mine would be, against a fence, anchoring it first with shrubs will take the eye down gradually from the height of the backdrop to the lowest plants at the front of the border. The drop, for example, from chimney to primrose is too steep, out of proportion; a shrub or more, setting off the graduated levels of perennials, in between high backdrops and the lower plants themselves, will cushion the drop. Even if the flower garden is to be a bed set off without a clearcut backdrop, in the middle of a lawn, perhaps, one or more shrubs edging or centering the bed will herald the space as important, in effect giving the viewer a reference point from which to measure and enjoy the garden that flows around it. Flowers alone aren't enough to reinforce the sense of enclosure that will make the garden all of a piece. Shrubs bolstering the flowers will do the trick. And, while perennials come and go, shrubs will stay green and predictably full all season (or longer, if you throw in a few evergreens), thereby anchoring the space no matter what is, or isn't, in bloom at any given time.

The mathematical formula for this principle is this: If you have a shrub that takes up five feet in a flower border, you'll get credit for five feet of garden. If, on the other hand, you have three perfectly placed (but hard to grow, except in Maine or England) delphiniums in a narrow border listing pathetically like sailboats in a storm, you won't get much credit for anything.

Bearing this in mind, I planned my mixed border, the mix to be composed of a few shrubs, lots of perennials, and whatever annuals were needed to patch the empty spaces.

With the last stretch of remaining fence as the back wall, this border was to undulate between five and eight feet deep for about forty feet, with the doomed catalpa the cut-off point at the shady end. The sunny end, shaded only a couple of hours a day by a tree next door, would stop at the place where the fence turned at a right angle into the back square. I chose an undulating shape because everything else on the property is so boxy—boxy house, square backyard, smaller square off the back, square inside the garden gate. A rounded shape, I figured, would be a softening relief from some of these hard edges. Had the yard been irregular, I would have taken the opposite approach: emphatic rectangular or somehow sharply geometric beds to give definition and corners to the property.

A garden in Brooklyn is finally what made me decide to anchor my border with *Buddleia davidii* 'Nanho Blue', a shrub with small, silvery leaves and lavish bluish purple spires that bloom from July practically through October. (I'm not making this up—they do bloom for the longest time.)

Nestled in a neighborhood with wonderful old brownstones and pocket-size yards, this walled garden is the simplest, most city-proof garden I've ever seen, perfectly in keeping with its setting. Through the locked wrought-iron gate (I've never actually been inside), the garden appears to be in two parts. Edging the grass in the front half is an array of well-trimmed ground covers rising up to some squared off privet and yews, and other evergreen shrubs, small box-leaved hollies maybe, and Manhattan euonymus, pruned in rounded shapes and used as specimens. The subtle combination of heights, shapes and shades of green make this small space seem sturdy and impervious to New York's harsh city air. Ivy climbs the walls; the garden is predominantly green all year. Just before the single step up that leads to the back half is a rough stone bench, very slightly off center, and resting on the ground is a perfect round stone ornament, about the size of a basketball.

Holding court in the center of the back half is a flowering fruit tree of some kind (a pear?); there are also other evergreens enclosing the space. Several roses impart color off and on throughout the season, and a mixture of perennials and annuals artfully dress up the shrubs all the way around.

To the right, though, at the sunny front of the garden as you look in, is a buddleia of one kind or another. Whenever I've walked by, beginning in July and continuing well into the fall, it casts forth long narrow blooms in a muted lavender. Against the silvery leaves, and in this green, green garden, the blooms are an accent and centerpiece all at once: They don't stand out too much, yet they draw the eye right away. They'd be just right, I decided, for the back of my border, and a little research told me that *B. d.* 'Nanho Blue' would be the right variety, its leaves more delicate than some of the other varieties, which would mix well with flowers.

From my point of view, buddleia had other factors in its favor as well. It's familiar here in my part of the country (so I knew it would do well), but not so overused as to be cliché. It's inexpensive (usually under $20) and troublefree: When you're warned against overfeeding, as you are with the buddleias, you know you've got an accommodating plant on your hands. I liked the idea, too, that one of its common names is the butterfly bush (the other is summer lilac), as it attracts butterflies (and hummingbirds, a friend reports). And here's one of the many cases where an artless common name is more lyrical than its proper one: the genus was named for the Reverend Adam Buddle, an English botanist.

Buddleia grows fast. Too fast, in the view of a friend who advised me against planting it in the border itself. He thought it might outgrow the space in scale, especially once there were flowers planted as well. 'Nanho Blue', one of the smaller-growing varieties, reaches eight feet even so, and with a generous spread but, weighing the pros and cons, I decided in its favor. It would be a last fadeout in the fall border, and it would, sooner than many other shrubs, give the impression of effusiveness, which was essential, since I was literally starting from scratch. If they got too big a few years down the road, well, that was a problem I could face later, by moving them if I had to—never an ideal solution for shrubs, but something that's done all the time, aesthetic possibilities outweighing practical risks. Some short-term pleasures, I decided, are worth a risk.

PLANTING IN ODD NUMBERS AND TRIANGLES
I drew three buddleia spaced far apart at the back of the border, the middle one just a little farther forward than the two at each of the ends.

It soon becomes second nature that when planning a flower border you plant the shrubs and perennials in odd numbers—threes, fives and sevens, rather than in even numbers—twos, fours and sixes.

This is one of those rules that seems puzzling at first, until you get down on your hands and knees and begin to understand how gardens grow, which is unevenly. When it comes to architecture, you can have two columns and two windows and a chimney on each side of a door, and if properly designed, the effect will be that of a pleasing symmetry. Try that in a run-of-the-mill garden, or at least one that's not constructed very formally, and you're doomed: Your garden will inevitably look crooked. An absolutely even, matched effect simply won't work, because the plants won't cooperate by growing in even, matched ways.

The odd-number trick will compensate for nature's waywardness on this point. If in a border you have two buddleia over there, close together, and one over *there,* it won't matter if they match up in height and fullness. The three shrubs will still be unified visually, as will counterpoint groupings of other shrubs or flowers, where you have, for example, one daisy over *here,* and two over there.

In addition to planting in odd numbers, it's a worthwhile design trick to plant with an overall deference to triangles, all sorts of triangles which, according to my dictionary and not my memory of geometry, are right, isosceles, equilateral, obtuse, acute, and scalene. A more useful way to think of it is to plant in big triangles, barely noticeable triangles, dramatic triangles, close-together triangles, and triangles so subtle and far apart that only you will recognize them as such. If you plant instead in rows or squares, the eye will go back and forth in dizzying straight lines, as if it were watching a Ping-Pong match.

By triangulating the border, on the other hand, you'll encourage the eye to seek out the matching bits and to roam. One lamb's ear at the front of a border with two equilaterally behind it give the illusion of depth, much more interesting than three in a row. Only to the knowing eye will the border look like a bunch of triangles overlapping and intersecting one another in a big scribble—which is okay, because the knowing eye already knows about odd numbers and triangles and will approve. To the casual observer, the garden will be full of surprising angles and edges, yet will seem drawn together in some mysterious way.

These triangles, too, will help you achieve those pesky *drifts* the catalogs and books are always talking about, masses of flowers tumbling and overflowing naturally and expansively, not placed in an overly orderly or regimented way. Planting in rows alone, however tempting, will ultimately yield a checkerboard. Later, when you're sick of triangles, you can break the rules, with a little row of this and one or two or four of that; a fully established border welcomes even more complexity and variation. In the early stages, however, planting in odd numbers and triangles will yield a garden that fits together seamlessly, with the groupings of plants sliding together like puzzle pieces, not just colliding with each other front to back.

So the buddleia served two purposes, lining the back of the border and also reinforcing the commitment to enclosing the entire garden in shrubs. They looked a little sparse, though, in my drawing, just the three of them back along the fence. I had read that buddleia needs to be cut back harshly every year around mid-April, and I thought that just when all the flowers, once I planted them, would be coming up, the buddleia would be down for the dormancy count; when it grows up each year, it does so fast, but late in the season.

So I drew in two other shrubs, spring-blooming ones, to make a triangle of five shrubs instead of three. Between the buddleia at one end and the one in the middle I found a home for my fragrant viburnum, *Viburnum Carlesii,* and between the one in the middle and the one at the other end, I drew in a *Philadelphus* × 'Beauclerk', if I could find one, or *P.* 'Virginal'. The fragrant mock orange, so-called because the blossoms look like and smell as sweet as orange blossoms, is a shrub I feel particularly sentimental about because it's one of the first I ever loved, absolutely beautiful and perfectly easy to grow. Two fragrant shrubs, each of which would ultimately reach about eight feet, blooming in the spring—and the mock orange might also bloom a little more here and there throughout the rest of the season—would anchor and perfume the border in the spring, and both would soon provide headily fragrant branches that I could cut to bring indoors. (If these varieties aren't readily available, make certain that you find another variety that's fragrant. Some aren't, and if you're going to plant mock orange, it would be a shame, pretty blossoms notwithstanding, to miss out on the scent.) Not long after the spring blooms would finish, the buddleia would take over the blooming chores, so that during a good part of the season there would be shrubs in flower at the back of the border.

And flowers in front.

I had coaxed my graph-paper garden into squiggles, flourishes, and more than a few smudges. Now it was time to coax a real garden into bloom.

$\mathcal{G}$roundwork

∿

A reasonably good-natured fellow, Michael had never expressed any interest whatever in gardening, beyond asking occasionally, "What's this called, again?" about the lilac that was already growing alongside our driveway. I had hoped that he'd catch the fever sooner or later, mostly so that there would be that much less work for me, and when I explained that I was about to turn over the earth to start planting the border, I took it as a promising sign when he volunteered to pitch in.

With the periphery of the entire yard to be cultivated, we had a huge chore ahead of us, and I thought that the prospective forty by eight-foot mixed border seemed as good a place as any to begin our tilling. One fine day (actually, it was hot, muggy and decidedly unpleasant, as I recall), we began tilling, or cultivating, our border, using our one spade and a borrowed one. The idea, I explained, was to dig up and turn over the dirt as far down as we could, then pull out all the grass and weed clumps.

As I handed Michael his spade, I gave one last fleeting thought to raised beds, an idea that someone had suggested and that I'd rejected, figuring they'd be too expensive or bothersome. I think a part of me was also daunted by the idea, fearful, maybe, that raised beds would imply I was really serious about this gardening business (and, therefore, culpable for my design gaffes), whereas planting at ground level would imply that, hey, this was a garden that just happened. I was wrong, and to this day I still think about changing a few things around and installing some raised beds, which can transform the contours of any garden, and are well worth considering at the outset.

Raised beds are like giant, garden-bed-size window boxes for the ground, about knee height, in any shape you want, and usually made from wood or railroad ties; sometimes beds are raised more elaborately and walled in stone or brick. Such beds elevate the garden, literally and visually, providing a stage into which the garden is planted. They can offer height to a monotonous flat place, or level off an uneven, bumpy space. And they look important, with the bed itself becoming a built-in structural element in the garden. Or you can use raised beds (even premade ones) more sparingly, two of them to mark an opening or pathway, for example, or as a way to set off one particular bed, like a rosebed or a raised bed of herbs.

Raised beds are also kind to gardeners. They're easier on the knees, for one thing; you can just sit on the edge and do the snipping, your tools, diet soda and other essentials right next to you on the edge. And there's less weeding to begin with, because you fill them with virgin topsoil that you buy at the store. They're also excellent for drainage, even though raised beds do dry out faster (and need more watering) than ground-level beds. But I'd imagined that topsoil would be prohibitively expensive, thousands and thousands of dollars. Turns out that a pickup-truck load of topsoil, which after all is nothing more than cleaned-up dirt, runs only about $40. With a carpenter spending a couple of days building simple raised wooden boxes and a few pickup-truck loads of virgin topsoil, I would have created a different garden entirely—a missed chance. Maybe someday, in my next garden.

With Michael standing there dubiously holding his spade, I also gave a fleeting thought to rototilling. Rototillers are either hand-held machines or larger ones you ride like lawn mowers, rented at hardware stores or garden centers or borrowed from friends, that loosen and chop up the earth—deeper and better than you can do it yourself—to make it ready for planting. Had Michael and I done it ourselves, or even hired someone to help out, rototilling this particular bed would have taken us a couple of hours instead of a day, and also warned us in time that I had probably picked the wrong place for the border. But no, for some primal (or foolish) reason, I wanted to turn the soil by hand.

Each third of the forty-foot border we tackled presented an entirely different, and barely surmountable, problem.

We soon learned that the back third, where we started, had once been covered by a small greenhouse, no more than five or six feet square, in which—I swear—plastic roses had been cultivated. Our spades hit against an immovable concrete floor, turning up dirt glinting with shards of broken glass, which were obscured by layers of weeds, tangled ivy and some twisted and deeply entrenched wisteria vines. Scattered among these ruins were the plastic roses, dozens of them, an occasional bit of broken crockery and the odd pinecone, painted red. We cleaned up as best we could, but even today, with the garden at the end of its second year, the ground often spits up more of these roses or pinecones, not to mention broken glass, which I find strewn about the plants I've tucked around the concrete floor of the former greenhouse, to try to hide it.

In the middle third of the border, our spades again clanged against something hard, but with a more metallic ring. An inch or two of soil covered a four-foot square of steel which, when lifted, disclosed a rather sinister underground room, at least ten feet deep, walled in brick and entirely empty—a bootlegger's storage vault? We now had a four-foot-square steel trapdoor as the centerpiece of our "border."

In the near third, closest to the house—stone again, a big square stone with a rusty ring on top under which we found an unused well, with water sloshing only a few feet down.

By the end of this, we felt more like failed archaeologists than gardeners, and needless to say, I had gotten over my urge to turn the soil by hand; rototillers from now on. As for Michael, he hadn't taken to gardening in the least.

Every friend I consulted said to move the border now, before it was too late. *Before* it was too late? To me, after all that work, it already *was* too late. We'd cultivated the border, and now it was time, or nearly time, to plant it.

There are, as the books and catalogs will tell you, all kinds of regimens and feeding schedules to know about each and every plant. Knowing this is intimidating enough to be paralyzing; no one wants to think that if he or she fails to care for a plant by the book, he or she will surely be the agent of its demise. Two years into my garden now, a garden with the most ordinary soil and sun, I'm still learning, still reading, still finding my way—yet most of the plants have stood by me, despite my benign neglect. This year, for instance, I remembered to feed my peony not only early in the spring, before it bloomed, but just after it bloomed as well, so that *next* year I'll supposedly have more actual blooms. Now I know, too, to add a little bonemeal to the irises when I'm cutting them up to make more irises.

But this kind of knowledge takes time to learn, and time to carry out; it won't sink in all at once. You can start your garden without it. The funny thing is, once you see the skeleton of a garden, the plants will take on a new significance. You'll *want* to learn to care for them properly, and you'll slowly accumulate the knowledge to do so. If well launched in a well-prepared bed, and barring unforeseen mishaps, they'll probably survive just fine till you catch up to them.

Think of a newly tilled bed or border as a brand-new refrigerator, just plugged in. Now you have to fill it with nutritious things to eat, and replenish it from time to time. Perhaps the orange juice cubby-hole will have to be filled more often than the mustard shelf—you can think about that later. For now, just a store of staples will do. Same thing with your newly tilled bed.

From the tilling stage on, just about every single thing you do in your garden will be subject to controversy. Opinions vary widely as to what, exactly, is the right thing to do in every case for the soil and the plants. There are organic gardeners, and those whose gardens are so teeming with chemicals that it might be dangerous to light a match nearby. There are people who use only store-bought fertilizers (and never bother with manure), and those who use *only* manure (and find store-bought manure horticulturally déclassé). There are people who plant only by the moon, and those (like me) who plant only when it's convenient. I once quarreled with a friend about whether to cut daylilies all the way back to the ground in the fall; she said no, and I said yes. It wasn't much of a quarrel, though, and she stuck to her guns, I to mine; both sets of daylilies, I'm happy to report, are doing just fine.

In gardening as in most things, I usually take the middle ground, distilling information and acting on what's easiest and what sounds most logical and pleasant. As for anticipating problems, why kill yourself over problems that might *never* arise? Just get things started, without doing too much troubleshooting before there's trouble.

The arguments actually start with tilling itself, as natural an instinct to gardeners as breathing. Some gardeners even recommend that, after an overall tilling to set the bed in place, you should never again cultivate (or till or turn over) the soil. The advantage to cultivating is that you aerate the soil that way, and can dig in fertilizer as you turn the earth over. The disadvantage is that the particles of untilled soil meld together to form what are called peds, which have something to do with spores and which, once formed, are beneficial to the soil. Tilling breaks up these peds. The middle ground: A little tilling every spring, and certainly when you're planting, to fold in some nourishment can't hurt too much and might help some.

As to preparing the soil, here again there is absolutely no one horticulturally correct way, so I again stick to the middle ground. To prepare my border for planting, I bought peat moss, dehydrated cow manure and, just to be on the safe side, some standard, all-purpose-granular fertilizer: 10-10-10, ten parts each of nitrogen, potassium and phosphorus.

Peat moss is the accumulation of mosses that build up in soggy layers in bogs over centuries, ecologically speaking as important to the Northern Hemisphere as the tropical rain forests are to the Southern Hemisphere. The peat we see in the stores is usually labeled sphagnum peat moss; sphagnum is a kind of moss. Peat moss, dried and pressed, is the perfect planting medium—and that's the trouble.

Peat enriches the soil as it decomposes and, when it's folded in correctly, acts as a sponge to help the earth, and therefore the plants, hold water. It's great, too, for mixing in with the soil when you're first planting shrubs or perennials. (Too much of it, too close to the surface of the soil, however, can also act as a sponge, but one that keeps moisture *away* from the roots of plants.) The problem lies in that the peat bogs, which take thousands of years to replenish themselves, are being depleted, fast. It's a tough call. Nurseries and farming centers still carry bales of it, piled high every spring, as if it were in infinite supply, so it's hard to make oneself worry about it too much; and no way around it, there's no easy substitute for peat (not so far, anyway, but marketers are working on low-peat and faux-peat products). Yet it seems wrong to pretend the problem doesn't exist.

My own compromise has been to dig a fair amount of it into each newly made bed as I dig it, and then to use it sparingly, only when planting shrubs or good-size perennials. By a fair amount of it, I mean that I spread an even layer of it, about two inches thick, over the soil, or an inch of it into a hole dug for a shrub, or just a sprinkling for a new perennial. In new beds, I follow the peat with another layer of dehydrated cow manure (dehydrated for me because, without going into the pros and cons of dehydrated versus nondehydrated, I have read that nondehydrated manure can burn the plants more easily), spread thinner than the peat moss, scattered in handfuls, so that the darker manure lets the lighter peat show through. Then the sprinkling of fertilizer. One ten-pound bag will more than cover my border; instructions on the bag will tell you how much to use. Compost would have completed the preparations, but it takes a far better planner than I am to put in a compost pile *before* a garden. For me, compost would come later. Having spread all this over the border, I then went back and turned the whole mess over again with a spade to dig in the peat, manure and fertilizer; this process of preparing the soil is called top-dressing. Lonely, tedious work, this; Michael had long since fled.

But I had my three buddleia to plant, to anchor the back of my forty-foot border.

I dug the first hole at the back edge, where the fence diverts at a strict right angle; my hope was that the buddleia there would make you think the border extends even beyond where you can see. Six feet in from the other end went the second shrub, with the thought that I could plant other things under and around it, so that the border would slope off and not end too abruptly. To complete the buddleia triangle, I brought the third one about three feet forward, maybe six feet to the right of the exact center of the border; thus these shrubs draw the eye out-in-out, rather than forcing it to slide in a straight line across the back. The triangle is scalene, technically, with the longest line at the back of the border. I placed them before I planted them, and they looked right, close up and from a distance.

To plant shrubs, dig a hole bigger than the pot the plant comes in. Scatter an inch or so of peat in the bottom of the hole, then dig some more so that the soil in the bottom mixes with the peat; otherwise the peat will work as a flat sponge and the roots will become waterlogged. Then throw in some superphosphate, a compound that encourages fast root growth, sprinkled as if you were sprinkling sugar on a cereal you didn't like very much: a thin coating lightly covering the top. (If you've already prepared the bed with manure and fertilizer, the shrub, once planted, will also realize those benefits.) Stir again.

Sometimes, if you're lucky, the plant slides out of the pot fairly easily; otherwise you have to jiggle it around, pulling carefully so as not to smash the top. If it's big, you may need two people, one to hold the pot and one to ease the plant out sideways. The potting mixture in which the roots are bound will probably be tight enough that the plant can stand erect, as if it were still in the pot. Roll the root-end of the plant around on the ground, inserting a spade or trowel into it about four or five times to loosen the roots. You'll have to jam the spade or trowel in pretty hard, but don't worry about that. Spread the loosened roots around the bottom of your hole. If the rootball comes wrapped in burlap, not in a pot, cut the cord that's wrapped and tied around it and see if the burlap is embedded into the plant. If the burlap pulls off easily, loosen and remove it, ease the plant into the hole and position it upright. If the burlap holds tight to the rootball, leave it in place when you slide the plant into the hole; it will decompose on its own.

Now you can fill the hole up with soil, making a kind of moat or well—as in a child's sand castle—built about four or five inches around the circumference of the base of the plant; this will hold water. Then water the shrub, by dribbling water from a hose till the moat stays full, and keep watering nearly every day for the first two weeks and, especially during the plant's first season, every time it seems to be drying out (when the soil looks gray and dried out on top, that is, when it looks dry when you turn it over with a trowel and especially when the plant itself is visibly wilting: You'll be able to tell all too well).

Repeat procedure with every subsequent shrub.

Over the course of that first spring and autumn of planting, we rototilled and prepared a shrubwide band of earth around the periphery of the yard, planting as many shrubs as we could, and leaving room for more later. Within a few years—I concede a five-year plan, give or take—the garden would be enclosed and cushioned with shrubs, divided into all the rooms and moods this quarter of an acre could contain. From the beginning, though, the buddleia looked reproachful, all alone in the big border. They were waiting for flowers.

3
Planting the Garden

Picturing the Border

There are a few exceptional gardens that I visit at least two or three times a season, to enjoy them, to study them, to feel inspired (if a little defeated) afterward. As often as I visit, though, it's hard to get my bearings, because these gardens change so much from year to year, when their "choreographers" execute whatever new ideas excite them at the moment. Paths become ponds, small separate beds join to become big beds, and gates and plant-lined alleyways pop up where they weren't before. Good gardens evolve and change. One constant I've noticed, however, is that somewhere in all these gardens, no matter how intricate or sophisticated, there's a lavish supply of daylilies.

I've also noticed that every time I visit these gardens, the daylilies, sometimes hundreds of them, seem to have been whisked to a different place.

I can easily see why. Daylilies (the genus is *Hemerocallis*), with their abundant, strappy leaves that move easily in the wispiest breeze, are pretty all season, especially when in bloom. They bloom over a long period of time, maybe three weeks or a month, one daylily per day, which dies off to be replaced the next day by the next bloom. If you plan well, and introduce early-, mid- and late-season varieties, you can have daylilies in bloom, in a range of pinks, peaches, salmons, reds, yellows and oranges, for just about the whole summer, with the leaves holding their space handsomely the rest of the season. The tags at the nursery will specify the height, color and blooming time.

Their care is simple: They don't mind some sun, and they don't mind a good deal of shade, although they don't bloom as well in deep shade. Okay soil is fine. In the spring, you fertilize them when you fertilize everything else. After they finish blooming, they like to be cut back, stems and leaves both, or mowed, on the highest setting, after which their leaves come back again just as they were before for the rest of the season. After a couple of years, they multiply; just dig them up, pull the root clumps apart, replant them and suddenly you have twice as many plants to play with as you did before.

Still, there *is* something about daylilies that makes you want to move them. Perhaps it's because they're almost too reliable, or too familiar, for the mixed border. If that's to be the centerpiece of your garden, the effect you want is the equivalent to bringing out the best china for company. Pretty as they are, daylilies feel more everyday or casual in spirit, a little too at home in the garden to feel like special-occasion plants.

Daylilies are among the perfect "starter perennials." They're pretty and full all season, they'll get your garden growing fast and, if you want to replace them, you'll always find a new spot that suits them fine: as starters for a new bed, surrounding a tree, circling a birdbath, in an exuberant clump edging a fence or a gate.

In the lexicon of plants, *starter perennials* are those that are hardest to kill, most readily expand into the "drifts" that will make a border feel full, are beautiful and respected plants that have, over the horticultural years, achieved the status of classics. With standard care, they're about as foolproof as plants can get. On their own they're steady and not necessarily very glamorous. Taken together, however, they add up to a garden.

HEIGHT

The front of the border, the midborder and the back of the border are the height-driven areas into which you'll want to introduce starter perennials. For once the rule is logical: shorter plants go in the front, the tallest plants line the back, the rest spread out in the middle.

The front of the border can be a little worrisome: Do you want ground-hugging plants, or higher but still low-growing plants or a mixture of both? A selection of plants all the way along the front growing up-down-up-down can look silly. Undulating the foreground, on the other hand, with plants of slightly varying heights curving up or dipping down—slightly taller plants, for instance, at the far ends, so that you can see them from wherever you're standing—can look wonderful. You don't want the whole border, front to back, to rise up *too* evenly, like an empty set of bleachers. You want it to look like bleachers once they're filled: thematically intact with people (or flowers, in the case of the garden), but alive with the natural variations in height, color and texture that occur within the theme.

Same with the midborder. By midborder, does one mean astilbe, about a foot tall with plumes that rise above it, or lythrum, closer to three feet? The nursery tag or catalog or seed copy will usually give you a ball-park ultimate height—two to three feet or three to four feet—but that won't necessarily be much help; the difference of a foot is a huge one in the border. Moreover, a plant about to (or in) bloom is not even necessarily the height and spread the plant will achieve at its peak. After a couple of happy years in the garden, your reliably two-foot tall plant could soar like a teenager at puberty and throw everything else off kilter.

It's not an absolute rule that every midborder plant has to be of uniform height. A few lower plants tucked behind some slightly higher see-through plants will sometimes work in your favor, causing the eye to seek out hidden treasures. But let the hidden treasures be those you choose to hide, not those buried or strangled by other plants around them. Don't let the midborder become the Bermuda Triangle of the garden.

By this point, it should come as no surprise that the background plants, the back-of-the-border plants, may also fall prey to the issue of relative size: How big is big? Big enough to show their faces behind the midborder selection, one hopes, but how do you tell? Be careful here of relying too much on the size of the plants you see at the nursery early in the spring. If the tag says they will, these plants will shoot up impressively over the course of the summer. Take a late-season visit to a nursery and you'll see the tallest perennials—hollyhocks, for instance—tumbling out of their pots and staked to within an inch of their lives. These huge plants were tiny little things just a couple of months before. You can't rely on your eye. Rely on the description on the tag.

If you start by staggering your plants in triangles, allowing them plenty of room to stretch and spread at the outset, you'll soon see whether the placement by height seems right, at least for now. One difference between shrubs and perennials is that most perennials are much easier, and safer, to move. You'll miscalculate height from time to time; everyone does. And you'll get new ideas or change your mind about placement. Any arrangement that's simply all wrong can be rectified easily by digging up the plant (in early spring, *after* it's bloomed or in the fall) and moving it to a place that suits it better. It's not cruel to move perennials to get the effect you want, but do it carefully.

COLOR

Color is another consideration, since a border, like a room, should have enough—but not too much—color at once. My own preference is for soft colors (pinks, blues, lavenders, whites), accented by the occasional brilliant splash of red or yellow. You may want more yellow or more red, but be careful: Reds can clash, and too much yellow can glare. Vita Sackville-West's famous white garden at Sissinghurst notwithstanding, a monochromatic border—all purples, say—is usually not a good idea. If you love one color, set it off in a bed of its own. For the mixed border itself, a blend of blooms in softer colors tends to harmonize more willingly.

For my garden, I was after a traditional Giverny palette of pastels, defined by the colors of the flowers and, more important, the color and texture of the green that buoys most perennials. Yes, I wanted color and spectacular blossoms. Nevertheless, no matter how sensational perennial blooms are, they're fleeting, here today and gone tomorrow, or at best in a couple of weeks. In the end, it's the foliage, the green part (or occasionally crimson, or bluish) of the plants that holds the space longest; if the greens set one another off well, they'll accentuate the contrasting colors and the garden will be a success. Most of any flower garden is green most of the time, so if you choose the greens well, with regard to texture, staying power and nuances of color—silvery green, deeper gray green, shiny bright green, whitish green—they will set off the other colors of the garden better, in addition to supplying color on their own. When you're collecting plants, try to imagine how they'd fit into the garden if they never bloomed at all. If they're pretty anyway, they're very likely the plants you want.

MOOD

You can go any which way with mood; it's your garden, after all. I always think of flowers with up-and-down stems and petals all around—daisy-like flowers, that is—as having a sensibility that's particularly cheery or perky. While perky might be nice on a good day, perhaps you don't want a garden entirely full of relentless cheer. Flowers that grow in a slightly rumpled way, like daylilies, feel casual to me. The muted foxglove is statelier, more formal, whereas the drooping bleeding heart, is melancholy—but pleasantly so, like a poem by Emily Dickinson.

Because this method of rating plants in a hierarchy of moods is a purely subjective matter (in fact, I may well have made the system up), each gardener will have to choose his or her own mood mix according to individual tastes.

My advice, though, is to mix the moods. I once saw a sprawling flower border that edged a sunny open yard. It was laid out very formally, with everything neatly in its place. What seemed strange to me was that all the plantings were those that one usually finds in wilder, more unkempt settings—plume poppies, sunflowers; I remember a lot of *big* things. Even more odd was that somewhere in the middle of all this was a formal-looking small tiled pool. The effect was formidable, at first glance. But the homespun coarseness of these plants all grouped together in front of this small-scale pool made this quasi-formal garden seem spiky to me, not restful or soothing. A one-mood garden would, I think, be as dull to live with as a one-mood person.

THROUGH THE SEASON

Sequence of bloom is another phrase the gardener is advised not to ignore; time is one of the important elements to consider in planning a garden. Sequence of bloom means that you want to plant some things that will bloom early in the season, in the midseason, and late in the season—plus all the times in between. If all the perennials you plant are meant to flower in June, your garden will be hopeless in April, May, July, August and September. Spreading the bounty by spreading out the ETB (estimated time of blooming, a private acronym I share with my neighbor) will give you something in bloom nearly all season,

which will be more effective, and far less embarrassing, should anyone pop in unexpectedly to see the garden, than if you peak for one
shining moment in June.

In the chapters that follow, "starter plants" are included for all
three levels of the border—front, middle, and back. I've tried to
address color, mood and sequence of bloom, and have tried to keep
the Latin to a minimum, although some is unavoidable.

I shocked a gardening friend when I told her that I wasn't including lupines among the "starters"; she happens to be a great fan. I am,
too, I told her—but I simply can't get them to come back the second
year. Nor can many other gardeners I know, which suggests to me that
it's best to leave lupine, along with a lot of other perfectly desirable
plants, for later. For starter plants, the odds for success have to be
overwhelmingly in the gardener's favor. To fill in the garden, in addition to perennials I've also sneaked in a few easy—and pretty—biennials and reseeding annuals, which make the job easier. After that,
you can plant all the lupine you want.

The Front of the Border

Once I started planting things in my border, I found that I spent more time looking at it than actually working in it. Looking with pleasure, with dismay or just watching it mindlessly, I could stare for hours. I could never weed for hours. Apart from staring, I spent, still spend, another significant amount of time shuffling unplanted plants around the garden in their pots, trying to imagine where this plant or that plant would work best to hide some other plant's flaws, to enhance that plant on the left or to see if some new arrangement would make the whole thing come together magically at last. I am as adept at shuffling pots as the card sharks on New York City streets are at dealing hands of three-card monte to naive tourists.

I don't know if other gardeners spend time staring the way I do, or where they stare, but I do most of my staring at the front of the border, where I find that any little traces of soil showing through, not covered by some gardenlike item, is a violation. I know gardens take time to fill in, but I also know that you're supposed to see garden in a garden, not dirt. Needless to say, some plants provide better coverage than others.

Over time I've noticed that a *blur* should be the overriding effect a garden imparts, because blurs do a better job of covering up dirt. And better blurs, in my experience, come from smaller flowers jam-packed onto stems growing closely together than they do from the one-flower-per-stem kind, however lovely they may be. I think this is what Henry Mitchell means when he says it's one of the "commonest" mistakes to "ignore the tremendous effect of small flowers massed." Phlox, with each stem a mass of tiny blossoms, will make a stronger impact taking up a large space in the garden than skinny-stemmed dahlias; the impression phlox leaves behind is of *abundance,* a haze of color and coverage.

The blur rule holds especially true for the front of the border, where the right effect is that of a blanket of foliage and flowers, with as few patches of bare dirt and, well, naked air as possible. A little breathing room farther back won't be nearly as noticeable or distracting.

Primroses (the genus name is *Primula,* suggesting the first flower of the season) and pansies (actually a viola, but asking for pansies will get you there) are about as sweet and basic as you can get in choosing plants that will bloom early in the front of the border, so they were the first flowers to go in mine. I had bought several of each at a greenhouse when it was still too cold to plant them outside, so I displayed them in baskets indoors, where they last a fairly long time and bring spring right into the house. Late in April, when it grew warmer and the plants began to flag indoors, I stuck them in the border.

The primroses, which had already bloomed indoors, sputtered out almost at once. The pansies, however, lasted well into June, because I kept pinching off the finished blooms to make way for new ones. You have time to do things like pinching pansies when they're pretty much the only things you have planted. Pansies, too, are small enough to tuck in anywhere there's a tiny patch of dirt. As it happened, neither came back very extravagantly the second year, although that might have been because my dogs trampled them almost to oblivion. The failure of the primroses to return in force was maddening, both because they had done well for me in my first garden and also because my neighbor has dozens of them growing close together under her flowering cherry tree, and they're lovely, tiny bouquets of blossoms nestled in curving, crinkly leaves. It might not have been my dogs' fault, after all; primroses like filtered shade, and perhaps I planted them in too much sun. Worth a try in any case, especially if you get some indoor mileage from them during the last days of winter.

But primroses and pansies were the warmup plants. I knew I wanted the front of the springtime border to feature the unforgettable blue of the forget-me-not, and I bought three first thing; the tag said *Myosotis* 'Sapphire', and they seemed to me to last a very long time.

They prefer filtered sun to full, and moist conditions, but with forget-me-nots, these are preferences, not demands. They do fine even here in eastern Long Island, where we're prone to droughts and very hot summers. Start a clump somewhere along the front of the border, let them go to seed (that is, get leggy and spindly and lose their flowers), then cut them back nearly to the ground; the odds are pretty good that you'll have many more forget-me-nots next year, from the seeds that have fallen at random. They bloom from midspring into early summer—from mid- to late April to early to mid-June, depending on what kind of a spring we're having—tiny flowers (an actual blur of them) in the most romantic blue. The first autumn after I'd planted the store-bought ones, I sprinkled two seed packets of them here and there between other things in the front of the border; they're very easy to grow from seed. By the second spring, I had all the forget-me-nots I'd ever need. And even though the foliage that remains after the bloom (what little there is of it) is thoroughly unattractive, it's easy enough to nestle other plants around them, so you won't even notice. The forget-me-nots violated the "rule" about choosing perennials for their foliage as well as their blooms, so to make up for it, I planted some artemisia and lamb's ears, more valued for their season-long silvery foliage than their flowers.

The foliage of *Artemisia schmidtiana* 'Silver Mound', the variety one sees most often in nurseries, seems to shimmer, lighting up the border, and does indeed grow (at least at first) puffed up in the shape of a mound; the genus, named after the Greek goddess Artemis, is a mismatched one, and also includes the herb tarragon, among other things that don't look anything like this silvery mounded stuff. These artemisia, though, should be planted right next to each other because they never grow much bigger than the size you find them in their first year. I was warned against the 'Silver Mound' just in time, however, by a friend who had found that the mound "deflates" in the middle by the second or third year, and so it does, which makes it more irritating that so many nurseries carry only this variety. Unless you like the pancake look in plants that are supposed to be mounded, a better choice is *Artemisia ludoviciana* 'Silver King' or the slightly lower *A. l.* 'Silver Queen', which reach up and out, no mound-shape about them.

They still offer the shimmery silver, and they'll spread out, at least a little bit, each year. Both are readily available in catalogs.

Similarly, *Stachys*, lamb's ears (touch them to find out how it got its name), are another silvery addition that will help define the front of the border. They spread out from year to year, dying off at the center and spreading politely*—but not aggressively—from the edges, so don't start with too many and give them some elbow room. *Stachys lanata* (now sometimes called *S. byzantina*) is the species you'll usually see, and descriptions will tell you that if you don't like the rather sinister-looking, eighteen-inch-high flowers, which come in July, you can cut them off when they appear; with lamb's ears, the leaves are the main thing. Better still, see if you can find stachys lanata 'Silver Carpet', especially bred *not* to produce flowers.

Other silvery choices are a low lavender hedge (*Lavandula latifolia* grows only a foot high), snow-in-summer (*Cerastium tomentosum*), and candytuft (*Iberis sempervirens*). They'll all flower beautifully, the lavender mostly in lavender and the other two in low lush hazes of small white flowers early in the summer. Although the latter two go dormant later, they do so so gradually you hardly notice; the silvery lavender foliage remains all season. All these silvery plants need a solid half day of sun or more. Snow-in-summer spreads persistently, too, so you might economize and buy fewer than you'll eventually want.

The ubiquitous lady's-mantle (*Alchemilla mollis*) is another polite spreader and is often described as a "prolific self-seeder." I'm embarrassed to say that I never had much luck with it prolifically self-seeding in my first garden, although every single other gardener I've ever met has it tumbling and trailing through his or her garden; a friend of

---

*To describe a plant as one that spreads "politely" or "persistently" is to describe the ideal starter plant, a collection of which will give you maximum garden as soon as possible. There's a fine but important line between plants that spread readily, as do most of the starters mentioned here, and those that are invasive. Invasive plants behave like invasive armies: They come in where they're not wanted, they conquer the land and it's very hard to get them back out. Persistent or polite spreaders, on the other hand, are easy enough to thin out if they stretch beyond their boundaries. You just dig out a clump where you don't want it, move it somewhere else or give it to a friend.

I used to love the idea of aggressively invasive plants, thinking they'd be the perfect solution to filling up a garden in no time; plant them, I thought, and *let* them take over. Why not? Because the more "threatening" invasive perennials tend to be deep rooted and almost impossible to contain.

It was the gooseneck loosestrife (*Lysimachia clethroides*) that taught me to be cautious about

mine even has it growing, welcome if unbidden, up through the gravel of her driveway, in three-quarters shade. The grayish green leaves are pleated at first, then open in such a way as to cup stray drops of rain or dew; the flowers themselves are yellow, long lasting and delicate for cutting to make tiny bouquets. I experimented with one plant in my new border, which thankfully came back the second year. It has yet to become a prolific self-seeder, but I'm hopeful; I'd love as many more as possible.

Several of the low-growing roses known as 'The Fairy', perhaps because they grow as if governed by a magic wand, went in next.

There's a whole (somewhat discouraging) chapter on roses (later in this part), but the ones discussed there are roses for devoted and responsible gardeners, hybrid teas for the most part that need special care throughout the season to keep them in top, or even middling, form. 'The Fairy', a small shrub rose, is different: self-reliant and proud, it asks very little from a gardener. In fact, apart from an occasional feeding (rose food or standard fertilizer two or three times a season), an occasional watering if it gets very dry, and lots of sun, they ask nothing at all, and will bloom profusely in pink from sometime late in June all the way up until the frost. What is more, the roses seem to grow in perfect bouquets, so that with one stroke of your clippers, you have a minibouquet to display indoors. They grow about two feet high or so, and you'd do just fine having nothing but these roses as a low hedge in the front of any sunny bed.

The rose known simply as 'Sea Foam' is another easy-care choice for the front of the border, and this one, unlike 'The Fairy', will also climb or trail if you direct it to. The 'Sea Foam' is fragrant, and also blooms most of the season in ivory with a pale pink tint.

In a different spirit, *Lamium* and *Aegopodium* are basic starter plants of a whiter shade of green, and I was lucky enough to be able to

---

blithely encouraging plants with invasive tendencies. There was a small patch of these funny white blossoms (they look like upside down swirls of ice cream—the soft kind that comes out of a machine—and they bob in the slightest wind) that bloomed in the midborder late in the summer in my first garden, then an alarmingly larger patch each subsequent year, marching over whatever was in their path. The roots went straight down a foot or more, and were virtually impossible to dig up. I like the way they look, and would plant them again if I had room for them to roam free, but I don't. There may come a time when I'll go to the considerable trouble of putting down some metal edging, six or seven inches deep, in effect a pen to hold them in place. There may also come a time when I read the whole of Proust.

poach a few clumps of each from friends. More often thought of as groundcovers (plants, that is, that can be massed to cover up any area—under a tree, in fairly deep shade, along a slope, lining a walkway) than actual perennials, these two are useful for their foliage only; the flowers are barely worth a mention.

The only aegopodium I've ever seen is the sun-or-shade *A. podagraria* 'Variegatum', with light green leaves edged in white; the lamium of choice is *L. maculatum* 'Beacon Silver', which likes part or mostly shade and which again is variegated in green and white. No doubt some would disagree, but to me both of these are pretty and formal enough to mingle with flowers, providing at the same time a foreground carpet between or among them. They both spread fast, aegopodium especially. If you get a clump of either, you might break it up into a couple of pieces, and set them out in different sections of the edge of the border, just to see where they grow the fastest. Then move the slower growing clump to join the winner, if you want, or just leave it where it is if it looks all right. After two or three years, when you're not so garden-poor and your other plants have stretched out, you may want to replace them, but in the meantime they'll fill in fast. When the time comes to move them, they're easily dug up, and there'll always be another unfinished place for them.

Two other possibilities, one blooming early and one blooming late, are saponaria (the common name is soapwort, because some species have been used in making soap), and plumbago, or *Ceratostigma plumbaginoides*. saponaria likes mostly sun, and plumbago can take a little shade. The flowers of the saponaria come out just after the forget-me-nots, which they resemble, but in pink. Their habit is to trail. Where I live, saponaria has only recently been available in the nurseries, and the only variety I know is *S. ocymoides* 'Splendens', which looks delicate but is surprisingly tenacious. Plumbago, an excellent border groundcover, blooms in vivid blue, late in the summer, and keeps blooming even while the green leaves are turning a dark red in early autumn—its best time. Not a transport-you-to-heaven plant, but sturdy, reliable and handsome—and it spreads nicely.

For a last-gasp bloom in the early autumn, *Sedum spectabile* 'Autumn Joy' flowers in August in pink, deepening to scarlet and later, over the course of a couple of months, to deep brown. It's not joyous at all, but stoic and somber, as if in deference to the coming cold weather. Traditionally, the blooms are not cut back but left alone at the front of the border over the winter—dried flowers, more or less, to keep outdoors. The next spring, the new foliage growing underneath the dried blossoms is wonderful to see. Remember that it's 'Autumn Joy' you want, however, because there are about 250 varieties of sedum, most of which have a succulent, desertlike feel: they creep along the ground rather than grow up, and they like it where it's sunny, hot and dry—in an herb or rock garden. 'Autumn Joy', which also needs mostly sun, is a little more dressed up and formal.

Digging the holes for these plants, in soil that was already prepared, proved easy: Dig the hole, ease the plant out of its pot, sprinkle in a little peat (four handfuls, say, for a perennial in a gallon-size pot), chop the peat into the soil, put the plant in, tamp down and water. The hard part was: should 'The Fairy' roses go there or *there?* Try them several different ways first, stepping back to see how they look each way. Stare at them for hours if you want, then plant with impunity— and resume staring, this time with pleasure.

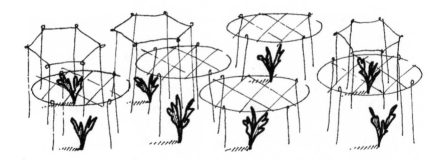

The Middle of the Border

If I introduce the middle of the border by talking first about irises, someone will surely protest that irises belong at the front of the border, not in the middle. The protester will have a point.

Each plant you place requires a judgment call, and nowhere is this truer than in the midborder, the middle area between the front, lined with the shortest plants, and the back, lined with the tallest. Everything in between goes in the midborder, at its best a study in color, form (some rounded plants, some that reach up, some that droop), texture and size, with the plants rising up gradually, not in an abrupt stair-step way.

I didn't place my irises at the front of the midborder behind 'The Fairy' roses, for example, because the roses grow bushy and tall, relatively tall, that is, for their front-of-the-border situation. But planted just behind the lamium, so that the low-growing lamium wends its way loosely around the bases, the irises looked good. It's helped me to think of the midborder as being two levels—front (holding plants two feet high, give or take) and back (plants a foot higher). Otherwise, it'll be oblivion for the slightly shorter plants.

Besides, during that brief period in late spring when the bearded irises are in bloom, the stems rise high, three feet or more, and look better with even a little distance from the front. You want to feel as if you could reach out and touch the flowers, not as if the flowers were coming to get you.

Lately, the Siberian and Japanese irises, with dense, narrow-leaved dark green foliage and blooms that don't rise so high, have come into favor—or maybe I'm just noticing them for the first time. In either case, it's true, they're leafier, they wave around in the wind and their blossoms are more delicate than the bearded irises. Me, I still prefer the old-fashioned bearded varieties, and I'm not choosy about the colors in which they bloom—blues, purples, yellows, white; they look fine together in a big iris jumble, which is what I'm aiming for, because most of my irises came from various gardeners who gave me dividing privileges my first summer. Even better than the blooms is the military bearing of the upright leaves, their grayish color, the way they stand erect, at full attention, all season, heat, rain or drought notwithstanding. And their flowering time is unmistakable. The stems rise high, eventually disclosing their blooms, big, slightly gaudy and worthy of endless study (how *do* they manage to look like that?). The blooms of the Siberian varieties, on the other hand, tend to get lost in the shuffle of the leaves. Whichever your preference, a few starter irises, tucked just behind the lower front-of-the-border plants, will soon be ready to be cut up into a few more, and then a few more after that.

When you buy irises, try to choose those with bigger rather than smaller bulbs (or corms, which are simply another kind of bulb!); the bigger the bulb the quicker the potential for more irises. The bulb itself often shows through the planting medium, and looks like the ginger root used in cooking.

Irises should be planted just at the surface of soil you've already prepared in the usual way. The soil can also be additionally enriched with a little bonemeal, sprinkled (like sugar on cereal) into the shallow hole before you plant. Take care not to pull out the tendrils coming out of the bulb—these will grip the soil once the plant settles in.

If you're lucky, you'll have bought an iris big enough to divide the first time you plant—at least four inches long and a couple of inches

wide; an iris with a heft to it. If that's the case, you can easily slice the bulb into two bulbs with a sharp kitchen knife, the way you'd cut fresh ginger; each "slice" should be at least two inches long. Plant these the same way, at the surface of the soil, with a little bonemeal sprinkled in first; then tamp down. (You can divide irises in this way every few years to increase your stock after they've bloomed—in early summer—or else in the fall, and don't complain if the new transplants don't bloom the first year after you planted them. You'll still have those wonderful leaves all season.)

Next to go in, also tucked behind some lamium, was a clump of *Nigella*, or love-in-a-mist, also donated by a friend. I was happy to have it. Though I see the seeds sold everywhere, I hardly ever see it growing, which is a puzzle because it's simple to grow and pretty, particularly when it's established and allowed to wander a little on its own.

With fuzzy foliage in bright green covering the upright foot-high stems, nigella grows in a graceful, weaving formation among other plants, colonizing itself easily. The blooms are subtle; they remind me of eyes winking out through that fuzzy foliage. Although it's an annual, it seeds itself so well it behaves like a perennial, which earns it a place in the mixed border. The seeds I usually see are mixed colors, pinks, purples, whites, but you can also get seeds in pure blue, *N. hispanica* or *N. damascena* 'Miss Jekyll'. These flower for a long time, starting in June. They're like perfect guests at a party; they move straight to the empty spaces to fill any awkward, gaping hole. Certainly worth the cost of a pack of seeds to start a patch.

In counterpoint to the straight-backed posture of the nigella, cranesbill are rounded in form, and delicate. Cranesbill is their common name; the genus is *Geranium*, but they look about as much like the more familiar annual geraniums (which are actually in the *Pelargonium* genus) as you or I do. These grow to about two feet by the second or third year, with smallish, quiet, cup-shaped flowers with five petals each. If they receive full sun, they'll flower extravagantly in pink, blue, white or purple from early to midsummer (a very long flowering season, which makes them doubly valuable), with the foliage keeping its shape for the rest of the season. I chose *G. himalayense* 'Johnson's Blue', which I thought would look nice next to the nigella, and which blooms in a deep, purplish blue, and grows in more vigorously every year, but without really spreading much.

If you have a bit of part-time shade, you can transform the front of the midborder into instant lushness, by planting bleeding hearts, columbine and astilbe. These are three of the perennials I was drawn to at once in my shady first garden, and I couldn't imagine not planting them again, even if I had to provide the filtered shade myself with an umbrella for a part of every day—which I might yet have to do: They were supposed to get their shade from the catalpa.

The Latin name for bleeding hearts is *Dicentra,* and the only minefield in choosing it is deciding which foliage you prefer, and whether you prefer your hearts to bleed in pink or white. *D. exemia* (more readily available in pink, but sometimes you can find white) has fernlike foliage, which is perfectly fine, but it seems mingy to me compared with the *D. spectabilis,* which has three-pronged leaves and a bushy form about two feet high; the blooms themselves, easily found in both pink and white, strung as carefully as pearls in an arc, begin earlyish in the spring. After the blooms fade, the foliage sometimes turns yellow; cut it back and new growth will appear to take its place—until midsummer, when the plant grows dormant, disappearing till the next spring. (*D. exemia* fans will point out that its foliage doesn't disappear the way *D. spectabilis*'s does.)

If bleeding hearts, with their hoopskirt form, bring the eye around and down, *Aquilegia* (from the Latin for "eagle"), or columbine (which means "dove"), planted nearby brings the eye back up: The puzzling and incredibly beautiful flowers do seem to float above the foliage, which may explain the plant's names, although that's the only birdlike thing about them, as far as I can tell. These are among the first plants to push their way through the soil in the spring, and it's thrilling every year to see the tiny leaves emerging.

These are technically not perennials but biennials, which means they complete their life cycle in two years, flowering the second year. Plant them anyway. When they go to seed, the little black dots fall all over the garden (sometimes you can shake the seeds out of the plants), or the birds move them around, so that new columbines are always popping up near the old ones, usually placed uncannily well; nature has a good eye. Start with a few and the chances are good you'll have plenty for years to come. As for color, you can seek out creams, blues, or purples, but most are mixed hybrids in pale colors that, without much planning, mingle comfortably. Again, after the bloom, the foliage may turn yellow; if it does, cut it off and wait for the new growth unfurling below to replace it.

An acquaintance of mine once hired a designer who discouraged her from planting astilbe; too boring, the designer said. As soon as the designer was out of sight, I overruled her and planted nine of them, filling up a fairly shaded area in her border. They looked fine—still do, five years later.

The name *Astilbe* comes from the Greek word meaning "luster-less," presumably because the prehybridized leaves were of a matted quality, without shine. Not true anymore; some now have a luster and some are tinted almost crimson. The common name for astilbe is gar-den spirea, owing perhaps to the plump midsummer plumes, in pink, white or salmon. These plumes are lovely, the leaves catch the light in a nice way and there's really not much you can do to destroy astilbe—except buy the wrong color. My first spring I carelessly threw in one that blooms in russet among others that bloom in salmon, and it still looks like a what's-wrong-with-this-picture lesson when it's in bloom.

I once made another mistake in my first garden after planting Japanese anemone, or *Anemone × hybrida*, a later-blooming choice for up front in the midborder. The year I planted it, I pulled the stringy stems out of the garden, roots and all, when I was doing the autumn cleanup. Because I hadn't seen a single flower, I chalked the plant off as a loss. I thought it had failed for lack of sun, but anemones can in fact take a little shade. Instead, it probably failed only because I pulled it out and threw it away. This is not the best instant-gratifica-tion plant: They take two years or more to really kick in. Once they do, though, they're prolific. Had I left mine in place in that earlier garden, there would surely be a solid mass of memorial anemones by now, delicate flowers that are sturdier than they look, in shades of pink and white. I include them here among starter plants because the sooner you start them, the sooner you'll *have* them.

Aster × frikartii is another late-summer classic, with flowers that look like daisies only less scraggly. They're also known as the hardy aster, which I particularly like the sound of; hardy always makes a lazy gardener rest easier. For romance, aster means "star" in Latin. The blooms are available in white, pink and lavender. The lavender always seem to me artificially dyed, like Easter eggs; but, having said that, I should also confess that the first year, I planted three of each color, lavender included.

Every time I go to the shopping mall near my house, I'm upset to see how the landscapers have "decorated" the sunny entrance and median strips between parking lots with *Lythrum,* one of the great back-of-the-midborder plants of all time. You know it's sturdy if the pros plant it where it might be run over by errant shopping carts; even so, seeing so much lythrum adorning the one-hour photo shop and the supermarket dampened my enthusiasm. Less is more, I decided on behalf of my own garden. I had planned to stagger close to a dozen of the purple lythrum in the border, to bloom all through the middle of the summer, but instead I planted three of the 'Morden's Pink' variety, to get away from the shopping mall deeper purple.

Peonies, on the other hand, could never become a cliché. *Paeonia,* named for Paeon, the physician to the Greek gods (a hymn to him is a paean), is breathtaking; it's the saddest thing when their short, and early, blooming season is over. They're relatively expensive, so choose carefully, and don't settle for any that aren't fragrant. Single blooms or double, lighter or deeper pinks or golden or red—a matter of choice. I don't even know what kind I have; they're light pink and deeply scented, and they were in bloom when I bought them. That was enough for me.

For all the talk of peonies being difficult, they aren't really. They're said to be a bit agoraphobic, and don't like to be moved if they can avoid it. Support hoops, which keep the heavy blooms from falling over, may seem like too much trouble, but they're optional. If you can live with falling-over blooms (or bring the falling-over ones inside), great. And you'll never have to weed under a peony. The foliage, which is nice enough if not breathtaking, stays in place and intact all season, at perhaps a few inches under three feet high. To me, their only disadvantage is that the shrubby plants take up a lot of room, while the blooming season is so short; if the garden is small, fewer of them than you'd probably like will have to do.

Where partial-to-deep shade muffled many possibilities in my first garden, my start-from-scratch garden has plenty of sun (more so now that the catalpa's gone). Because I'd first learned to garden in that cool shade, it took me a while to accept the fact that most plants like direct sun beating down on them all day long. Perhaps, because of the depletion of the ozone layer, we've come to distrust the sun. Besides, plants seem so fragile, and so lovely, that I wondered how they could bear up under that relentless heat. But they do. You can see it most vividly if you plant a sun-loving perennial in dappled shade: It'll reach forward or sideways to seek out all the extra sun it can. A gardener has to trust the beneficence of the sun, and I'm learning this from the sun-loving plants now coming up.

The first to go in was *Artemisia bachonia,* picked up that spring at a nursery on a whim; I'd never seen it before. It doesn't remotely resemble the front-of-the-border artemisias (which is why you have to remember the *bachonia* part), but has matted (not shimmery) silvery leaves that face up like palms, and offbeat flowers, whitish silver, that look like beads. They spread well and are unusual enough to work in a curious but pleasing contrast with practically anything else you might want to plant.

And now, with this sun, I could have lilies, the oldest plant in cultivation.

I used to think of lilies, or *Lilium,* as fussy plants belonging to an earlier generation, reasoning (defensively) that any plant that did so well growing in greenhouses would immediately keel over under my on-again, off-again care. Not the case at all. Unless you have rabbits, moles or more than the run-of-the-mill number of those disgusting slugs, you can have lilies.

Lilies are as confusing to buy as they are easy to grow, as there are literally hundreds of varieties around, and those available vary from nursery to nursery even in the same area. Just be certain of the color, height and particularly the fragrance. A label that says Asiatic lily won't give you a clue about what you're getting; there are as many Asiatic lilies cultivated as there are Hatfields and McCoys in the American South. The lily I've discovered and stuck to are the cultivars of *L. regale* (which are Asiatic, as it happens, native to China). They're easy to grow and don't need staking. The man who early in this century "discovered" them growing by the tens of thousands along the Min River (previously unexplored by Westerners) was Ernest H. Wilson of America's Arnold Arboretum. He didn't gather enough on his first visit, went back for more and almost lost a leg in an avalanche. He limped for the rest of his life, but still thought the effort had been worthwhile: It was.

Most lilies like full sun, but there are some that will do fine in a little shade; excellent drainage is the more important factor. Even the sun-lovers, though, like a little shade close to the ground, around their feet. What works to this end is to plant seeds of the annual *Gypsophila,* or baby's breath, around your lilies in the spring, as they begin to push their way up through the soil, or when you plant them for the first time. By the time the heat of midsummer kicks in, the baby's breath is growing up all around them, the tiny white flowers, pretty in themselves, making a built-in bouquet.

The perennial gypsophila, which comes in big pots at the nursery, are well and good, but I've found them unusually expensive, heavy stemmed, and likely to topple over. A tip from a friend made me switch forever to the annual gypsophila. The seeds for the annuals, at maybe a dollar a packet, are foolproof. Sprinkle them soon after the danger of frost is past, and they'll come up with the lilies. I've also found that the tiny white flowers of the annual are more assertive, and the stems are less likely to collapse.

Another good thing about lilies is that it's important to cut the flowers before the plants produce their berrylike seeds. So keep them in the garden till they're just past their peak, then cut the blossoms to bring indoors, where they can last up to another fragrant week. This is always a good week to have an elegant dinner party.

Foxgloves, or *Digitalis* (source of the heart medicine), which can tolerate a little bit of shade, are also back-of-the-midborder essentials. These bloom in midsummer, and usually turn up at the nursery rather late in spring, because that's when they like to be planted.

Like columbine, foxgloves are technically biennials that are used in the garden as if they were perennials, hope springing eternal. They multiply readily if not prolifically, so if you plant a couple both the first and second years of your garden, you can expect (well, the odds are about sixty-five–thirty-five in your favor) a few more foxgloves to turn up for several years or more beyond that. The leaves look like big tongues, but the blooms are as delicate as can be: a series of fox-paw-size mittens in the palest colors lining the stalk. Cut them back as they fade and you have a good chance (sixty-forty) of a second bloom later on that same season.

Malva sylvestris, Monarda, and *Centranthus ruber* are three additional choices, high summer bloomers and unusual enough that they suggest you know something about gardening even if you don't. They're all easy, and if they have to, they'll all put up with a little shade.

Malva, which comes in white or pink, is tall and graceful, with blossoms that look like a Victorian watercolor of what perfect garden flowers should look like. When the plant starts to come up in the spring, you should find groupings of little seedlings at the base. You can pluck them off and plant them, so that you can increase your stock, fast. (If you forget, nature might do the job for you.)

Monarda (common name: bee balm) isn't nearly as rare as malva, but at least I haven't seen it in shopping mall parking lots. In pink, blue, purple, white or red ('Croftway Pink' is soft and pretty), bee balm blooms spunkily, spreads easily, keeps blooming if you dead-head and is thoroughly satisfying; it's a friendly plant, not a formal-feeling one.

Centranthus ruber, which comes in a strange cotton-candy pink or a sparkling white ('Alba'), carries several common names, among them keys of heaven, for reasons I can't begin to guess. The bloom actually looks like a snowball of tiny knots, impressionistically dotted rather than bold. Rabbits hate them. They've naturalized so well in England that they're thought to be weeds. I'd love to have such weeds in my garden.

Garden phlox, or *Phlox paniculata* (there are other groundcover phlox, called *P. sublata*), is an old-fashioned, yard-high classic that, once planted, you'll scarcely have to think about (except to divide them, which means digging them up about every four years, cutting them in half hard with a spade and giving the half-plants more space to breathe); they get stronger and thicker every year, and the more you have outside, the more you have for cutting to bring indoors. In white, pink, red, or an odd—but nice—violet color, they come into brilliant flower as if on cue toward the end of July where I live, just as the garden would otherwise be going into an August funk. And the flowers last a long time, three weeks or a little longer. If you plant different colors near each other, I'm told that you might end up with a mongrel third color, but I wouldn't mind that so much.

For an accent touch of yellow, I planted both *Lysimachia punctata* and the biggest of the coreopsis (*Coreopsis grandiflora* 'Early Sunrise'). The first turned out to be kind of boring in this setting; I later moved it to my bed of herbs, where I liked it much better. It spreads easily, it's dependable and well, yellow. The coreopsis, on the other hand, worked fine. Flowering in buttercup yellow, the unassuming flowers bob in the wind and look thoroughly at home in both formal and casual settings. Coreopsis has a particularly long blooming season, all the better because the more you cut the flowers, the more flowers it will produce.

In contrast, the Oriental poppies, like *Papaver orientale* 'Brilliant Red', are startlingly dramatic for the brief period they bloom early in the summer; they elevate the garden. Oriental poppies have a stand-offish air about them, as if they want to distance themselves from their neighbors. Let them. Give them a space of their own, because when they *are* in bloom, nobody would notice their neighbors, anyway. Once they've finished, they don't drag out their good-byes: They just leave the garden, disappear, vanish, and you can fill their space with annuals. Dormant throughout the summer, the foliage, which looks as if it needs a shave, appears again in the fall. Supposedly they hate to be moved, but I got mine from a gardening friend two towns away, and they've done fine.

If Oriental poppies are aloof, tulips are gregarious, announcing spring in the midborder. There will always be room for tulips, which come up early, and disappear early, leaving plenty of space for later-summer perennials still waking up from the winter. Real diehards think of tulips as having a season of their own, and every autumn they plant a variety of bulbs to bloom on the early and late sides of tulip time as well as in the middle. This extends the tulip season for three weeks at best, but it's a distinction that means very little to me. I don't like to plant different kinds of tulips; I like a stronger showing of just one (pink, mid-height, so it won't topple) variety, or maybe two, if I throw in a few white ones.

Thoughts of tulips, however, could wait till the fall, when it was time to plant them. The border was rising up, with the front and mid-border plants drawing the eye in to admire the different colors, textures, sensibilities. I tried to memorize it at this moment, but couldn't; it was already changing and growing as fast as an infant. Now I wanted the border to rise higher, to a new level somewhere above the height of the stock fence. I wanted to be able to look *up* at at least a few grand-scale perennials.

The Back of the Border

Try as hard as I could to act nonchalant about it, I was thrilled to see the three buddleia I'd planted to anchor the back of the border begin to shoot up, right on schedule. The viburnum and mock orange, too, were showing signs of growing, more slowly, but also right on schedule. Where the foreground and midborder had been empty, reproachful spaces, here I didn't have to start planting perennials from scratch to fill the area. As promised, these shrubs anchored the border, and although there was room between them for some tall perennials, there wasn't *that* much room—a huge relief both to my aching back and to my budget.

The back of the border is the line where the garden meets the sky, and the shrubs anchoring it will give weight and importance to that horizon. Perennials in between will lighten and soften the space, so the shrubs won't look too heavy in comparison with the graduated layers of flowers in front of them. They'll also underscore the blur of greens and flowering things throughout established with the lower plantings in the front and midborder.

All of which is to say that to fill up the border, in my garden at least, there are only a few more starter plants to go.

Because perennials, like anything else, need time to grow tall, I can think of only one back-of-the-border choice that reaches its full height and blooms early in the season: *Thalictrum* happens to be beautiful, which is fortuitous because it has little competition so early in the season. It's shrublike in form, but feels ethereal, and has leaves similar to columbine's and small hazy blossoms rising above. The common name is meadow rue. There aren't very many species within the thalictrum genus, and the one most easily found is the tall *T. rochebrunianum*, which grows to five or six feet and is also known as lavender mist; the others are lower growing and belong in the mid-border, not the back. With lavender mist, one trap to avoid is thinking that because the foliage is so delicate it won't grow as high as promised. Wrong. I've made the mistake of planting them too far forward, and thus have had to move them back to where they belonged in the first place, and where they're surprisingly easy to grow.

The only danger (this genteel sport, with all its "dangers," is beginning to sound as risky as parachute jumping!) with thalictrum is that because these plants are so delicate they might list after a really heavy rainfall. If they do, sometimes you can just tilt them back, hard but not hard enough to break the stems, the other way, and they'll come around. Otherwise, attaching them to a temporary stake will help them right themselves.

Appropriately, many back-back-of-the-border plants are flamboyant or oddly shaped, as if to call attention to themselves so far back: "Hey, look at me!" You will.

Filipendula and *Aruncus* are perennials as weighty as good-size shrubs, both rising up high and flowering not long after the thalictrum in a fluffy way, like giant astilbes. They're just as easy, too, and with a bold form even when they're not in bloom. Filipendula likes sun up in the north and a little shade farther south; aruncus can take a little shade even up north if it has to; they're not very fussy. Be cautioned, though, that they take up a *lot* of room; both grow to five feet or even more. I didn't have the space for masses of both, and chose to plant three of just one, the slightly smaller and tighter-growing filipendula rubra 'Venusta', which blooms in pink and has leaves that seemed slightly more graceful to me than those of the aruncus.

To add a counterpoint to their fluffiness, I also planted three *Cimicifuga racemosa*, despite the dreadful name; it's easiest if you order them by number from a catalog, so you won't have to say it aloud. The name, all hard c's, even the one in *racemosa*, is Latin. Cimex is "bug," and fugo means "to repel"; there's a species (not this one) that smells bad enough to drive away bugs, and everyone else. The common name is bugbane. These take a fairly shaded situation, which I found in the shade of our neighbors' tree that hangs over part of the fence. The flowers look like giant white candles, rising two feet or more above the foliage, and the plants can eventually rise up to six feet tall in midsummer.

Here, as elsewhere in the border, I was trying to address every gardener's challenge—sequence of bloom, which (I was now finding) is much easier to orchestrate on paper than in reality. Seeing the garden actually blooming was to see how difficult a smooth sequence is to achieve, all those subseasons and microseasons crashing into one another or missing entirely. If the catalogs or books (including this one) tell us that a plant blooms in midsummer, does that mean between July 6 and 14, or between July 18 and 27? Plants surely won't peak at the same time for someone who lives in Georgia, where it's hot, as they will for someone who lives in New Hampshire, where it's cooler and things bloom later. How do you get the sequence right?

The most honest answer is by trial and, unfortunately, error. You can never know exactly what will bloom when in your own garden until you've actually seen the thing in action, and seen what adjustments have to be made, with more or less of this or that, and with shrubs, annuals and good lush foliage to compensate for the various perennials' down-time. You'll be off to the right start with a relatively equal dose of plants that promise to bloom early, midseason and late. To start dividing the season now into early-early, mid-early and late-early turns a midsummer night's dream into a nightmare, so to speak. Just let the garden take its course, and figure out where to divert it when there's a need to. Or make careful note of the barren spells for next year, and plan your summer vacation to coincide with them.

In general, that microseason between late midseason and early late-blooming season is an all-around dry time in the garden (at least in my garden), the midsummer counterpart to that first moment in early spring when winter clothes seem too heavy and spring clothes too light, and you feel so gloomy you just want to stay in bed all day. I've never had the right outfit to solve the sartorial problem, but I've solved its counterpart problem in the garden by planting hollyhocks, which bloom just before the phlox in front of them, one tier down.

Native to the Holy Land, or so one theory goes, hollyhocks take their common name from "holy" and "hoks," an old and inexplicably unattractive word for flower. The genus name *Althaea* is confusing because it can be spelled (or misspelled) Althea or Alcea, but once you've seen one it hardly matters; you'll never forget a hollyhock from then on. There are only a few species, but many cultivars; generally one buys hollyhocks by color, and by whether you prefer single blossoms or the fluffier doubles. Rising up to six feet and blooming in every possible color except purple or blue (some even bloom in black), hollyhocks need full sun and bloom at just the midsummer moment when you need them; possibly they are holy, the flowering patron saint of exasperated gardeners. The flowers look like the tissue-paper flowers I used to make in high school for homecoming dances, but better.

There are some who might argue that hollyhocks are a little erratic to be considered starter perennials, but to me they signal a garden to be taken seriously; besides, I've found them easier to grow than I ever thought I would, and if there's a little risk, the satisfaction quotient more than makes up for it. The stems are fat so, if you're lucky, they'll hold themselves up without staking. I had one topple over once after a storm, though, to a forty-five degree angle, just as the buds were about to open. Since I view staking as a last resort, I came up with an alternative solution. The plant was growing against a shingled wall, so I hammered a small nail, like a large pushpin, into it, and looped a rubber band from hollyhock to nail. That hollyhock stayed in place (its posture like a West Point cadet) just fine all through the blooming period, while the rubber band, hidden under a flower, remained invisible.

Just as the hollyhocks fade, give or take a week, *Rudbekia maxima* (the maximum rudbekia), which grows up to six feet high in a sunny spot, will start its long blooming season into late summer/early fall, producing cheery yellow blossoms, much brighter than the smudged yellow of its more familiar relative, the black-eyed Susan. And just as *that* begins to fade, *Boltonia asteroides* 'Snowbank' comes into bloom, the last back-of-the-border show before the gardener begins longing for winter.

Unassuming when not in bloom, this boltonia variety is called 'Snowbank' because when covered in its tiny white blossoms, it's supposed to look like a snowbank—it doesn't, but it's nice anyway, the kind of plant the eye skips over at first, then goes back to to study. And it offers plenty of tiny daisylike flowers for cutting.

If I've made it seem that these starter plants can be planted and will grow full in no time, then I've exaggerated. My border still has a long way to go. But most of these plants went into the new border, some the first year, some the second. At first I planted sparsely, so as to see how these plants I loved would fare. If they came back strong the second year, more went in. That process can be repeated for years. And then, of course, you come across more and more new or different plants you want to try.

Still, I can remember, after the first flurry of planting, gazing down at my infant garden and feeling utterly disappointed: after all that work, nothing more than a few nosegays here and there and, of course, those shrubs growing in the back—or that's how it looked to me. There were many empty spaces at first, and more than a few remain. Eventually, I got around to all the practical solutions for disguising these empty spaces: movable container plantings, an infusion of annuals—and giving time a chance. Time will heal a host of horticultural wounds. The empty spaces will be fewer each year.

The Herb Garden

With the sketchy perimeter of the garden finally in place and presumably growing, the space inside looked a little drab. It seemed time to begin coloring in the middle, so that the garden would begin to work from the inside out as well as from the outside in.

Because I like to cook, and because I'd particularly wanted herbs from the beginning, planting an herb patch was the next logical step for me. Herbs are both fanciful and, if you want them to be, functional. If you plant them, you won't necessarily have to cook more, or even hang them artfully to dry upside down in your kitchen or porch. But your garden will be a richer place. Herbs are to gardens what fine tweeds are to wardrobes: richly textured classics that, in their simplicity, make everything nearby look better.

Pay no attention to those intimidating warnings in some of the garden books about digging up herbs to create an instant herb garden in your kitchen to use all winter long. If you go to all that trouble, you'll just have a bunch of dead plants in your kitchen in November. (Rosemary, the expensive exception, would definitely be worth digging up and potting, if you have tons of sun somewhere inside.) For the most part, herbs are a cheap and easy-to-grow combination of annuals and perennials. Having a little (or big) patch of herbs imparts fragrance, texture and also an important sense that life isn't really out to get you, after all. Maybe they do have healing properties; in any case, herbs always make me feel *safe*, as if the world really might be a predictable place.

Classic herb gardens are formal affairs, often with herbs arranged to grow in the shapes of knots, interlocking circles, or geometric designs, like the clasp on a Chanel or Gucci bag. Needless to say, this approach is risky; if you get distracted during the execution, the bag won't stay closed or, in the case of the garden, the perfect design in your mind's eye might look lopsided and pathetic when translated to the soil; knots require absolute care and precision, and the results, when they work, show it. (Perfect knots also require a book more advanced than this one.)

I've recently seen several herb gardens that are easier variations on this wildly ambitious theme. In each, the herb garden was set off in an enclosed area by itself, and coming upon it was a surprise. The gardens themselves, but not the plantings, were geometric in shape, two of them perfect squares, one a little over twenty feet square, and one carved into a perfect circle about twelve feet in diameter. If you choose this route, the herb garden should have a sculptural center-piece—a weeping fig tree, *Ficus benjamina* (which would have to be dug up and brought inside, if you live in a place where the winters are cold); a bay laurel (*Laurus*), which also can't take extreme cold; a spectacular hybrid tea rose, if you're willing to take care of it; a topi-ary; or an ornamental fence post with a wonderful vine growing over it. The beds within all three gardens were defined as if by spokes of a wheel, so that the round garden had beds carved out like slices of pizza, and the square gardens had beds that were triangles of different shapes.

The narrow paths between the beds were covered variously in crushed white stone, brick and mud. The stone and the brick looked fine. The mud was more puzzling, until my gardener friend explained that what he had been aiming for were thyme paths, modeled after the legendary thyme lawns in England. After he'd explained it, I could see, here and there, small shoots of drowning thyme. But the experi-ment, like every single experiment with thyme lawns I've ever heard of, was a sad failure—just too difficult to achieve. Once that was clear, he covered the paths instead with a healthy layer of wood chips, not expensive, and now they look fine.

For me, there was no question of setting off beds with paths for the herb garden; I simply don't have the room. Not that I felt particularly heartbroken about it: I almost prefer the herb garden to be informal, with the herbs sprawling and rumpled-looking, inviting daily use. I also prefer herbs close to the house, and the kitchen, for the sake of convenience, and because they look so homey. Many of them start coming up early enough in the spring that they can almost be considered part of the spring garden. Even the spring after I'd first planted them, my new chives came up with the daffodils, and signaled the season to me just as much.

You can do a lot with herbs in just a small space, but choose a location that's sunny, since most of them will prefer sun over shade any day. I chose the wall of the back porch and a little beyond, and I already know I want to expand the bed, it's so easy and useful, and it's doing so well. I knew I was taking a chance: The site could have been problematic, because the drainage pipe from the gutter on the porch flows onto one edge of the bed, making a rather noticeable hole (which I kept from getting bigger by lining it with some good-size rocks). But the soil in that bed is on the sandy side, which helps drainage. And I hoped that the hole would be obscured soon enough when the plants started growing in, which for once is exactly what happened.

You first cultivate the soil in the standard way, by turning it over and enriching it with manure, peat, and the prescribed dose of a standard fertilizer.

And then, before you start imagining the fragrant and tasty herbs you'll cook with all summer, you start thinking about herbal plants

you *won't* cook with. Among herbs, some have culinary uses and some don't. As it happens, many of the nonculinary herbs are "dressier" in demeanor than the culinary herbs; even if you don't use them to season foods, they'll spice up the herb bed and keep it from being unremittingly green and, well, edible.

PICTURING THE HERB GARDEN

Herbs, whether used for cooking or not, are subtle, low-growing and green for the most part although the perennials do flower, mostly in a ho-hum way; they're valuable more for their textures and uses than for any showiness. (As for the annuals, you have to keep snipping away at them so that they *don't* flower; once they flower, they'll go to seed and be worthless in the kitchen, and the garden.) But to even out the effect of the garden as a whole—that is, to make the garden all of a piece—a plot of culinary herbs growing by themselves might seem a little dull, particularly if off in the distance you see a relative rampage of color in the border.

This is not to suggest recreating the colors and plants you've put in the border in the herb garden; there are plenty of different plants to go around, and the more plants the better. The idea instead is to anchor the herb garden, in the same way the border is anchored with shrubs, with herbs or other plants that do something a little more exciting than turn up in soup.

Because herbs are low-growing, the scale of the herb garden has to be low as well; you wouldn't anchor it with a giant maple tree, for instance. If the bed is fairly small, around ten feet long, say, and three or four feet wide, an anchor plant about four or five feet high will do the trick, bringing the eye up and back down in scale with the herbs. If the bed is bigger, it's worth considering anchoring it on either side.

An anchor plant too spread out or too coarse will work against the softness of the herbs and take up the whole bed; what you want is a plant that's delicate enough in demeanor to match the herbal sensibility, but strong enough in stature to serve as a visual correlative.

Where a run-of-the-mill maple wouldn't do, a dwarf specimen or Japanese maple (*Acer* is the genus name), for example, would do fine. Low- and slow-growing, the pretty leaves, in golden-green or a reddish copper, which eventually form a canopy extending down to the ground, would seem almost to protect the herbs growing around it. Try this approach only if you have room to expand the bed slowly over time, so that the herbs can be pulled out from under the tree's canopy as it grows. An elegant boxwood (*Buxus*) would be an excellent and classic evergreen choice, growing in a perfectly rounded form.

If you want a flowering shrub, and your herb bed is tiny, try a *Perovskia,* or Russian sage, a shrublike perennial herb, silvery leaved with purple blooms late in the season; it grows in an exuberant **V,** about three feet high. What you don't want is a shrub that flowers too early to set off the herbs, which won't be at their best till high summer.

Because I know I want to expand my herb garden, and am not yet sure in which direction, I haven't yet chosen a centerpiece. Two years into it now, and I still don't know where the center of the herb patch will ultimately *be*. Where the center is at the moment I've put a small orange tree in a big terra-cotta pot; a sculpture or ornament could also serve as anchor. The orange tree was a gift, and although I can barely keep it alive in the winter, it revives each summer when it's placed outside after the last frost date. A container planting can be a permanent anchor, if it's elaborate enough to make a statement and in scale with the rest of the bed.

There are other plants that mix and match well in the herb garden, that look as if you might eat them even if you shouldn't and that will make the space seem replete right away. *Nepeta,* unless you have a cat, is one of the best.

The choice was a toss-up for me: Do I put nepeta in the border or the herb garden? The herb garden won.

Technically an herb, nepeta is also called catmint—or catnip. Cats love to roll around in it; it makes them giddy. It's risky to plant it if you have a cat (or if other neighborhood cats have access to your garden) who would take pleasure in flattening it. Otherwise, it grows like a dream if it's given full sun.

I started a little nepeta "hedge" with three of these lovely plants, whose etched leaves are silvery green and whose habit is shrubby. I planted the variety called 'Six Hills Giant' which, by nepeta standards anyway, is big; it sprawls to about two feet, with the grayish foliage remaining vigorous all season long. The flowers, which come late in spring and last a long time, are spires of bluish-purple, and if you cut the blossoms back when they fade more to grayish and fertilize the plants at the same time, they'll bloom again in the fall.

I was lucky, too, to inherit a few more of a different and slightly smaller variety, *N. musinii,* whose leaves are more silvery that the 'Six Hills Giant'. My neighbor had learned about catmint the hard way— from her cat, who had indeed flattened it to the ground.

Certain of the "border rules" can be relaxed or forgotten about in the herb garden. Curves and rows, I've found, in this setting can work better than the traditional border triangles. Because the herb garden is low, you'll usually find yourself looking *down* at it, at what amounts to the tops of the heads of the plants. In fact, the easiest way (and prettiest, I think) to think of planning an herb garden is to think of a series of minihedges, some curved, some straight, flowing into one another, in relaxed, lazy gardener's knots. Viewed aerially, from the perspective of your height, these juxtaposed or intersecting hedges will ebb and flow the way farm fields seem to do when viewed from a plane. You'll see the plants themselves, and also the arcs in which they're planted. These hedge rows can be effectively broken up by plantings of one or two of something else—a clump of parsley to break up a long row of chives, for instance. With herbs, it looks a little decadent to have *way* more than you could possibly use. The kitchen garden, even if it's herbs and not vegetables, should be in scale with the kitchen and the rest of the house and garden.

Nepeta 's leafy branches spread out wide; a good contrast plant is the upright *Santolina,* both the green and the silvery, so in keeping with culinary herbs that I often see them displayed in the herb section at nurseries. They look softer and lacier than the smallish junipers, grow in full, almost two feet high, and with tight, pretty yellow mid-summer blooms that are like feisty fists; you keep expecting them to open more, but they don't.

So in went three santolina surrounding a tansy (*Tanacetum*), which I bought because I liked the old-fashioned Shakespearean sound of it. Like perovskia, it grows in a lush inverted V, bringing to mind a big, unself-conscious fern for the sun, with flowers, also yellow, that come in perfect sequence, just as those of the santolina are fading. It would even be effusive enough to anchor a small bed of herbs. It spreads on shallow runners, soon supplying several tansy off-shoots. One cautionary note: By the second year or sooner, with no special care at all, it'll be a yard high and just as wide. You might as well allow it that much room when you plant it.

I also couldn't resist another "hedge," a row of rue, *Ruta grave-olens,* a self-reliant herbal perennial with feminine, silvery gray leaves coming out of a thick, stoic trunk in the middle, like a tree to shelter a dollhouse. Again, rue, pretty in itself when viewed straight on, enhances the aerial view as well with its unique color and form.

Thus sketchily outlined, the horticultural dots of the herb garden were ready to be connected with kitchen herbs.

PLANTING THE HERB GARDEN

A bold curve of chives came first.

Chives, in the *Allium* genus, grow in big, clumpy bunches; the more established, the fatter each chive, and each clump. You can buy a fat clump in four-inch pots, but save the money; they grow so fast, you'll do just as well if you buy them in the skimpier clumps in the little six-packs and plant them six inches apart. By the end of the first season, you'll have a hedge. By the second season, you'll have a fat hedge. Stagger the hedge a little if you want, plant chives in the shape of a wedge or use them as the edging to the herb border. In late spring or early summer, chives produce their cloverlike lavender blossoms—thoroughly edible, but if you want your chives to spread, leave the blooms in place. As for the chives themselves, there are a million ways to use them. If you cook, you'll find yourself snipping a bundle a day. If you're a reluctant cook, you can approach them warily: Try cutting a few (with any sharp scissors) and throw them whole into a salad, or drop them like pickup sticks over meat or fish as you're finishing cooking or grilling them. They melt right in.

Don't skimp, on the other hand, when you're buying oregano and thyme (*Origanum* and *Thymus,* to be official about it). With these, the bigger the plants are to start with, the bushier they'll grow in the garden. One big oregano plant will grow like a shrub, a foot or more high and wide, and will give you as much oregano as you'll need to cook two or three Italian entrées for four per week all season. One big thyme plant will provide the same yield, more or less: enough thyme to make fish, chicken, or sauces more fragrant a few times a week all season.

Oregano is pretty much oregano, but with thyme, there's a choice: yellow-tinged lemon thyme, variegated green-and-white thyme, or plain old green garden thyme are all easy and handsome, and all useful in the kitchen. The grayish hairy-leaved thyme that spreads flat, not in a shrub form, is thyme-lawn thyme, fine in the kitchen but much iffier to grow. Give it a try if you want to take a gamble. Me, I'd rather invest the money in lottery tickets. Or in fennel.

The tiniest fennel plant (the genus is *Foeniculum*), either with bronze-tinted or lime-green fronds, will surprise you by how fast it turns into a knee-high fennel plant, sprouting up like a geyser. Its pattern of spreading is whimsical, as if it were following a hopscotch board of its own devising, but it's easy to pull out where you don't want it. It's a great backdrop for the herb patch and, even if you don't much like the taste of fennel for cooking, a big bunch of the top foliage is a fragrant and pretty way to decorate a platter.

Mint, or *Mentha,* is an evocative summer herb; sprigs of it in fruit salad, iced tea or lemonade are almost essential enough that you notice if they're missing; it's not a bad garnish for lamb, either (though rosemary is better). The smallest, cheapest mint plant you can find will be more than enough; it's notoriously invasive and not very pretty—it gets leggy—after its first flush of green. Pick a patch where you'd like it to grow. Then put a ten-inch pot on that very spot, fill it with soil and stick in your mint plant. You'll have plenty in no time. What is more, the pot offers a quirky, informal counterpoint to the ground-bound herb bed, and it also serves as a barrier, preventing the mint from getting out of hand and taking over the whole bed. An alternative method of planting, if you want your mint growing in the ground, is to sink a section of open-ended ceramic piping, like sewage piping, into the ground, leaving the lip of the pipe a couple of inches above soil level. Plant the mint, one tiny plant per two or three inches of pipe, inside the piping, and it will be unable to roam.

Upright sage, a *Salvia,* and the floppier sorrel, in the *Rumex* genus, are quieter herbs, worth growing only if you really intend to use them. (I don't use fresh sage very much, but I'd always choose to grow it anyway; I'd miss it if I didn't have it, the leaves are so satisfying to run between your fingers.) If you like sorrel soup, or sorrel with shad and shad roe, plant sorrel and don't give it a second thought. Sage is trickier, and not always reliable as a perennial, at least, not where I live. The variegated and purple sage are generally available along with plain old green (my own preference is the green; the others, even when thriving, look a little sickly to me). Even if you have to treat it as an annual and plant a few every year, as I usually do, it's worth it to find a corner where sage can grow politely and unobtrusively.

Rosemary, or *Rosmarinus,* is a special case of herb. Even the pros curse at how hard rosemary is to grow from seed; that's why it's so expensive and so worth saving from year to year, if you have enough sun to bring it inside. (If that's the case, plant it outside in the spring right in its pot, then dig up the plant, pot and all, come autumn.) My own reasoning for buying a big plant every year is that, expensive or not, I use it enough for cooking from May through December, when it finally gives up outdoors (where I live, that is; it'll survive just fine outdoors farther south, till just about freezing level), that by planting a big, healthy rosemary, I'm actually saving money by not having to buy sprigs of it at the vegetable stands all the time. Another justification: Try rubbing fresh rosemary into your hands, as if you were washing them. Then smell—the fragrance is heavenly, for hours.

If you cook at all, you actually *will* save money by filling in your herb garden both with annual herbs and with perennial herbs that either might or might not come back from year to year, depending on where you live and how lucky you are. Tarragon (*Artemisia dracunculus*), marjoram (*Origanum marjorana*) and chervil (*Anthriscus cerefolium*), for instance, are well worth having, even if you have to start anew each year; all are supposed to be perennial herbs, but never have been for me. I've never had much luck with dill (*Anethum graveolens*), either, because it needs a lot of room to spread out. A few sprigs of it in my small herb bed just feels wrong; the plant will seem to be gasping for air. This herb is used in abundance in cooking, and needs to be grown that way, too, if you have full sun and the space.

Save a big spot, though, for the parsleys (genus *Petroselinum*, but just sold as parsley), both the flat-leaved Italian and the curly. Many cooks have recently abandoned the curly in favor of the Italian, but the curly is actually more flavorful and prettier to grow. Three little six-packs of each, planted only two or three inches apart, so they'll grow tight, like a bouquet, in rows or filled-in circles, will give you a bushy, cheerful and usable crop of parsley well into the fall, for under $10.

When I first began to grow basil, basil was basil. The genus is *Ocimum,* and basil—*basilicum*—is the species name, after basilica and meaning "princely." Nowadays there's the purple-leaved basil, the miniature mounded basil, and half a dozen other new varieties. Designer basil, I thought at first, who needs it? But seeing a row of the miniature mounded basil in a friend's garden (and, more persuasive still, tasting it at lunch there one day, snipped over fresh tomatoes) made me rethink the issue. Now, in addition to the plain old basil, I have a few miniatures, planted mound to mound, which I love. The only disadvantage is that both get leggy by August anyway, no matter how faithfully you keep snipping them.

While I don't mind a few empty spaces in the border, I hate empty spaces in the herb garden. I want it to look profuse, like a big tossed salad. Nasturtiums make great fillers, especially now that you can find those that bloom in pink, instead of the more common orange. The seeds look like Kix, the children's cereal. Soak them for a few hours in a bowl of water, then push them an inch or so into the soil. Within two weeks you'll have their round leaves, and soon after that you'll see the blossoms (both good to eat in salads, and for tiny bouquets), trailing casually around the garden. Even better, so as to avoid letting them clog the herbs around them, plant a separate pot of nasturtiums, and let them trail.

Perhaps it takes a while to get used to the subtleties of growing herbs, learning their different textures, fragrances, and tastes, seeing beauty in these simple plants grown to heal or nourish. If the border is nurtured to be looked at and admired, the herb garden is grown to be touched, sniffed, tasted, and *used*—without having first to pull off the plastic wrap.

Learning to Love Cleome: Some Uses of Annuals

I was so awed by every plant that grew in my first perennial border that the idea of actually *cutting* a flower to bring indoors to display in a vase was unthinkable. Whenever I tried it, the naked stem that remained seemed to me like an accusation; I noticed every missing flower. I compromised by working all day in the garden, then going to a flower stand nearby to stock up on cut flowers for the house. Someone else's naked stems never bothered me very much.

Because I learned about perennials first, the wondrousness of annuals hit me by surprise: Here are plants that you can cut and many of them will simply come right back again all season; their batteries don't run out till fall. They're inexpensive. They're not all horticultural cop-outs, like impatiens and geraniums. You can tuck some of them judiciously into the perennial border or the herb garden and nothing bad will happen. Some of them will even, as advertised, grow from seed, with equipment no fancier than your hand.

The miracle of annuals was driven home to me one year when a friend who was going on vacation asked if I'd go over to her house

once a week while she was away to cut the flowers in her cutting garden. As a *favor!* Her cutting garden is a fenced-in realm away from
her formal border with flowers growing in rows, climbing the fence,
draped over trellises. These flowers *need* to be cut so that they won't
go to seed and stop flowering. Needless to say, I was happy to comply,
and the thrill of gathering all those flowers every week was tantamount to that of watching my own perennials come to life every
spring. As a result, blossomless stems now seem to me as much a sign
of renewal as of death.

You can use annuals in myriad ways. Two years ago, the spring I
started my present garden, for instance, I completed round one in the
border and the herb garden, then got ambitious one day and prepared
another small bed in a good deal of sun for planting; it was a blah corner by the driveway that was really getting on my nerves. That's as far
as I got, until on a whim I bought two flats, or trays, of cosmos, and
the space came to life. Not the way I wanted it to forever, but for that
year (which turned into two years, since these so-called annuals
reseeded themselves and came up again like perennials before I had a
chance to think about the bed this year), the five-foot tangle of pink,
deeper pink and white flowers, excellent for cutting, looked casually
effusive. It was a one-note cutting garden, but it was my first, and I
loved it for its simplicity.

The cutting garden need not be a permanent, fenced-in affair like
my friend's. Lacking that kind of space, I like to think of it as
portable, like a horticultural picnic: You pack the cutting garden up
and move it around each year. The process is incredibly simple: The
minute the annuals arrive at the nursery, when it's warm enough to
plant them, scoop them into your car, take them home, dig holes big
enough for them (which is easy; they start small), put them in, cover
them up with soil, sprinkle the bed with fertilizer and water. That's
about it. With my own yard several beds shy of the garden I hope it
will be one day, my plan is to move the annual bed every year to a
spot where its extravagant color will balance, and enhance, the whole.
That is to say, you don't want the cutting patch, with its brighter colors, too close to the border, where the colors are muted; that would
detract from the border. Nor too close to the quiet herbs; they would
be diminished even more. Color way off in the distance, which pulls
the "horizon" of the garden in closer, is one approach. Another is to
separate the cutting bed entirely—off to the side of a garage, maybe,
but never out of sight entirely.

For those who harbor a compulsive need for order, the cutting bed will be a relief from the triangles of the border and the colliding rows and curves of the herb garden: Here is where nature can be lined up in tidy straight rows, graded according to height—cutting flowers are, in effect, a *crop*, to be harvested all summer long. The bed can be of any size; even six feet by four feet in a sunny spot can yield a couple of big bouquets a week all summer, and look pretty on its own besides. The most pleasing beds I've seen are the simplest: a few graduated rows of annuals, planted close together for a massed effect, but with a spin to soften the rigidity of the rows—a splintered fence post with a climbing vine in the middle, an off-center clump of something at one end to belie the uniformity of the straight lines, even a few staggered flowers encouraged to break formation here and there.

WHAT EXACTLY IS AN ANNUAL?

Learning by doing is the best way to figure out how specific annuals work in your area, and how they don't. The trick is to remember that annuals live for one year only, produce seed (every plant is biologically compelled to reproduce itself) and then die. If the climate is favorable, new plants will spring up every year from the previous year's seed. If it's too cold, new seeds or new plants will have to be introduced every year. With perennials, on the other hand, it's the same root or bulb, year after year. However simple this fact seems, I never really understood it until I visited a rain forest in Puerto Rico and saw impatiens in their natural setting: just growing, all over the place, all by themselves. Nobody had to replant them from the tiny six-packs every spring.

The lesson in this is that you can't always rely on guides to annuals to tell you which plants will come back and which won't or which are annuals and which aren't; it all depends on where you live. All the guides to annuals I've studied include plenty of plants I think of as perennials, even as far north as Long Island. Not that I'm averse to mixing a few perennials in with annuals or vice versa. Here again, though, at least when it comes to the more imaginative choices, you're better off trusting your nurseries and your neighbors to see how so-called annuals will fare in your own garden. The worst that can happen? You plant what you think is an annual, and it behaves like a perennial, blooming for only a short time. The best? An annual you like takes hold, naturalizes in your garden and becomes a perennial fixture.

Plants that reseed themselves are called volunteers—a wonderfully comforting concept, free help in the garden. The phrase *reseed themselves* usually suggests that the new plants pop up here and there, sometimes more of them, sometimes fewer of them. Plants that reseed themselves (or reproduce themselves in some other way, as on underground runners) en masse into colonies, on the other hand, are said to *naturalize*.

PICTURING THE CUTTING GARDEN

If you have a secret streak of deplorable taste (and who doesn't?), the cutting garden is the place to air it; a slight gaudiness here is almost expected. My own particular weakness is for gladiolus, I'm only slightly embarrassed to admit. I know, everyone knows, the flowers are funereal. And yet, maybe it's the name, after the Roman word for "sword"; the gladiators' flower of triumph was the gladiolus. They're increasingly available in less, well, appalling colors, they're as easy to grow as can be (shove the corms to the depth of your forefinger into damp soil), they're stately when they're growing and they only bloom once, so you can't be accused of bad taste all summer long, unless you decide to plant several rounds of them a week apart, to have more of them to bring inside. You can sneak them into a corner or toward the back of the cutting bed, and they'll only look like gladiolus when they're actually blooming; the rest of the time they'll look like irises, or *Crocosmia*. Supposedly they naturalize, but I haven't yet been so lucky (or unlucky, depending on how much you hate them). If you're too embarrassed to buy them at the nursery, you can usually buy the tiny corms at supermarkets, so no one will have to know.

"Marigolds, how *could* you?" a friend of mine asked, when she saw me planting my flats of common yellow marigolds, of the *Tagetes* genus, and another annual "weakness." I reminded her of her zinnias, which I would never even think of planting. Her defense: Her zinnias are a dwarf variety. Alas, I've no such defense. My marigolds are the fat yellow kind, musky-smelling in vases and pitchers all over the house, where they last a week or more if I remember to change the water every few days. Outdoors, they're perky all season, and among those flowers you *have* to cut to keep them blooming.

With marigolds and zinnias, along with the common snapdragon (*Antirrhinum majus*) and even, increasingly, cosmos, you can't just buy a flat casually, and assume you'll get the plant you want. More than ever before, growers are playing around with larger and smaller versions, so it's important to make sure that the annuals (however gaudy) in your mind's eye match up to those before you in the nursery flats. I'm still new enough to annuals that usually I want the largest, showiest varieties possible—instant horticultural gratification and sensational to display indoors. Maybe later I'll become more discreet.

After having chosen your annual vice, there are plenty of other annuals to subdue the cutting bed, and give it some real character, so that it won't look like a New Year's Eve party the day after, with the remains of streamers and party hats.

I have friends who take their dahlias very seriously, and I can understand why: The flowers are so primary somehow, like a child's drawing of a flower. One dahlia in a bud vase, where it lasts a long time, is perfect. They remind me, too, of colored snowflakes, each one slightly different. On the other hand, they require a fair amount of care—staking (except for dwarf varieties), which means tying them to a stake to hold them up. I object to this on principle. They also require lots of pinching new buds, to direct the plants' nutrients to just a few strong buds (those narrow stems can't nurture very many blossoms). Also, you have to dig up the bulbs each year to store over the winter, since they can't stand the cold. Still, every year when I see everyone else's dahlias I'm always sorry I didn't plant them.

Not that sorry, though, because there are other compensations. This year, for example, at the back of a friend's cutting garden, I saw *Tithonia rotundifolia* for the first time. I'm determined to have it next year, even if I have to grow it from seed. The flowers have that same kind of child's-drawing clarity as dahlias. They're daisylike, black or yellow centered, and grayish orange or yellow and have the amazing texture of velvet. They're somehow lighter than dahlias, taller (up to six feet) and fuller, on sturdy stalks about five feet high that don't need staking.

There are softer choices available, too, with a homespun appeal that, mixed up in bouquets, feel like they've been grown in a gentler time. Rocket larkspur, or *Consolida ambigua,* in violet, pink or a dusky white, is terrific mixed in bouquets with just about anything; the spires, made of numerous tiny blossoms, are slightly pointy at the top. Poor man's delphiniums, to which they're distantly related, they need full sun. Lupine, that recalcitrant perennial, can be grown as a cutting annual, but it will *act* like a perennial, refusing to bloom all season. *Campanula medium,* annual Canterbury bells, with demitasse blooms that look as if they had been inflated, lasts longer than you think it will in water, whereas the equally beautiful but more delicate *Eustoma grandiflorum* (often called *Lisianthus*) tends to droop the minute it comes into bloom; mine do anyway. There are numerous annual verbena hybrids—higher and lower, some pink and some blue, some spiky and some rounder in form—that are classically pretty to look at both inside and out.

Whenever I think of statice, or *Limonium*, I always think of static. These unmoving flowers, which seem dried even when they're not, don't do much for me, except to grow well and easily, alas. I've never grown them, and yet I find myself buying a few bouquets each year. The papery everlastings, or *Xeranthemum*, feel dreary to me in the same way—useful, thrifty, and long- (ever-) lasting as they are. Sunflowers, the *Helianthus* genus, on the other hand, are summery and spirited. Few of us have the room to plant the giant *H. annuus* species (which only look right if they're planted en masse), but there are several other species, in pale yellow or dusty ivory, that feel as much at home in an expansive country garden as they do in a small village plot. *H. annus* 'Italian White', for instance, grows to about ten feet, but more delicately and daisylike than the big-stalked sunflowers; it also reseeds itself. I've seen it growing in cracks in the embankments of the expressways leading into New York, which gives you an idea of its hardiness. And *H. annus* 'Autumn Beauty' looks like a sunflower but smaller; it grows only three or four feet high.

If you're going to plant cosmos, think beyond the plain old mixed pinks and white, which is called *Cosmos bipinnatus*, but you won't need to remember that; it's everywhere, come spring. Cosmos is also increasingly available in pure white and in dwarf varieties, which don't flop around so much. Even prettier are the several varieties of yellow to orange cosmos, *C. sulphureus*, now more widely available, at least in seeds, with blooms that are fluffier than those of the traditional pink and white; among the C. sulphureus varieties are 'Bright Lights' and 'Sunset', which answer to the common name Klondyke.

One garden designer I know told me about a little plot she had done for a client, with huge bunches of cosmos "staked" with *Cleome*, whose sturdy stems are strong enough to keep the sprawling pink-and-white mixture in line.

It took me a long time to like cleome, the funny spider flower, with its spikes and impressionistically dotted blossoms; I had a hard time telling when it was coming into bloom, at its peak, or past it. An acquired taste maybe, but now I'm a fan: to watch cleome grow is to learn to love it. Each plant branches off into several stems, and each stem into bloom after bloom. Spider flowers might or might not reseed themselves and look more natural when they plant themselves than they do when you set them out, no matter how carefully, although they can entrench themselves more than you want, requiring you to spend hours of work to thin them out. I tried it that first summer in a makeshift bed on the driveway side of the garden gate, planted among some *Salvia farinacea* 'Victoria', which also grows four feet high or more. The endless series of purple blooms on long stems against dark leaves looked incredibly lush bordering the cleome every time I walked from the driveway to the gate.

A permanent annual bed is not the oxymoron it sounds. If you know for sure that one spot is right for your cutting garden, then you can make even more of the space by including a few perennials, vines, a flowering shrub perhaps—anything to give the bed a less transitory feel. Annual daisies are all right, nothing wrong with them at all and they're fine for cutting, but perennial daisies, of which there are numerous kinds to choose from besides the floppy shasta daisy which you see all too often, feel more grounded, and will seem to make the lighter annuals around them feel less ephemeral. (On the other hand, *Felicia amelloides*, the annual blue marguerite daisies, also feel grounded, and they go on and on, whereas perennial daisies don't.) Any of the rudbekia species and varieties will also help ground the cutting bed.

OTHER PLACES FOR ANNUALS

A few low-growing annuals here and there can also liven up any remaining empty spaces in the herb garden. Not too lively, though, or you'll undo with garishness all the subtlety you worked so hard to create. But there are annuals, some of them herbaceous, that look good enough to eat. *Heliotropium arborescens* 'Marine,' for example. Musky and fragrant, and botanically an herb, it looks to me like a plant with a secret. The low pink verbenas aren't simply fill-in-the-blanks plants; they seem to belong with herbs. *Verbena × hybrida* 'Pink Bouquet' is really pretty, for example, and not too showy mixed among herbs. *Lathyrus odoratus,* the mixed sweet pea, easily grown from seed, which will curl its way up a metal grid or a low fence as a lacy backdrop with nice light blobs of mixed color, is another good choice.

As for the perennial border, I would never again buy flats of sweet alyssum. (The name in Greek means "not madness"; it was once thought to cure rabies.) As my neighbor once pointed out, sweet alyssum planted from flats looks like plugs of hair transplants that never quite blend in. Planted from seed, on the other hand, a week after the last frost date, it looks like a soft full head of sweet alyssum hair and, annual or not, often comes back from year to year. (Don't worry about thinning out after germination, which the directions will tell you to do. Just leave them alone.)

Once you've planted the actual seeds of sweet alyssum (a process like that for planting baby's breath, the annual *Gypsophila,* which amounts to scratching the soil to one side with a fork, sprinkling seeds into it and pushing the scratched-up soil back to where it was, in a kind of sweeping gesture with your hand) and seen how readily they grow, you'll be able to fill up empty spaces at the front of the border every year, if it comes to that. To be on the safe side, you can plant a second set of seeds two weeks after the first; sweet alyssum sometimes peters out during very hot spells, and a second round of seeds ensures a summer-long blooming season.

Sequentially planted seeds will also guarantee you an array of Shirley poppies in the front of the midborder from late spring through early summer.

On the thinnest stems, these annual poppies (the genus is *Papaver,* but they're sold in seed packets simply as Shirley poppies) are so astonishingly delicate, you're almost afraid to touch them. But they're tougher than you think. They require cold weather to germinate, so begin planting them in late February/early March, or sooner or later if you live farther south or north. Plant a couple of packets of seeds a week apart for a longer season of bloom; they'll keep coming till the weather gets hot. And then forget about them, which you'll do anyway, because they take a long time to turn up. But when they do, they'll take your breath away.

Among the other annuals great to sneak into the perennial border is the tallish and delicate *Verbena bonariensis,* on which small clusters of mid-range purple flowers float five feet high on thin, thin stems. These are wonderful to tuck here and there toward the back of the border. *Viscaria* (which has been renamed *Lychnis,* but I still see it listed mostly as viscaria) is shorter, front-of-the-midborder height, pink flowers growing in a V, but these can pretty much peter out in extended midsummer heat. The soft blue flowers of *Browallia speciosa* can serve in the front of the border where it's fairly shady; *Nierembergia,* of a deeper blue, belongs slightly farther back. The salvia farinacea, which accompanied my cleome, will instead go into the border next year; it's lovely, lush, and shrublike, and goes on well into the fall.

Budget-breaking is a relative term, but a station wagon full of annuals will be cheaper than, say, a station wagon. Cheaper, too, for that matter, than a station wagon full of groceries. If that thought makes you feel thrifty and virtuous, and if feeling thrifty and virtuous makes you want to splurge, buy a *Mandevilla,* that tropical climbing annual vine with big glossy leaves and dozens of pink or white blooms as pretty as orchids. Installed in a big pot, it'll climb a trellis, trail over a terrace or mark a doorway and look like a million dollars. It won't *cost* a million dollars, but if you're going to splurge on one, shop carefully: This year I saw plants of the exact same size ranging in price from $17 to $45! I bought a $17 one, and looking at it every day, I know I got a bargain.

Roses, According to Bob

Every year for Mother's Day, my college roommate's husband gives her a rosebush. Apparently he once saw a magnificent rose garden somewhere, which lives on in his memory, and had hoped to replicate it in their backyard—or more precisely, had hoped that his *wife* would replicate it in their backyard. The roses he gives her are Hybrid Teas, and they take a lot of work.

My friend has been a mother for eight years now, so I did some quick calculating: "So now you've got eight rosebushes, right?" "Oh, no," she said, "only two. Every year I plant the new one and throw away a dead one. And every year we get maybe one rose." Hardly the rose garden her husband had in mind but then, as she points out, she never promised him a rose garden.

Maybe there's a Darwinian rose garden in our collective evolutionary memory as well, because every spring, it seems that every store—grocery stores, hardware stores, nurseries, discount stores— give much of their floor space over to these Hybrid Tea roses, which seem to get bought up fast enough before vanishing by the following spring, when the stock is set out all over again.

Where do these roses go?

Having bade good-bye to several roses of my own, I'm beginning to understand where they go, which is to that big rose heaven in the sky. Why they go there is a sadder matter. They go there because we kill them: Rosacide is a much more serious threat than black spot and all the other dangers combined to which roses are prey.

The verdict, in most cases, for rosacide would be accidental manslaughter or extreme negligence, and if the punishment were just, the Hybrid Teas would be given a restraining order to keep most gardeners at least a hundred feet away from them. Instead, they're put out again every spring for the slaughter.

I had always heard that Hybrid Teas were a lot of trouble, but this kind of trouble was a concept I'd never really grasped. When I planted my border, I bought three 'Queen Elizabeth' plants, stuck them in, poured some rose food around them and thought that because they seemed to be leafing out rather enthusiastically they'd be fine. I congratulated myself on not having bought into the myth that roses are labor-intensive and went about doing other things as one of my poor roses began to die, a long, slow decline that would be completed by the following spring.

When I met my friend Bob Schider, a colleague at the nursery, and when he came to see my fledgling garden, I began, finally, to understand, even to feel ashamed of, my cavalier attitude. Roses, after all, are living things, and I shouldn't have them if I'm not going to take care of them. Bob has won twenty-one ribbons and two silver trophies for his roses, plus two best-in-shows in the Southampton Rose Society competition; he's also a member of the American Rose Society, whose magazine, he says, has been a great source of help to him. He devotes a good part of one day a week to tending his three hundred roses—three hundred! With scarcely a bloom to show for myself, who was I to tell him about my considerably easier, though clearly less effective, methods for cultivating roses?

It was Bob who carefully explained to me that Hybrid Teas are a horticultural category all their own. If you want roses and don't want to put in the time, he says, plant lower-maintenance shrub roses— 'The Fairy', *Rosa rugosa*, the historic Gallica shrub roses, and 'Sea Foam'. These are all actual shrubs, actual roses, and most of them bloom once per season, although you can keep the bloom going longer, sometimes much longer, by feeding them rose food from time to time. 'The Fairy' and 'Sea Foam' roses, those front-of-the-border choices, go on longer, starting late in June and lasting till the frost. Some are fragrant, and none of the shrub roses requires the intensive maintenance that the Hybrid Teas do. These shrub roses can go anywhere sunny in the garden.

But if you love roses, and dream of a real rose garden, the chances are good that those you have in mind are the incomparable Hybrid Teas. Their care begins early every spring and ends after the last frost: hard work. The rewards? Beautiful, fragrant roses. All summer long. "The most important thing is that you have to love roses," Bob says. "You can't just like them. You have to love them, because you have to dedicate a couple of hours a week to roses alone." And yes, you can *learn* to love them.

Hybrid Teas are best set off by themselves, because their care is so specific, although (he admits grudgingly) they can be incorporated elsewhere into the garden. Having seen huge vases full of Bob's roses, however, I am determined to move my second generation of 'Queen Elizabeth' roses to a bed of their own and add to them some of Bob's other recommendations for "starter" roses: 'Broadway' and 'Chrysler Imperial', both really hardy, and 'Double Delight' and 'Heirloom', both very fragrant. Some way or another I'm going to find room for an arch or a small pergola, so that I can grow 'New Dawn', a Hybrid Tea climber, over it. No one knows why, but for some reason, yellow and white Hybrid Teas are the least hardy. I'll keep away from yellow and white.

And, while there are as many formulas for growing roses as there are recipes for making meat loaf, I'm going to follow Bob's instructions, imparted here, to the letter.

PLANTING THE ROSES

If you look closely, you can see that a Hybrid Tea is actually grafted onto another root stock—the graft is literally visible down by the crown. This is important to remember because in winter, you have to cover the crown, and the graft, so that they won't freeze; bandaging the scar, so to speak. In the summer, on the other hand, the crown, which is that little ball on top of the rootstalk, belongs exactly at ground level; the graft should be touching the soil. Planting roses too deep or too shallow dooms them from the start. So does damaging the roots, if you start by planting bare-root roses. The roses in boxes, available just about anywhere for about $10, are the safest way to start: You plant them, box and all, to the depth of the top of the box, where the crown will be showing through. Slashing the box (*only* the box) a few times when you're planting will encourage faster decomposition.

Okay, phew, the roses are in the ground.

The best way for a rose to grow is with only three major branches, called canes, coming out of the crown of the plant. After you've planted it, trim away all canes facing *in* toward the plant. If you don't, the canes will cross over each other and fail to produce any flowers; any extra canes will also impede aeration, which is crucial to roses. At this time, too, knock off any extra nodes (those little leafy bits that haven't had a chance yet to become canes) to prevent them from turning into full-fledged canes—again to ensure air circulation, and also because the sun, again critical to roses, has to be able to get in.

Okay, three canes.

CARING FOR ROSES

Feed the roses when you plant them, first with a cup of Epsom salts around each plant, to provide the magnesium they need. Don't water the Epsom salts in; the plant will absorb it slowly on its own. This step's easy; the Epsom salts goes on only once a year, in the spring.

Then apply a dose of rose food according to package directions or, after the plant has absorbed the Epsom salts, substitute manure tea. Here's the recipe: One-quarter manure (any kind of processed manure) to three-quarters water, about a gallon per rose in total. Mix it up, let sit till it turns the color of tea, then pour it slowly around the plant. Remember that the Epsom salts goes on only once a year, but the feeding gets repeated every couple of weeks until mid-July, following the directions for timing and quantity for the rose food you've bought.

In early May, plus or minus a couple of weeks, depending on where you live compared with Long Island (where Bob lives), the follier feed begins. By this time, God willing, you should begin to see new red growth, which will indicate that the plant is healthy. That's when you start spraying with fungicide and insecticide. There is work being done to develop natural fungicides and insecticides—seaweed, for instance, is supposed to be a natural fungicide—but most serious rose enthusiasts still capitulate to the commercial products, some of which are combination potions, so that you at least don't have to be mixing up fungicides and insecticides. Given that you'll be repeating this ritual more times per summer than you probably want to think about, a backpack sprayer contraption, or one you carry around with you, is a good investment. You'll also want to wear a mask, which along with the backpack will make you look like a scuba diver.

In the same container, add fish emulsion to the fungicide and insecticide. ("Fish emulsion?" I asked pleasantly, hoping that Bob had, in fact, said something more recognizable than *fish emulsion*. He saw what I was up to. "Yes," he said. "Fish emulsion.")

Fish emulsion feeds the plants various salubrious oils and nutrients systemically, which is to say it goes directly through the plant's system and is absorbed by the leaves when you spray it all over. Like an IV, in effect, shooting directly into the bloodstream, the emulsion will encourage follier growth (foliage), which is what you want early in the season. Measure the fish emulsion carefully, according to the directions, as too much of it can burn the roots and really hurt the plant.

Another timid question: What if you've already veered from the program and installed your roses among other plants? Will the fish emulsion hurt them? "Not at all," says Bob. "They'll love it. It's already broken down and they can take it in right away." So once a week you spray the bushes all over with the combined fungicide, insecticide and fish emulsion.

Until, that is, the weather starts to get very hot, at which point you cut out the fish emulsion. Earlier you wanted foliage growth; now you want budding. Moreover, if your garden is prone to fungus, the fish emulsion will, as the season wears on, encourage *that* as well.

Keep up with the regimen of spraying the fungicide and insecticide, though, until mid-August. The time to spray is very early morning before it gets hot, or late in the day before the sun goes down. Too much heat on the stuff you've sprayed will cause spotting.

In sum: Feeding-insecticide-fungicide-fish emulsion or, to give it an easily remembered acronym, FIFF.

By the time you begin to get bored with all this work, you'll have your first of the season's roses, which will give you your second wind. Just keep going. The first year you'll have a few roses and the second a few more. The third year, you'll have a rose garden.

When you see your first roses, cut them.

The beauty of Hybrid Teas is that you *have* to cut or deadhead the roses to have roses flowering all summer, or the plant will go dormant prematurely. (Cutting shrub roses, too, will encourage more blooming.)

The rose's mission in life is to produce a seedpod—a rose hip, those round balls that look like giant beads. And it will keep producing flowers until it produces those seedpods, at which time it will begin to go dormant. So if you get your first roses late in June and do nothing about them, you'll get your rose hips a couple of weeks later, a signal to the plant to start switching into the lazy dormant gear of hibernation. If, on the other hand, you cut the roses, the plant will go into high flowering gear, and keep producing flowers until it's permitted to form its hips. (No, Bob assures me, this isn't cruelty to roses; it's more like giving them a healthy aerobic workout.)

CUTTING YOUR ROSES

Naturally, there are rules for cutting roses.

First, never use an anvil pruner, which will crush the cane to the point where the wound from the cut won't heal, on roses. They require a scissors cut. (Bob adds that real rose nuts—no, no, he isn't one!—protect the wounds with hot wax poured over each one.) Bottom line: Use scissors pruners, those with blades on both sides.

To cut the roses (or to deadhead any that fade before you've gotten around to cutting them), look down the stem. First you'll see a number of leaflets grouped in threes, then you'll come to one with five leaflets—really. Those with five are those that will produce blooms, so you want to cut or deadhead just above the five leaflets.

CARING FOR YOUR ROSES SOME MORE

Meantime, you're still FIFFing. And watering.

As damp, cool spring turns to hot, dry summer, roses need an inch of water per week. They also don't like to be watered from overhead, preferring to take their water from drip or soaker hoses. Midsummer, every couple of weeks, you'll also have to get down on your hands and knees to look inside the roses to trim any new growth coming in inward.

You'll also start being on the lookout for any yellow leaves, which you'll have to, pluck by hand and get rid of—not on a compost pile: Never put rose clippings on a compost pile. Should there be a trace of powdery mildew or black spot, they'd contaminate the entire compost pile. And rose canes themselves don't decompose very well. Dispose of rose clippings with your regular household trash.

If, after all this, you do happen to come across a rose with black spot, the symptom for which is black spots all over the leaves, you'll probably want to move to a high-rise apartment with no garden anywhere near it. Failing that, pick off all the leaves by hand, then spray the plant and the soil around it with a fungicide three times a week, until clean new leaves come in.

Stop cutting the roses in mid-September, finally to give them the chance to form their hips and go dormant. You can stop FIFFing at this point, but you can't go dormant yourself, until after the first frost.

When the roses are hit with the first frost, and all the leaves turn brown, cut them back to knee height (foot to knee is about two feet), gather up all the leaves that have fallen to the ground and get rid of the clippings. This is the time to apply the mineral gypsum, according to directions. This helps leech out extra salt in the soil, which can accumulate from the water you're using, and it also lightens the soil up to improve aeration. Now apply one last dose of fungicide, to the roses and the ground around them. Then get fresh bags of topsoil—weed- and disease-free, and sterile. Mound the soil halfway up the exposed cane, covering the graft. Climbers would rather be wrapped in burlap, three feet up from the ground.

Come the following March, prune the plants to remove all dead wood. At the end of April, remove the soil and burlap that protected the plants over the winter. Take all the topsoil out of the garden, so as to avert the chance that extra soil will find its way around the crown of the roses.

Then go back to the beginning of this chapter, take out the Epsom salts and start all over again.

"Shortcuts?" I asked Bob hopefully. "Surely there must be some shortcuts. . . ."

"No."

"But what if, you know, you want to maybe take a summer vacation?"

"I take my vacations in the winter."

Other Gardens, Other Moods

I used to believe that a garden should be created to give the settled impression that it had always been there, that it happened almost by itself. A meadow garden should turn up in what was already a meadow; a rock garden would only look right in an area where there were rocks strewn about to begin with; a water garden required preexisting water.

That point of view, I've grown to see, is too narrow and restricting. Any garden, by definition, is unnatural, an attempt to tame and enclose nature, and to change it around. The gardener's objective is not so much to make the garden fit the place as it is to make the place fit the garden. Any garden, so long as it's executed well and with deference to the scale of its site, can go anywhere. If it's the right garden, it will soon sink into the landscape and draw its surroundings around it like a cape.

PLANTING A MEADOW GARDEN

A gardening friend of mine once offered to design and plant a garden for some neighbors of hers who were determined to have a wildflower meadow somewhere on their half-acre suburban plot. They had a funny little protrusion of land, only eight feet wide and maybe twenty feet long, jutting off to the side of their property, between the curve of the driveway and a fence, away from their flower garden behind the house itself. This plot, she promised them, could become their small meadow. Early that spring she took me along when she sowed the seeds for their "wild" perennial garden. She wanted trusty, and meadowy, perennials—coreopsis, *Gaillardia,* shasta daisies, and lupine among them (although I still don't believe lupine are trusty perennials). For instant effect, she also planned to throw in a few bachelor's buttons (*Tanacetum parthenium*) and corn poppies (sold as corn poppies). Knowing that the perennials wouldn't kick in until the following year, the bachelor's buttons and poppies, which are annuals, would, she knew, foreshadow in the first year the permanent look the meadow would achieve in the second.

The bed was neatly rototilled for us and free of weeds when we got there. I carried the seed mixtures, in three separate envelopes, a small one for the shortest plants, a big one for the midheight plants that would predominate, and a third for the tall plants she wanted to line up along the fence. All the seeds had been "diluted" with sand, so that when they were scattered, they wouldn't land in clumps too close together.

"Wouldn't it be easier to use one of those meadow collections that comes in a can?" I wondered aloud, looking—as usual—for the easy way out. Not really, my friend said. One danger is that there won't be enough perennials in them to get a bed established and, while annuals often reseed themselves, you can't count on that when you're doing the placement. So while meadow mixtures are getting more sophisticated all the time, you still might find yourself replanting every year. Also, those mixtures often include various grasses as filler, and my friend didn't want grasses; as filler, she wanted clover, and had included some seeds for clover in each of her envelopes. Her third objection was that while, like the ingredients in prepackaged foods, the seed content is listed on the can, it's often listed by *weight.* So even though you might *think* you're getting a good percentage of what you want, it may just be that the seeds you like are heavier. If you have a one-pound premixed selection, for example, which lists yarrow as making up 2 percent, you'll have about 55,000 yarrow seeds; 2 percent of lupine in that same mixture, however, will only provide you with 450 seeds.

We wandered through the bed like Johnny Appleseed, scattering the seeds (on average, two ounces per 150 feet of each plant you want, so that if you wanted five plants in the same area you'd scatter about ten ounces, two of each, or a cup and a quarter), which also included some white yarrow (Queen Anne's Lace would work just as well, but it blooms later), golden marguerites for the front and some annual hollyhocks for lining the fence. Not too many selections; the plot is small, and the jumble had to be *controlled.* After that, we retraced our steps laying no more than an inch of compost over the whole bed. A thorough watering, and because it remained a rainy spring, that was that.

The first year the showing of annuals looked a little sparse, it's true, but to drive by that tiny meadow now, three or four years later, is to see a tangle of summer-long color, with the perennials alive and growing lustier, and the annuals crowding into spare corners. To enable you to get closer, a lawn mower occasionally weaves a slim mowerwide path down the middle, so that, if you walk through it, the flowers brush softly against your legs. The bed requires work—the usual weeding, dividing the perennials, replacing those that don't come back (lupine, probably) and the yearly addition of some new annuals. But these meadowless people wanted a meadow, and now they've created one, right there in the suburbs, where meadows are essentially a thing of the past. The garden, with clover inching its way into the gravel driveway, looks as if it predated the development, and somehow survived. Incongruous as it sounds, it now *belongs* where it is.

What makes that meadow work is the scale. Had these people turned their entire backyard into a meadow, with a swathe of a path down the middle, it would have looked ridiculous in a neighborhood where everything more or less matches. Instead, their small-scale touch is imaginative and whimsical. While it calls attention to itself, it doesn't shriek.

"PLANTING" A POND

I first began to see how many gardens you can have in one when in my first garden, we decided we wanted water. I was dubious about it at first: Would water look right in a village garden where there was no running stream in existence to begin with? I was overruled, and a crew of water specialists was brought in to create water; I have since seen many do-it-yourselfers create the same effect on their own, much less expensively.

The water specialists brought their shovels and dug a pond.

Ours was a pond about four by five feet, and two feet deep, dug at the bottom of a slight slope, so as to create a trickle of a waterfall flowing from the slope itself. Having dug the pond, they lined it in a huge sheet of thick, heavy-duty black plastic, the color of choice for fake pond bottoms.

Then they brought in some good-size but liftable rocks, which went around the edge of the pond, anchoring and obscuring the plastic. They next installed, into the slope, a pump connected to a length of narrow hose, only as round as a pencil. More rocks were piled into the slope to hide the pump. Because sooner or later the pump would surely break or the hose would clog, the stones weren't mortared in a permanent way. Instead, they were piled up like building blocks dropped into a natural-looking pile, to give us access to the innards of the waterfall. Once the pond was filled, the pump circulated the two-foot high waterfall continuously, down the strategically placed rocks, winter and summer long; circulating water won't freeze, and won't get all murky and disgusting. The goldfish we introduced, which easily survived the winter, also helped keep the pond clean.

The sudden appearance of this combination pond and rock garden did of course seem strange at first: there was no way that nature could have put it there. But plantings softened it—some Japanese irises growing submerged in the water, trillium, Solomon's seal (*Polygonatum*), different kinds of ferns. The area was shady, and we kept it all green, with a little variegated white to lighten the area. Rock gardens have the advantage of being made mostly of rocks. No weeding, no maintenance. I was thrilled. And the soothing sound of that trickle of water transformed the garden, making me understand, finally, as many gardeners know all along, that a garden isn't complete without water.

Even the most primitive "display" of water makes a difference. One friend of mine bought a few black Fiberglas cattle troughs of different sizes, all of which come with a drainage hole at the side, by the bottom. He unscrewed the plug, inserted and affixed a hose on the outside, and buried the troughs and hoses here and there in his garden: instant pools. A quirky designer I once heard about buys up old bathtubs. Copper, if she can find them. Otherwise she buys porcelain and has them refinished in black—and sinks those into the gardens she creates. Two matching bathtubs with a "bridge" of stones or planks between them, and you've got something of a river.

In a flowerless Japanese garden, and making the most subtle statement imaginable, I recently saw a stone basin, a yard in circumference and no more than five inches deep, sunk into a bed with two clipped, ground-hugging cotoneasters. There were about ten black pebbles at the bottom of it, off center, and it was filled with water. Against the cotoneasters—great low-growing shrubs shaped like a ripple, which produce early flowers and late berries—the simple basin looked like a work of art, and the still water inside it, with the pebbles refracting in the light, was simplicity itself, quiet and lovely.

Having no water yet in my own garden, I tried to imitate that effect by taking apart my birdbath, using both the basin and the pedestal in the border, the basin at the front, and the pedestal farther back, with an indoor fern summering outside on top of it. The basin looked pretty stupid, and the fern fell off the pedestal in a rainstorm, and I abandoned that strategy when Michael asked me why on earth I had taken the bird bath apart.

One suggestion a friend had was that I revive the unused well that's under the border, turning it into an ornamental well and building a well-house over it. I finally rejected that idea as too dangerous and not watery enough; all you'd see would be the well house. No, I want a real fake pond, or at least a stream. And where? Near the house, when we get around to creating a new terrace, to make maximum use of the sound and sense of water. Next year, I'm going to start with cattle troughs, the galvanized steel kind which come in several sizes, *above* ground, painted green on the outside to match the trim of the house. They're pretty on the outside, and the larger ones are big enough to hold fish and a couple of water lilies. If you can have raised beds, why not raised ponds? (Henry Mitchell also writes about using them throughout his garden, even finishing them sometimes with stucco, although omits telling us what happens to the fish in the winter. I suppose you have fish inside in the winter.)

As I've said before, the more moods in a garden—soothing water, bright annuals, the muted border, healing herbs, shrubs to draw you in—the better. Even now, with the roughest outlines of my garden in place (at least in my mind), I can see that I'm still several moods short of the garden I want. How, for instance, now that my one tree is dead, and my garden feels too glaringly sunny, am I supposed to find a corner of cooling shade?

PLANTING FOR SHADE

To me, one of the greatest garden pleasures is to be standing in the hot sun, in the middle of a garden, and looking toward shade. Trees are the only things I can think of that actually beckon, and a big shade tree, with a bench or a swing in its shade, is such an elemental focal point it needs no other adornment, except for perfect grass or, even better, mounds of spongy moss underneath.

Lucky for you if you already have such a tree, but if you don't, there are two ways to create shade.

One is to buy a mature shade tree, and to have it professionally planted, which will usually cost a percentage of the cost of the tree, give or take, depending on how many people it takes to transport and plant the tree. This is of course a wonderful solution if you can afford it.

The other way is to create the *illusion* of shade.

If you haven't the means to buy a big tree, one or several small ones, preferably bought and installed in the autumn when they're on sale, will provide height, movement and pools of shade underneath, all the glories of a big tree, only smaller. Because my garden is small and because I can't afford a big tree anyway, I'm not going to get a small version of a big tree but will one day buy a good-size version of a small tree: an ornamental cherry (*Prunus*) or flowering apple tree (*Malus*), both of which flower brilliantly in the spring, and both of which, even before they're fully grown, will fit the scale of my cottage-type garden; I'll plant it where the catalpa was. I'll also arrange for a nursery to plant it, since many nurseries guarantee trees they've installed for the first year. Further down the line, I'd also like to add a few elaeangus, silvery-leaved, which will also remain in scale. The trees won't provide big shade, but several areas of small shade do add up. A pergola covered in vines would do it, too, but where? Or maybe a summertime canopy over part of the new terrace, whenever we get around to it.

Shady or not, every garden has at least one dark corner, or at least a corner that's darker than the others. Most people, I've noticed, tend to ignore such corners, figuring that no one walks over to them or around them, so why bother? A lesson I learned from an interior designer, however, made me see that dark corners can be an invitation for the eye to take a break from the sun and cool down. Dark corners, especially those winding toward the side alleyways of houses, or those anywhere within view of the main areas of the garden, should be played up, not played down.

This interior designer was given the job of decorating a fairly grand, high-ceilinged apartment, but one that, from a design point of view, had a fairly obvious flaw. Upon opening the front door, you came not into the imposing foyer you would have expected but into a narrow—really narrow—hallway, which extended about thirty feet, with a couple of doors opening off of it, until you reached the living room, which was lined with a wall of windows and as bright as you could have wanted. The previous designer had tried to brighten the hallway, with celadon-and-white striped wallpaper and lots of high-wattage sconces along the walls. A sisal rug, the kind you often see in sunrooms, covered the floor. The effect was garish, like a dressing room in the bathing-suit boutique of a department store.

This decorator, however, had a different point of view. You can't turn something that's dark into something sunny and light, she thought; instead you have to enhance the dark. Her solution: navy blue wallpaper, with a small, copper-colored design on it. She used the same sconces but put in fifteen-watt bulbs. A dark gray runner, well cushioned, lined the floor and served to muffle sound, which also accentuates darkness. The effect was darkly, warmly inviting; you were being called down a softly lit tunnel to the light at the other end.

The principle of emphasizing the dark works just as well in the garden. Evergreen shrubs such as weeping hemlock, groupings of ferns, or a semicircle of the deep, bluish green hosta weaving around a dark corner will lead you to think that if you followed these plantings around the corner, you'd be enveloped by the cool darkness of a clearing in the forest, even if there's nothing back there but your garbage bins or the woodpile. You can "illuminate" such a corner, too, by planting aegopodium or variegated ajuga as a groundcover, for example, or a couple of variegated hosta, a climbing variegated euonymus or white or pale pink impatiens: anything with white that can prosper in some shade will provide the lighting and make a dark corner seem to glow.

I like to think that over the years, as the garden evolves, I'll get better and better scores when I play a kind of garden game I made up for myself. Imagine standing in the middle of the garden where there's a spinner, like that on a game board; spin it and see where it comes to rest. If it points to something in the garden that pleases, I win the point. If not, that becomes the next area to transform. Not that anyone will stop in his or her tracks and exclaim over every little bit of garden; for visitors, it's the effect as a whole that counts. It's only the gardener who sees the garden bit by bit. But then it's only the gardener who loves the garden bit by bit.

$\mathcal{D}$ecorating the $\mathcal{G}$arden

∽

A few years ago, an acquaintance of mine, who had just put in his garden, proudly asked if I'd come to see it. We couldn't find a time when we were both free, so I said I'd stop by to have a look one morning when he was planning to be out, then call him later with my full report.

I was especially curious to see the garden, because he'd created it on the tiniest bit of property I'd ever seen. He'd recently bought the house, a comfortable, newish Cape Cod–style saltbox, with a big square wooden deck, opening out from glass-paned doors at the back of the kitchen. The deck was too large, proportionally, for the small backyard, which was only about fifteen feet deep, deck included, with a fence around it and not much else. His first thought had been to make the deck smaller to give himself more garden, but dismantling the deck proved as dishearteningly expensive a prospect as building a new one. He had greeted my counter idea, that he turn the deck into an adjunct garden, with grudging enthusiasm, but the more he got into designing and planting his garden, the more excited he became.

I arrived on a sparkling morning in May, and was charmed by what I saw. Beds lining the fence on all three sides of the yard were bursting with fat yellow tulips, white bleeding hearts, nepeta, and lamb's ears, which already were stretching out from their neat beds toward the sun. There were still plenty of empty spaces, and a few nursery pots, with cranesbill and irises, stood at the edge, ready to be planted.

He'd built benches around three sides of the deck, with "end tables" at the corners, each of which had a round hole sawed into it to accommodate a big pot for annuals. Along the fourth side, he'd begun putting herbs into a built-in bed; chives and thyme so far.

Even at this early stage, the place had clearly improved substantially, but what struck me even more than the pretty plantings (perfectly scaled to the small yard) and the upgraded deck were the unmistakable signs of the gardener at work, lovingly bringing his garden to life. The gardener's presence was palpable, even in his absence.

The new wooden table and chairs, taking pride of place on the deck, were not yet painted. Even so, the table bore the remains of the gardener's breakfast—folded newspaper, a stoneware mug with a little coffee left in it, a hand-painted plate with a crust of toast. There were also a few horticultural magazines piled on the edge of the table, anchored by a jar of strawberry jam; a dark gray cat rested on a chair, sleeping on a lighter gray sweatshirt.

Scattered around the garden itself was other evidence of the gardener: clippers and a trowel, a few terra-cotta pots, crumbs of topsoil falling out of their plastic bag. There was an Italian bike leaning against the garden gate. It felt as if the gardener were there, just at the edges of this pleasing still life. And these traces of the gardener made this humble garden feel lived in and vital.

Ever since that morning, I've been more sensitive to the simple human nuances that give each garden its soul. It's true that the garden is more important than the gardener, but it's also true that a garden—however ambitious—that doesn't offer any clues as to who cares for it feels lifeless.

So how do you make a garden feel lived in?

Same way you make a house your own: You decorate it. This is not to recommend flocks of pink flamingos, or even one—less is more.

With a house, you bring everything—furniture, houseplants, paintings, personal effects—from outdoors in. With a garden, you reverse the process, bringing a little bit of yourself from inside the house out to the garden. A garden is meant to be lived in, and if you don't have a few of the accoutrements of living at hand, it'll feel like a furnished model apartment, adequate but strangely sterile.

FURNISHING THE GARDEN

Furniture is the obvious starting point: a table and chairs for dining, chairs or chaises longues for relaxing or benches for repose; it's all a matter of taste and space.

But you can vary even the obvious. For the past couple of years, whenever I've gone to a yard sale or flea market, I've been on the lookout for a small, classic wrought-iron two-seater bench to put in the back courtyard off the barn. Happily I've never found one, because it occurred to me only about a week ago that no one would ever in a million years sit on such a bench in that small courtyard. It would look stilted and fake. I suddenly saw that what I want instead is a plankwide crude wood bench, three or four feet long. I might easily sit on that bench, while studying directions on a seed packet, say. Or I might set my gardening tools or gloves or books on it. I know I want to paint it bluish gray, and I know that it will look exactly right.

Arches, gazebos, decks, terraces, and pergolas are the doorways, rooms, and hallways of the garden. Usually the site choice for decks or terraces is close to the house, but if you're starting a garden from scratch, it might be wise to wait a bit before choosing where you want your arches, gazebos, or pergolas. The more you garden, the more you'll *change* your garden, and expand it; what seems logical at first may feel all wrong later. Spend the round-one money instead on enclosing the garden. And then put in all the structures you want, within scale and reason. Even a prefab child's playhouse, well adorned with flowers and small shrubs, can become a part of the whole of the garden.

Any other movable furniture or fixtures, however, belong in the garden from the beginning. Not long ago, I ran into a man I know leaving an antiques sale and triumphantly carrying, with the help of several of his friends, a heavy, *L*-shaped alter railing. At first, it seemed like an unusual thing for him to buy. I remembered, though, that he lives in an old church that's been converted into a house. The alter railing, he said, would become the partition between his living and dining areas, which take up the big former sanctuary.

That got me thinking about the new bed I want to expand, where I recently planted two lilacs, a bed that would run parallel to (and help obscure) the front of the barn. And that got me thinking about the junkyard in our village.

Sure enough, there's a curving wrought-iron banister (in fact it's a whole wrought-iron staircase, but in pieces) sitting in the junkyard which, if I dug it into the curve of my planned new bed, might (if it doesn't curve too sharply) lead to an arch for the climbing roses, and set off another garden "room." That's one possibility.

GARDEN ORNAMENTS

And then you can decorate the garden rooms themselves, with artfully placed urns, a millstone, if you can find one, and other indoor-outdoor ornaments. Just walk around rooms of your house, imagining what might look pretty outside, new ways to connect the indoors with the outdoors.

If you have an outdoor dining table, give it an indoor center-piece—a painted pitcher, a bowl or basket of plums and peaches ripening, a vase with cut flowers from the garden itself, a candle protected against the wind by a hurricane lamp.

If you have a fence, think of it not as a fence but as an empty wall. I once saw a simple stock fence on which the gardener had mounted one of those wooden shelves you can buy at a lumberyard and screw in anywhere. Resting on the shelf in the middle of the garden were three antique colored bottles, which looked odd but nice. That gave me the idea for mounting a useless, scrolled, wrought-iron *thing* I spent way too much money for one day when I was feeling madcap or temporarily insane and that had been in the cellar ever since. Hanging on the fence, where ivy is beginning to curl around it, it looks fine.

Or try walking around the yard with a few cans of brightly colored spray paint, to bring some (restrained) whimsy into the garden—paint the odd fencepost red, or a trellis navy blue. One man I know has a guest room with a beautiful doorway jutting out into his garden. He paints the door and the lintel above it a different bright color each year, making his garden look like a different garden every year: The parade of colors offsets the plants around it in a new way each summer, heightening the transition from garden to house and back again.

WINDOW BOXES AND CONTAINER PLANTINGS

You can also, paradoxical as it sounds, use plants to decorate the garden. Window boxes, for example, don't belong only on the front windows, facing the street. For that matter, they don't even necessarily belong on windows; they can be mounted on any wall that needs softening. On a garden tour this year, I saw a smallish garden that sloped down two terraced levels, below a two-story house. From the lower tier of the garden, the house could have looked like a skyscraper, as if it were bearing down on the garden. The designer, however, had foreseen this, and installed window boxes under the windows of the second story of the house; the gardener would open the screens upstairs to tend them. White petunias (well tended; petunias look terrible if they're not pinched severely several times a week) tumbling out of these boxes softened the imposing lines of the house, and made it all of a piece with the garden. In the same way, window boxes filled with impatiens (which don't need any pinching) can brighten dark windows stuck on the shady "wrong side" of the house, away from any garden view, but pretty from inside.

Container plantings—movable window boxes, in effect—can impart a wonderful complexity to a garden or a terrace, and can obscure a fair number of mistakes besides. Even in the formal border, a few container plantings set next to a dying-back perennial (not on top of the root system, or it'll strangle the plant) can bring that area back to life, visually speaking, again. Then move the containers into the next spot that peters out.

If the container is big enough and provisions are made to water it regularly (plants in containers, like those in raised beds, dry out faster—much faster—than plants in the ground), you can grow anything in them: perennials, annuals, roses, herbs, even evergreen shrubs or topiaries for a permanent effect. Even common geraniums, especially the new trailing hybrids, look cheerful and optimistic in big pots on the terrace. It gets expensive, though, buying big pots, saucers, potting soil, and finally the plants themselves. Plus terra-cotta planters have to be brought indoors during the northern winters, or they'll crack.

One cheaper way out is to buy big planters in plastic made to look like terra-cotta, and from a distance, they do. Earlier this year, I read that if you rub these planters with yogurt, then leave them in the shade, they'll emerge looking as if they have some facsimile of moss over them. So I bought two big planters, covered them with yogurt (I only had vanilla on hand, so maybe that was part of the problem), and left them in the shade. They did turn sort of greenish brown after a while, but it wasn't very pretty. I hosed them off and planted, among other things, variegated myrtle around the edges of the containers; the myrtle trailed over the sides nicely, so that only a mean-spirited person would notice that the containers were plastic. Nicer pots are important where they really stand out, and are as much a decorative element as what's planted in them; plastic is perfectly fine for out-of-the-way corners. (Fiberglas containers, which are really pretty, not to mention lightweight, bear watching, too; perhaps they'll get a little cheaper if there's more of a demand for them.)

A friend of mine keeps a row of carefully chosen but mismatched pots on the brick wall surrounding two sides of her terrace, filled with perennials in bloom. When the perennials have done their thing, she transplants them to the garden for next year, and puts in the next perennials coming into bloom. Usually she tires of this by early July, though, and the pots stand empty for the rest of the season, but even then, lined up in a neat row, they look like an expectant display.

MOVING YOUR HOUSEPLANTS OUTDOORS

Another annual decorating ritual is moving the houseplants outdoors for the summer, like sending your plants to camp. Wait till after the last frost to bring them out, and bring them in long before the first frost in the fall, after having sprayed or at least washed them thoroughly, so as to prevent bringing bugs or fungus inside. If you have any water in the garden, or even if you don't, papyrus, which grows on long stems like drinking straws and produces green, spiderlike foliage on top—most exotic—is one of the best indoor-outdoor plants you can choose. If you tend to overwater your plants, then papyrus is for you. You *can't* overwater it because it has to be *submerged*, literally, by putting the pot it's planted in into a bigger pot filled with water. Outside, it can go directly into a pond or a small pool, or it can simulate the cooling impression of a water garden when you set it into a tub of water. Inside, it needs lots of light (though not necessarily direct sunlight), and just as much water. Ferns, which often grow ragged by May (mine do, anyway) when kept indoors, seem to get a special infusion of energy just from being set outside, in dappled sun-shade.

The aesthetic trade-off for bringing your houseplants outdoors for the summer is that you can fill their spaces by bringing the garden—cut flowers and branches of flowering shrubs—indoors. Another trick, too, is to give plants meant for the border a few days inside before you get around to planting them in the garden. A plumed astilbe or a fox-glove in bloom on the mantle in a pretty basket or a coreopsis in the kitchen brings the garden inside, and you'll find yourself studying such a plant's beauty in a new way, viewing it out of the context of the garden. You also buy yourself a little extra time before you have to plant it.

VINES AND GROUNDCOVERS

There are garden plants, too, that I think of as finishing, decorative touches: You don't notice if they're not there, but they make the garden look complete when they are. These are the less-is-more plants that are wonderful when used with restraint, but veer, when overused, toward the cliché. Take vines, for instance.

A climbing honeysuckle (*Lonicera*) winding up a trellis, a silver-lace vine (*Polygonum abertii;* it grows incredibly fast, about fifteen feet a year) overtaking a fence, a trumpet vine (*Campsis*) or climbing hydrangea filling a wall, a wisteria making its way across a sloping roof. . . . As much as shrubs, vines give the necessary sense of enclo-sure to a garden—and most grow to cover posts, pillars, walls, and trellises—and a lush presence that draws the eye up. The only design worry with vines is that too many per garden can be claustrophobic, making the walls of the garden look as if they were covered with clashing wallpapers.

If you want to mix vines, to cover, say, a long, boring fence, you're best off keeping the theme consistent—evergreens, like climbing holly, plain old English ivy or *Pyracantha,* called firethorn, which produces subtle white flowers in the spring and huge clusters of red berries in the fall—and thorns.

If you like twining, flowery vines, clematis, which won't choke a wall, is to the garden what a perfect accessory—a silver candlestick, an antique clock—is to a room. Clematises are expensive at the out-set, but when they take hold, they grow dramatically better with each passing season, cascading over walls or fences or fenceposts or tree trunks but with a restraint that can best be described as well bred: a solid mass of blooms up and over whatever is in their path.

Many books (and gardeners) will tell you that clematis is easy to grow, but others I know have had only so-so luck with it—enough, though, not to get too discouraged. I've lost enough myself, and had enough work, to know.

Usually there are two choices when it comes to buying clematis:

the spindly looking varieties climbing on metal grids stuck in their pots, which cost about $20 and the twice-as-thick varieties, which cost nearly double. If you possibly can, select more expensive plants; you'll improve your odds by a lot if you plant the biggest clematis you can find, which will be about three years old. Clematis like full sun at the top, and cooler roots. When you plant them, sprinkle and chop some peat into the hole, tamp the plant in carefully, then cover the earth three inches or so out from the stem—a sprinkling of gravel, a thick mulch or bricks in a V-shape around the plant will do the trick. Then leave it. Don't prune it for the first few years, as it will leaf out and bloom over last year's growth. Just fertilize it in the spring when you fertilize everything else, keep it watered when you water everything else and don't touch it. Even if you think it's dead, leave it in place; don't pull it out and throw it away—it may surprise you next year. And hope for the best.

There are about a zillion different clematis species and cultivars, the hardiest of which are the *Clematis* ×*jackmanii* cultivars. Hardier still is the sweet autumn-flowering *C. paniculata*, or *C. maximowicziana*, which any idiot can grow; however, pretty (though commonplace) as it is, *C. paniculata* doesn't have the flair of the summer-flowering species.

The poor gardener's clematis is the morning glory, which I've always loved but never had much luck with, probably because I never read about growing morning glories until this year, when I didn't plant them. They germinate easily from seed when planted outdoors as soon as it starts to get warm: That much I know. But here's where the concept of nipping in the bud comes in. You're supposed to nip them in the bud, whereupon, slightly annoyed at having been nipped, they fragment themselves into two buds, and then, assuming you keep nipping, more after that. Then their little tendrils wrap around whatever you give them to climb on, and then you supposedly have morning glories, which actually can be glorious all day long, from late June through September. Often they'll come back year after year, and when they do, they can turn into an aggressive vine, strangling plants around them. "How picturesque," a friend of mine said to herself, when she noticed morning glories climbing a pine tree at her new house. Until the asphyxiated pine turned yellow and died.

If vines take the eye up the walls of the garden, sooner or later the eye has to come back down. When it does, it should rest on a horticultural carpet.

Grass is the obvious carpet of choice, though I've never understood why. It's hard to grow. The chemicals and weed killers it
requires are harmful to the water table. It requires more watering than
most plants. In a hot summer, it gets brown and dormant in July, and
doesn't recover till October, when you hardly care anymore. One of
my aims is to reduce the percentage of grass in my garden a little bit
each year, replacing it with beds of shrubs and flowers, and surrounding petticoats of groundcovers, until I have just a small, perfect bed of
grass the size of a swimming pool.

Less grass means more garden and, for a gardener, that's the
whole idea. If you have a row of shrubs, pull the row—and the garden—out with plantings: ferns if it's shady, an arc of hosta here and
there (just avoid long, straight, unbroken rows of hosta, unless you
want your garden to look like a median strip), patches of ajuga, delicate variegated ivies or myrtle (if you've got the patience; it's very
slow growing). Think of layering: Plants under plants under plants, so
that groupings of shrubs taper off gradually, softly, with plants that
keep them afloat all the way down to the ground.

It's a combination of human and horticultural flourishes that
makes a garden unique, and that makes it lived in, like the rooms in a
well-used house. Just as such a house takes time to settle into its
foundation, so, too, does a garden take time to settle in. But seasons
go surprisingly fast; you notice it more when you garden. It's startling
to see how much richer the third-year garden is than one in its first or
second year. By then the garden has a history, a presence. And by
then, you'll be offering to friends as well as accepting from them gifts
of cuttings and clippings of your favorite plants.

The only thing I'd have to offer now, my second season, is
aegopodium, which spreads so abundantly that I wouldn't miss it if a
friend needed to dig up a clump. And it was only last year that I got
my first little bit of it—amazing. Mostly, though, I'm still the recipient
of those clumps and clippings. Recently I got such an offer from a
gardening friend who was dividing her phlox; she had some extras and
wanted to know if I wanted some. Yes, of course. "Just come by," she
said. If she wasn't in the garden, she'd be inside the house. My three
clumps of phlox were in a box resting in the shade when I got there,
and the garden looked perfect. Right by the back door were her
muddy sneakers, gloves and some clippers, as much a sign of the garden as the phlox themselves.

4

Tending the Garden

$\mathscr{A}utumn$

Iceboating season, a friend of mine maintains, begins in the summer. Every June he mounts his teak iceboat onto sawhorses and painstakingly sands and waxes his sleek boat, varnishing this part, waxing that one, rubbing the brass till it's shiny. That he can imagine and prepare for iceboating on a clear summer day seems to me an incredible affirmation of the future: Yes, before you know it there *will* be ice on the pond near his house, and he'll be ready for it when it comes.

In the same way, the gardening season stretches well beyond the few short weeks that signal the best time to plant—and even beyond the spring and summer months when the flowers and shrubs are at their peak. Starting a garden is a year-round commitment, with some months more labor-intensive than others. Maintaining a garden is as much work as planting one, but at least there are a few rewards along the way.

When does the gardener's year start? There is something about the garden in fall, when the light slants just so, and you keep putting a muddy sweatshirt over your T-shirt and then taking it off again as the temperature goes from warmish to cooler and back again. Hopeful, invigorating, a little sad nonetheless. Perhaps arbitrarily, I'd say the gardener's year begins here.

Autumn never feels like the last chance to me, though. It always feels instead like the real beginning of the gardener's year. This is because a garden exists as much in one's imagination as it does in the earth, and autumn is the time to plan, and dream. You can't be a gardener for very long before you begin to look ahead to grandiose future triumphs rather than dwell on the paltry stems of the past. What matters now is the garden you'll have next year, not the fact that, come to think of it, didn't you used to have three dwarf *Spiraea* and how come now you only have two? You learn to accept the losses, and to look ahead.

This fall, I moved the two remaining dwarf spiraea, along with some santolina and a few other things, to the lilac bed, which I enlarged with a rototiller. This new bed runs parallel to the front length of the barn, and curves toward the back, creating a path to the back quadrant off the barn. Mostly, I plan to keep shrubs in this one, or plants that act as shrubs, like the three rue that used to look nice in front of the "hedge" of chives until they got too big; now the chives can fill the space by themselves. Plus I'd like to give two shrubby *Potentilla* I got from a friend a second chance; they only produced a couple of white blossoms in his garden and may do better in new surroundings, although a lot of gardeners around here have trouble with potentilla. (Too bad, the flowers seem so feisty on these small shrubs, which—when they work—make a great low hedge.) I had hoped to buy that curved railing from the winding iron staircase I saw in the junkyard, to mark the curve of this bed, putting irises in front of it, but it turned out that I would have had to buy the entire staircase, which cost too much and would have looked ridiculous winding up to nowhere. Maybe something else will turn up.

It's thrilling that even now, with the garden completing only its second season, some of my plants are big enough to be moved around or divided (this may be because I still plant them too close together— even though I should know better by now—and crowd them), enough so anyway to get this new bed off to a good start. This new shrubby bed will be easy to maintain, I reason. But will it have enough color? Just to be on the safe side, in went three Japanese anemones, white ones, a few asters and a fragrant 'Sea Foam' rose, bought on sale. It'll mean more deadheading and more maintenance, but next year, with a nicer garden, I will (of course) be more diligent about all that upkeep. Gardener's resolution.

Bad planning, in a way, this new bed, but it's been on my mind to do it.

Bad planning because after a stellar moment in late July when I felt for a change that I was ahead, the weeds once again took the lead early this fall. Why start a new bed when the other ones are so ratty looking?

In another way it made sense. Plunging into a new bed always has spillover effects into existing beds: Digging a plant from here and a few more from there makes me weed a little around where I dig, thus clearing out more of the whole. Moving one perennial often starts a chain reaction of moving others that need to be moved or divided, like the jump-over progression in a game of Chinese checkers—which encourages even more clearing out. A clean new bed also makes the old ones, particularly if they're weedy, look worse, which makes me feel sorry for them and love them more and start weeding all over again.

Fall repeats spring in some respects, this flurry of planting and moving and rethinking the whole garden. It repeats summer, too, in that the last blooms of the season are as surprising as the first. Many spring- and summer-blooming perennials give off a faint echo of their full splendor in the fall with a little blossom here, a spray there, all the more beautiful, I think, for being unexpected and minimalist.

But there's an urgency to autumn. If spring chores slide into summer, well, it happens; and if summer chores slide, there's always the fall. Fall, however, stops short at winter—and that's the deadline. In part, the gardener's instincts in autumn are protective: As you come to love your plants, you want to tuck them in safely for the winter, the way you'd wrap up a sleeping child for a long ride home in the dark. In part, too, the instincts are *self*-protective: Any chores you leave undone now will be ten times more unpleasant to tackle in the spring. You'll spend the whole winter worrying about the garden, and you'll also spend it suffering from self-recriminations, which is even worse.

To get around those self-recriminations, I decided in the fall last year to start—finally—my compost pile.

CREATING A COMPOST PILE

I had long felt about compost the way I do about coming to grips with the pH factor: too boring, too complicated, a mental block. There was also the expense. Should I buy one of those compost barrels that you turn, like a giant version of the cages in which you mix up the numbers in a bingo game? Should I have someone come and build a compost setup? And where, in my small yard, would I put it? I also had trouble picturing myself running to and from the kitchen carrying orange peelings and leftover string beans; even though it's probably as old as agriculture itself, the compost ritual seemed, frankly, a little too New Age for me.

There was, however, the attraction of compost.

Early last summer, I'd stopped by to visit a friend whose Oriental poppies were in bloom, and meandered all the way back through her garden, which ends, beyond a vegetable patch, with the compost pile—piles, more accurately, because once you get it going, you keep at least two piles or bins, one holding compost-in-progress and one holding compost. Sprouting at the top of her compost were a dozen or more tiny shoots of columbine, their leaves newly green against the rich brown stuff, at once solid and crumbly, in which they were growing. The cycle of replenishing seemed to exist right there, in that bin, and suddenly, despite my applications of fertilizer, manure and whatever else, my own garden seemed badly depleted by comparison. Besides, I was sick of taking the garden debris off to the town landfill, to put on the big compost pile there, for someone else to use. I wanted compost of my own.

It struck me that no gardener I know, however fancy, has one of those compost barrels, and I decided to go the simplest route, ordering from a mail-order catalog two adjoining steel wire compost bins with lids (forget about protection from raccoons; I needed protection from the bigger of our dogs), which weren't even very difficult to assemble. While I know you don't *need* plastic liners, I ordered them anyway—anything to speed the process—which turned out to be a mistake. The plastic ripped, flapped noisily in the wind and had to be cut back. Some compost activator, for instant gratification, proved a worthier investment.

Equipment in place (in some, but not necessarily full, sun; compost needs heat), I started my compost pile and, from the beginning, I found the cycle really satisfying, one of those things that makes you wonder, once you've done it, why you never did it before.

Grass clippings are good compost material, and I'd vowed to start my compost pile while the lawn still needed mowing, so as to get a good base. Naturally I broke that vow, and had to start later, with dead leaves, which turned out to be fine.

To that I added clippings from the garden, trying to avoid including huge piles of weeds. Weeds in themselves are fine in the compost throughout the summer but, just as the columbine sprouted in my friend's compost, weeds will sprout, too, if they've set their seed. Many of them do so in late summer, so seedy weeds are best kept out. I also avoided branches, clippings from roses and anything else that looked too big or bulky to decompose readily; my bins are small, and I wanted compost by spring. Slowly, I got used to including leftovers from the kitchen (no bones, dairy products, meat or greasy things). A little compost activator, any extra soil, manure, the ends of a bag of peat and the like—the recipe is casual, like recipes for making stock from leftover bones, and after a while, when I ran out of it, I stopped adding the activator. I watered it well, turned it often (practically every day when I first got it and then, once the novelty had worn off, a couple of times a week) and was surprised to see how fast the level of the bin dropped from full to about a third full: I was making compost. By spring, there was a good deal of it to spread around the garden. An inch thick is about the right amount, over every bed, right up to the stems of the plants. Much more than that and the compost encourages excess foliage development, and less blooming.

If you're not ready to make a full commitment to composting, you might try *precomposting*, a term and technique invented by my neighbor.

The highway department sweeps up leaves in our village if you rake them into the street by a certain cutoff date, which she had missed. (I once missed it, too, and learned that if you sweep them into the street after that, they can tell they're your leaves, since they're right in front of your house, and someone comes by and yells at you.) Anyway, she raked her leaves into lawn-and-leaf garbage bags, added a little manure and a fair amount of water, poked about ten good-size holes into each of the bags on all sides and set them around the corners of her garden: behind a hedge, in unused weedy beds—places where there was nothing below to strangle. The bags piled up looked a little sinister, like body bags, but you didn't notice after a while, and covered with snow in the winter, they actually looked like shrubs. She turned the bags from time to time and, by spring, she had not only excellent compost but also a few weedless new beds; the heavy bags had killed everything underneath them. I wish I had known about this technique the autumn before I started the garden.

AUTUMN RITUALS

You'll get plenty of raw material from the autumn garden for the compost pile (or precompost bags), since most of the autumn tasks involve cutting back. Most perennials, for instance, should be cut back or nearly back to the ground, although, as always, there are exceptions to this rule.

Perennials go dormant when they're cut back at the end of the season, and the plants' remaining energies are all directed to the roots. They go dormant anyway, even if you don't cut them, but why permit their energies to be diffused? Plus there's always the possibility that a fungus might find its way into limp or soggy, toppled-over leaves. It's harder, too (to say nothing of depressing), to separate the spent growth from the new growth if you wait till spring. Some gardeners disagree, and argue that autumn foliage makes a good mulch or coat that can help protect the plants against being killed by a cold winter. For me the winning argument is that the spring garden will be a soggy mess next year if it's not cut back in the fall.

When you do cut your perennials back, don't slash away at them as if you were clearing a jungle with a machete. Some plants have already gone dormant, and you'll want to avoid disturbing them. Whenever I get too enthusiastic about weeding and clearing in the fall, for example, I always crash into the root systems of the same bleeding hearts over and over, poor things. They went dormant in August and no doubt would rather be left alone. Or maybe they're used to it by now.

Plants exempt from cutting back in the fall are generally aesthetic exceptions. Some plants, notably sedum spectabile 'Autumn Joy', astilbe, the ornamental grasses, and anything else that has faded naturally to look like an attractive dried-flower arrangement, can be left alone over the winter to mark various moments and places in the garden—built-in winter interest. Moved by the wind, or bowed and disguised by the snow, these plants will still attract the eye from now until spring. But everything else goes.

This means annuals, too, which are also a slimy mess to get rid of in the spring. If you're hoping your annuals will reseed themselves, they will have done so by now. You'll be surprised, actually, by how stoic they are. My cleome this year had stems so fat I could hardly fit them in my hand. The blooms just kept on going well into October, and beyond; it felt wrong to think about pulling them out. But cleome reseeds itself readily anyway, and failing that, it can be replaced in the spring with very little trouble. Most important, if my daffodils were to be planted, in that bed just by the porch door, the cleome would have to come out.

DEFERRED GRATIFICATION:
PLANTING IN AUTUMN

I have recently read that daffodils are best planted early, in September, but this was a surprise to me; I don't think I've ever planted them so early, nor have I ever failed to have them come in just fine in the spring. The tulips go in late, too, at the last minute; I aim for October, to give the roots a chance to develop while the soil is still warm. I've often put the planting off until Thanksgiving, however, if the autumn is unusually warm, and even so, the bulbs have always managed to come up somehow. (Except once when one of the dogs dug them up, ate them and got sick. The vet says his dogs do the same thing.)

With my daffodils from last year and the year before beginning to naturalize, I can count on some kind of spring showing just by doing nothing, which is reassuring, but a few more each year, planted the same time as the tulips, which are clustered farther back, in the perennial border, won't hurt.

Forget about following the instructions for planting bulbs. Plant them instead the way you want to see them growing. Usually the instructions will tell you to space the bulbs at least several inches apart and, if you do, that's the way they'll grow, not in the casual, here-and-there clusters that are so much nicer, and more natural looking. Plant bulbs to a depth three times their height, sprinkling a little bone meal into the bottom of the hole. As long as there is soil between them, to keep the bulbs from touching, they're far enough apart. A hole full of newly installed bulbs should look from above like a raspberry tart, with the raspberries spaced not quite touching so that you can see a little of the custard and glaze between each one.

Anything that's newly planted or transplanted will need regular watering for the first couple of weeks, which is easy to forget in the autumn, when the cool air doesn't make you thirsty enough to remind you that your plants might also be thirsty. To remember, think of how much warmer the water can be than the air; once you're swimming, you're fine. It's the same way with the soil—in the autumn, the air may be growing colder, while the garden soil still retains heat. This heat is drying, and new roots need moisture to grow strong enough to withstand the winter. If the weather doesn't cooperate, the gardener will have to provide the water.

So that's the drill: clearing out, cutting back, planting. The rhythm is slow, even a little melancholy.

There are a few chores that I didn't get around to—but should have—this fall. There are beds into which the grass has encroached, and that need reeding; I had thought I might get around to it in time, so that the lines delineating beds from lawn would look clean all winter. I tell myself that I'll get to it instead on one of those unnaturally warm days in January or February, when in fact I know that I won't get to it until April or May, when I get to everything else. Then there's the front of the house, to which I still haven't given much thought. Too late for this year now, I guess. Plus, I forgot that before the winter came I'd wanted to install a trellis (simple but nice wooden ones can be had for about $15), painted green to match the trim of the house, to support the climbing honeysuckle, which currently, with nowhere to climb, is tumbling all over the place. That'll have to be done first thing next year, because it comes up early and grows fast.

We don't have the room so I don't do it, but I like to visit a friend every year whose final autumn chore is an anticipatory one. She lives in a kind of woodland setting, lots of trees, even more saplings. Every year she clears out a few of these to create new beds, so that her garden is becoming full of secret places. Along one slope is a collection of pines, each one a former Christmas tree, bought roots and all for planting later. And every year around pumpkin time she and her young son dig and prepare a hole, before the ground freezes, into which this year's tree will go just after the New Year. They've always survived the January planting.

Autumn, too, is the time to lay in a supply of salt hay, a protective winter mulch, enough to cover your beds and border. Whenever the ground freezes, is the time to spread a generous layer of salt hay (enough so that what you see is the salt hay, with only a peek here and there of the bare earth underneath) over the garden. Winter mulch has nothing to do with summer mulch, which stays put forever; winter mulches are to protect the plants, and gathered up every spring. Somehow the salt hay blankets the garden and helps keep the temperatures in the soil from veering too wildly, and heaving the root systems around. I'm not sure I understand the concept entirely, but I like it, and I like the ceremony of putting it down when it's cold, as well as that of gathering it up the following spring.

As we were spreading the salt hay around this year, once the weather began turning bitter, I asked Michael which flowers he'd like to see more of. "Foxgloves," he said without hesitation, which stopped me in my tracks; I hadn't known he was paying attention. Suddenly I wanted to stop winter, to count up the foxgloves and plant more, to rethink the lilac bed, to move the crape myrtle closer to the herbs. Was the bamboo a mistake? If so, I'll never get it out. Would there be enough room for an elaeagnus one day? A flowering cherry? Meantime, with every passing day, my roots were trenching their way deeper into the earth. The more they established themselves, the more disruptive it would be to move them, and the more time they'd need to establish themselves somewhere else all over again. But perhaps I'd have to move them all, anyway. . . . The dark thoughts of winter.

The course of two years is a very short time in the life of a garden, of course, but now, like gardeners all over the world, I begin to revise that brief history, and to make a new garden in my mind. Sooner or later, I see now, the carefully planted lawn will have to go, to make room for pools and ponds, that rose bed, at least one other bed where I can squeeze in all the plants I like but can't grow in those I already have. I'll need to create more sun, and more shade. In the tiny alleyways along the dark side of the house, I'll finally put in those narrow paths, and achieve the grottolike look of a terrarium.

Should this garden in my mind ever match the one outside the door, it will be a beautiful place.

$\mathcal{W}inter$

I have planted many an avocado pit, into highball glasses and with toothpick supports, but without much faith that the pits would turn into new avocados for home-grown guacamole, and indeed, they never have. I'm fascinated by life regenerating itself on the sunny windowsills of other people's kitchens: jelly glasses with snippings of ivy taking root; a thriving pot of summer savory, whatever that is; one big maidenhair fern producing many smaller maidenhair ferns; children's seedling experiments that actually work. Intellectually, I know that big plants from little seedlings grow. In my heart, I'm more like a horticultural agnostic. I won't believe it until I see it.

It was a dark, stormy night late in March when I made my first visit, quite a number of years ago, to a real home plant "laboratory." It didn't turn me into a believer at once. I felt instead that I might as well have been visiting a voodoo meeting, because the rituals were so arcane.

The woman behind it, a meticulous, by-the-book, *very* good gardener—and, I now discovered, a mad scientist as well—had concocted in her basement a fail-safe system for growing plants from seed. Long wooden tables were lined up, with a number of flats (those shallow plastic trays for planting) on each one. Some of the flats were carefully covered in dark plastic wrap and resting on warming trays or coils ("germinating," she said). Others, and there were many of them, with tiny or slightly bigger embryonic plants in them, were lit, or not lit, by overhead growing lights set on timers; even in the few minutes we were down there, growing lights clicked on and off in a pattern that made no sense to me. At the far end, amid more clicking lights, were larger pots, filled with plant infants and toddlers who would be ready to venture outdoors in a few weeks' time. "I rigged it all up myself," she said, "for under a hundred dollars." The neatly labeled perennials growing there were worth, retail, a thousand dollars, easy.

No way, I said to myself. It looked like so much work.

And yet, the closer you get to your garden, the closer you want to get to the source. Savings aside—well, no, most of us can't really put the savings aside—there's also the miracle of watching a seed you've planted grow into a flower or an herb. Seeing my friend's lovely garden, after all the seedlings had taken root outdoors, is what began to turn me into a cautious believer. Nasturtiums, sweet alyssum, forget-me-nots, annual gypsophila, and Shirley poppies . . . having seen, too, how easily these could grow from seed, even for me, my curiosity (and greed) began to get the better of me: Growing plants from seed produces more plants for much less money, to say nothing of the satisfaction of nurturing real live plants from little black specks.

Spring travels up the Eastern seaboard (the Western seaboard, too, no doubt, and the Midwest) at a rate of fifteen miles a day, so the farther south you are, the longer (beginning earlier and ending later) the gardening season. I have friends in Virginia, for instance, who have cut their last peony in May before my first one comes into bloom. For them, winter planning for spring, and thus the launch of the gardening year, happens almost a month sooner than it does for me. I'm glad I don't live in Virginia.

There are gardeners who will happily fill up their year-round calenders with horticultural things to do, but this isn't really necessary. Winter is, for the most part, the gardener's resting time, and one of the reasons we should do all we can to fight global warming is to keep it that way. You don't really need to place your order for catalog items the minute the catalogs arrive in December or January; you can simply throw them all into a basket or drawer for a couple of months. If the supplier has run out of something you want, then maybe, knowing that so many other people will be growing it, you wouldn't have wanted it anyway. Or maybe it was hard to grow in the first place or the catalog company would have had more in stock. You also don't have to rush outside every time a branch falls, to move it. My rule of thumb is that you can get away with remaining dormant for as long as the garden does, and still have a perfectly fine garden.

WINTER RITUALS

Along with eating too many Christmas cookies and avoiding any fanfare on New Year's Eve, there are two winter gardening rituals I make myself do every year, and neither takes much effort. The first is pleasingly melancholy, will take only a few hours, and can almost count as exercise: visiting gardens—parks, arboretums, botanic gardens, whatever gardens you come across. Visiting gardens in winter is like visiting a darkened theater: The emptiness echoes, and the imagination fills in the kinds of scenes that might take place. Like neglected props, the structural elements of the garden are stark, unadorned by leaves and the frills of perennials, annuals, and groundcovers. Evergreens stand out. The shapes of the beds and borders are unmistakable. It's the only time you can tell exactly how roses are lined up in a rose garden, or the situation of flowering shrubs in a perennial border. It's also the only time that nature stops to give you a close behind-the-scenes look, and you'll come home with pink cheeks and a longing for a grove of pines, as green now as they are in June.

The second ritual is sprinkling the wood ash every time the fireplace needs sweeping out, thereby helping the garden and also getting rid of the ashes, which otherwise can be a nuisance to dispose of. Wood ash is a good source of potassium, which most plants (with the exception of those troublesome pH-dependent acid-loving plants like rhododendron, azalea, and mountain laurel) need to thrive. Spreading the ash is not a refined art. I just put it all into a paper bag and sprinkle it around the garden and lawn. A thin, even sprinkling everywhere is the object—too much in one spot is no good—but if you accidentally dump the whole bag in one place, you can just spread it around with your foot.

Those rituals aside, for me, on Long Island, Valentine's Day actually marks the start of the hands-on gardening calendar year, not because of the array of bouquets that come streaming in from my husband, who prefers to send flowers after a fight, but because the nurseries, closed for their abbreviated idea of winter, begin to reopen at about this time. One of the first things they display are the new seed packets, and the interesting seeds always disappear fast. (It's good to know, too, that many of the nurseries fail to reorder seeds once they're sold, I assume because they're such low-ticket items.) If you're going to order seeds from a seed catalog, or buy them from a nursery, this is the time to do so. You can then throw them into the drawer with the catalogs for a few more weeks, and go back to being dormant yourself till the third or fourth week in March, when it's time to germinate them indoors—the great winter gardening ritual.

SOWING SEEDLINGS: A TRIUMPH OF HOPE OVER EXPERIENCE?

My friend with her laboratory has the whole routine down pat, but there are less complicated ways to grow plants from seed.

The easiest way is to have someone else do it. I have a friend in another state, and she and the other members of her garden club have worked out an enviable system with a commercial greenhouse nearby, whereby they rent a corner of the greenhouse space, pay the nominal labor costs, supply the growers with the flats they need, the seeds they want grown and the planting medium of their choice. They bring the supplies over in February and pick up the ready-to-plant plants in late April or early May. For its part, the greenhouse is growing all kinds of stuff anyway; here's a guaranteed sale. For the members of the club, the entire cost is less that half of what they'd pay to get the plants at a nursery. This way, too, the gardeners are able to experiment with hard-to-come-by species that might not be readily available from their usual suppliers, from seeds they can order from anywhere in the world.

The second easiest way is to plant the seeds directly into the garden, in the spring for bloom not *that* summer but the summer after, or in the early fall for bloom the following spring or summer. They'll be growing, but roots first, so they won't do you much good right away.

Regrettably, if not surprisingly, the most effective way to grow plants from seed is to start the plants indoors, which is also, of course, the most difficult: there's nothing guaranteed about this method, even if you go to all the trouble my friend does in her home laboratory. Having managed, with occasional success, to grow plants from seed myself, I'd compare the odds favorably to those of soliciting a mail-order response, where a two-percent return is considered fine. With plants, I'm thrilled if I get ten sturdy, healthy plants from a hundred seeds.

GETTING STARTED

Do-this/do-that instructions for growing plants from seed are so mind-numbingly complicated that it's best not to know too much when you start, or you'll be likely to give up without trying. For example, I once read somewhere that it's best to moisten seeds (some seeds? all seeds? I couldn't remember) before you plant them, and this faint memory came to me when I went to sow some foxgloves. So I dumped the seeds into a saucer, a speckled Italian pottery thing, into which I'd poured water—and lost them forever. The seeds were so tiny they simply vanished. I kept the saucer around for a few days, thinking something horticultural might happen, but no such luck. Moistening seeds (not all seeds: some seeds) ahead of time hastens germination, but why not let them germinate at their own speed?

If you're starting in a small-scale way, the only equipment you really need are a planting medium—soil premixed with things to help the seeds get started—and flats. You can mix your own germinating medium, but it requires mixing sandy soil (which, to sterilize it, has to be baked!), with peat moss, perlite (ground mica), clean potting soil, vermiculite (volcanic matter) and fertilizer. The first time out, however, I'd recommend a premixed planting medium, which is much easier and costs almost nothing. (If you insist on starting on a grander scale, you might add to that list of supplies a more comprehensive book than this one on growing from seed.) You'll be surprised at how light the prepurchased medium is; this is because to germinate, seeds need plenty of air.

Many gardeners also like to use planting pellets, which resemble little disk-like dog biscuits; when you add water to them, they puff up into chunky blobs of mostly peat, encased in biodegradable netting; you insert the seeds into the tops of the pellets, one seed per pellet. The pellets then get lined up in the flats, and can subsequently be planted right into the garden. I haven't had great luck with these, although I find myself trying them again and again because it's so much fun to add the water and watch them puff up. But when they're all lined up in the flats, for some reason it's hard for me to water them evenly: Some seem to dry out, whole others end up waterlogged. And if I've accidentally put too many seeds into one pellet, the netting seems to get in my way and I have trouble thinning them out. Still, just because I'm a klutz, it doesn't mean you are.

So fill the flats with planting medium, to the point where it looks like a baking pan of brownies; then you're ready to sow your seeds.

One mistake I made in the beginning was to plant several kinds of seeds into the same tray, with the result that everything died. Each kind of seed is on its own germinating and growing schedule, and needs its own tray. For small crops, small trays are fine—and you can improvise. Try those tin-foil delicatessen trays with the plastic covers, the kind you sometimes get at salad bars. They make excellent mini-greenhouses.

You can sow the seeds into neat rows, or you can do it the easier way, which is called broadcasting: sending out the seeds all over the tray helter-skelter in the hope that they'll take. A trick to doing this is to mix the seeds, if they're small enough, into a salt shaker with an envelope of unflavored gelatin, which will send them off with some protein and nitrogen. (Better yet, see if you can find one of those bigger-holed shakers that hold herbs or red pepper at good pizzerias.) Sprinkle evenly over the whole tray, then tamp down very lightly with your fingertips. If the seeds are too big for the salt shaker, mix them with the gelatin into a bowl or saucer, then sprinkle by hand and tamp down a little harder. The seeds should be planted no deeper than their diameter, which in most cases is just slightly below the surface. The planting medium should remain crumbly in texture, not packed.

When you water the newly sown flats, use warm water, not scalding, but water you'd be willing to take a shower in on a cold day. What your seeds will do first is germinate, or sprout when the seed opens, begin growing their roots, and producing baby leaves—the equivalent of baby teeth—that won't resemble the leaves they'll get when they're mature. To this end, they need moisture, and warmth. The water can't just be dumped on, either, or your carefully planted seeds will be heaved all over the place. The flats usually have holes in the bottom, and by putting a pan of warm water underneath, the medium will soak up the water from below. To be on the safe side, mist generously with a sprayer (warm water again) from above as well.

Some seeds will germinate in light or darkness, others only if it's dark or if it's light; the smaller the seed, the likelier it is that it will need light to germinate. Unless you're told otherwise on the packet, assume darkness. What I do is to put the flat loosely into a dark garbage bag to make sure there's plenty of air inside, and then poke a couple of holes into the bag just to be doubly certain.

As to warmth, plants need temperatures of between seventy and seventy-four degrees to germinate. If you have a gas stove with a pilot light, the oven and stovetop are the perfect places, so long as you remember them before you turn on the stove. Or you can nestle the flats into blankets in a particularly warm room of the house—a bathroom, say. But it has to be warm enough day and night.

I'd always heard it said that getting plants to germinate is really hard, but when I began experimenting, that proved not to be the case. Germination is easy. Open the garbage bags every two or three days, to check that the planting medium is still moist enough—very important—and in a week (or two or three, depending on what you're growing), you'll see the little shoots beginning to push their way up: Corny as it sounds, it's incredibly exciting. But that's also when the process gets risky.

TRANSPLANTING

If you've successfully germinated your seeds in the pellets, you're in luck, because they won't have to be transplanted, so long as you've planted just one seed per pellet, to prevent overcrowding. They can just keep growing in the pellets till it's time to plant them outdoors. (That's why it's worth it to keep trying to get pellet planting right.) If you've planted instead in flats, when your germinated plants get about an inch high, they'll have to be thinned out and moved, transplanted into individual pots with replenished planting medium, like the plastic six-packs that annuals come in in the spring, and which you can collect and save to reuse from year to year.

Push apart with a pencil any plants growing close together, then carefully scoop out the plants and their root systems one by one, easing them into their new setting carefully. There's no way to explain it, really: The process is a gentle moving of this fragile thing from one place to another. Water with warm water, again from above and below (the six-packs should already have holes on the bottom). Then put them into a warm, day-lit place for a day or two, until they perk up again, recovered from the trauma of the transplant.

After this, sun is what they'll need, about six hours a day of direct sunlight. They should also be kept warm, day and night—again, in temperatures ranging from seventy to seventy-four degrees. That, and water; you should be able to feel a sense of dampness when you touch the medium in the pots, but never let them get soggy. Once they've recovered from being transplanted, you can feed them with a house-plant fertilizer as well. The fertilizer application, diluted according to the directions, can be applied every third time you water the plants, till they go outside.

A sunny window, if you have one, can supply the light, but be sure to move the plant away from the window to somewhere warmer in the late afternoon when it grows cold again. Windows are draftier than you think. Grow lights are more reliable; if you're starting in a small way, a couple of these could prove a good investment. With electric warming coils, specially designed to warm the plants from under-neath, you can also guarantee that they'll get enough warmth. (Do *not* try to simulate these coils by using a stovetop; it's dangerous and it won't work.) Or you can buy a heated cold frame that you plug in out-doors, which is glass on top and heated inside: a small greenhouse, in effect. On warm days, you open the glass windows, and keep the heat on the rest of the time.

My own method is more lax, but cheaper. I have a small car with a hatchback, and with back seats that fold down. On sunny days in April, the plants go out to the car, parked in the sun and with the win-dows rolled up: another kind of greenhouse. At night, I run hot water in a rarely used shower stall till it's steamy, then dry off the floor and make a bed for the plants with rags or old towels. With the door closed, the room stays toasty and damp all night.

Terrible things can happen, mildew, blights, mites and fungus, among them. There are remedies for these, requiring the application of soap concoctions or commercial preparations. I had some such weird thing happen only once, and simply took the flat (it was sunning in the car anyway) over to a nursery-greenhouse nearby, where they sprayed it for me when I agreed to buy two houseplants. Unless you're fully versed in blights, it's best to get the help and advice of someone who is, instead of applying the wrong concoctions.

THE NEXT STEP: HARDENING OFF

Hardening off is the process by which you help your plants accli-mate themselves to the real world by keeping them outdoors more and more hours per day, until they're used to the fluctuations in tempera-ture, before you actually plant them in the garden. It's a cruel-sound-ing name, but then, it's a cruel world. Start this toward the end of April (or earlier or later if you live farther south or north), and continue it until all the nurseries nearby are displaying their tender annuals, which means that the last frost date is safely past. If the nurseries have just set out their big hollyhocks, it's still too early to plant your tiny hollyhocks; they're not strong enough.

Whatever plants have survived this—and, sadly, the attrition rate can be fairly high—are now ready to be graduated to the garden. You've done all you can. Moisten the soil in preparation, plant them, keep them moistened for the next two weeks and hope for the best.

You may think, if you've read this section, that growing plants from seed is a time-consuming enterprise. Maybe. But not compared with what the garden requires of the gardener in spring.

$\mathcal{S}pring$

We always knew spring had arrived in my first garden when the marsh marigolds appeared, thousands of them, literally, surrounding the shrubs and spreading across the lawn in a widening spill of shiny green leaves first, then bursts of flowers in buttercup yellow every March, fading to a dull white by late April. "Oh, no, not again," a serious gardener friend would moan, every year, as if we had been cultivating typhoid flowers. She saw them as weeds, and perhaps some suppliers agree with her, because they're not easy to find commercially. (My nursery sells them, however.) I'd seen this before: One gardener's treasure can be another gardener's weed.

If you read about them—proper name is *Caltha palustris*—the descriptions will tell you that they'll grow in bogs or mountains, along the edges of streams, in loamy soils or where they're always kept damp or even wet. I never bothered to read about them; didn't have to. They just grew, at sea level, in ordinary soil, far from a marsh or bog, in sun or shade, lasting from year to year even through our notorious midsummer droughts.

Their downward slide—and complaints about them—begin when the blooms fade, the leaves turn slimy and yellowish, and it's time to cut or twist them to ground level; otherwise, they look truly disgusting until they melt away on their own, in a couple of weeks. Once you've cut them back, the garden looks bare, because they've been holding a kind of filibuster, not letting the plants that follow them in the sequence of spring maneuver their way up into the sun. But within even a few days, the other plants in the wings just behind them take over the stage. Marsh marigolds don't do any lasting harm.

The strange thing was that, even though this particular garden had marsh marigolds growing wild by the thousands, the gardens on either side had not a one.

Even stranger, when I moved into my own house, not very far away, to my amazement, in the wasteland of our backyard, I was greeted the first spring by marsh marigolds—hundreds, not thousands of them, but still. I'm a little more pragmatic now, though, and prefer not to have them competing with the other plants in our border, so whenever I find a stray clump of those recognizable bulbs, I tuck it into the grass. That way, they'll eventually bloom all over the early lawn, in counterpoint to the daffodils. The leaves will disappear, leaving the bulbs in place, the first time the grass is mowed, early in May. I like having this odd plant follow me around, ushering me into spring. These marigolds, together with that earthy *smell* of spring, lure me outside. For me, that's the signal.

SPRING RITUALS

Most of my friends confront spring more energetically than I do, beginning when it's still mitten-cold to start the clearing-up process. I usually start after I've mailed in my taxes (which is to say on the first nice day after April 15), with the marsh marigolds to keep me company.

The first step is to walk gingerly around the garden, to see what's peeking up and how much work you'll have ahead of you. The salt hay winter mulch that was applied in the fall will stay on the flower beds for a couple more weeks, until mid-April where I live, so the first chores of the season are tedious: an early spring raking, removal of damaged limbs of trees and shrubs, a pruning of the privet hedge nearly all the way to the ground, beginning to deal with the roses, the way I promised Bob I would. Before the grass really starts growing, too, it's a good idea to edge the beds with an edger for a satisfying sculpted effect between lawn and bed. You stand on the edger until it sinks all the way down, angle it away from you and scoop up the edger full of unwanted grass.

Some shrubs—notably the buddleias—need to be pruned back severely every spring; this is the time to cut the branches with your clippers or loppers to about eighteen inches from the ground. (This will seem like too much pruning, but it's not.) Other shrubs can be pruned lightly now, too, to remove any wayward branches. Deciduous flowering shrubs, like hydrangea and mock orange, bloom on growth from the year before and so shouldn't be pruned—which in their case mainly means pruned to shape only if necessary—until after they bloom. But if your deciduous flowering shrubs are older and a little worn out, which means they've become leggy and aren't blooming as spectacularly as they once did, prune them now as well, back nearly to the ground. This gets rid of the old wood, giving new wood more room in which to assert itself. The plant may skip a blooming season, but it wouldn't have bloomed too well anyway or you wouldn't have had to prune it so hard in the first place. By the second season, it will be as vigorous as it ever was. The sooner, too, you begin weeding in the beds of shrubs, the better. It's easier to maneuver among the shrubs now, before they fill out entirely with leaves and buds. While most weeds won't produce their reproductive seed until much later in the season, it's best, and prettier, to get rid of them now. Year by year, the weeding will diminish if you stick to it fairly rigorously. Gardeners who promise you that rigorous weeding will make your weeds go away entirely, however, are lying.

By mid-April, you can remove the winter mulch of salt hay. Salt hay is easily scooped up, and can be stored in garbage bags for reuse. Now the fun part begins, when you can venture cautiously into the flower borders and beds, and into the herb garden. This part's a miracle, seeing the tiny new shoots of your perennials returning. It will be a new garden every year, with fuller plants and surprises, where plants have reseeded themselves: wonderfully familiar, but new at the same time.

It's nearly impossible to describe what you actually *do* in the garden at this point. It's easier to describe how new the garden feels now, late in April. Not all the plants have yet reached the surface, but there's plenty of green coming up, that early spring green that seems lit from inside. You make your way carefully—here's where I use a child's rake, to collect stray leaves and debris that have fallen over the winter, to clean up as much of the beds as possible. Some of the plants will have the brown remnants of last year's growth, which should be snipped off carefully; sometimes you can just pull away the old stalks and leaves. What you want to do is to see what's there, and what isn't, in much the same way that you walk tentatively through your house after you've been away for a long time, feeling like a stranger and getting to know it again.

The most important task is going through all the beds, weeding, turning the soil lightly around the emerging plants and fertilizing it, in much the way you did when you first planted them, in all the beds, including those of shrubs and herbs. An annual application of manure—tucked around the plants but not directly on top of them (so it won't burn the roots)—is beneficial, along with a sprinkling of an all-purpose fertilizer like 10-10-10, or the special fertilizer for acid-loving plants. Using both manure and fertilizer may seem redundant, but it's not. The fertilizer has some nutrients that manure lacks, but its benefits last only one season (like a once-a-day vitamin) before petering out. Manure, on the other hand, not only enriches but also helps aerate the soil and aids in water retention. After sprinkling the fertilizer, which will eventually dissolve and work its way into the soil, a layer of compost, if you have it, one inch thick, should be spread over the whole garden.

TRANSPLANTING AND DIVIDING

Now is the time, too, before they get unwieldy, when, in general, perennials, shrubs and trees should be moved.

This is actually a tricky subject, since some plants don't like to be moved at all, while others don't mind but like to wait until after they've bloomed. Early autumn is another great time for transplanting, particularly because the plants will have gone through the summer cycle by then, so there's no danger of interrupting the blooming period by transplanting them too clumsily. But, unless it's a plant just about to go into bloom or already in bloom, if something's going to drive you crazy unless you move it now, move away, by all means—by digging it up with as big a root ball and as much soil around it as possible, having prepared its new site ahead of time. Water well afterward and check it for a couple of weeks to make sure it hasn't dried out (it will droop if it has), as if you'd just gotten it for the first time.

As for dividing, you're in luck if your garden is new, because your perennials won't, for the most part, need to be divided for a few years at least, and even then you can push it off for another season or two. The other way to look at it, though, is that by dividing your plants you double your stock: not a bad trade-off. As with moving, division is tricky, because some plants like to be divided in the spring, some in the fall and some, like irises, in midsummer, after they've bloomed. Others don't care at all whether they're divided in the spring or fall. (Check the Glossary for plants that are testy about this.)

And how do you tell when the plants *need* dividing? With some—hosta and phlox, for example, both of which prefer to be divided in the spring—the plants will simply *look* cramped and strangled after a few years. With phlox, especially, you'll notice that there are too many stalks too close together, preventing all of them from growing up and spreading out to bloom their best. Daylilies, on the other hand, which are best divided in the fall, won't bloom as prolifically as usual when they get overcrowded.

You have to play it by ear, or by hand, when it comes to dividing, which sounds daunting but won't be. With many perennials, the process is obvious: you dig up the plant, doing your best to get all the roots, and tug the clump apart into two, three, or four other, smaller clumps; if the root system is a loose one, it'll come apart easily. Conversely, with phlox and hosta, you'll be terrified. You'll dig up the whole clump, and notice that not even Hercules could pull it apart. You'll feel as if you're killing it, but cutting it apart, as neatly as you can, with a spade or a butcher's knife, is the way to divide, and pre-serve, it. With daylilies, you dig up the clusters of bulbs, which will be stuck together, gently pry the clusters apart, and replant.

If you could fix this moment in time, the garden would probably provide you with more joy than at any other time during the gardener's year: cleaned out beds with early buds beginning to open, and the sil-houettes of other plants etching themselves stronger on the landscape, for bloom later. It's all promise, now.

Seeing the garden this way always makes it easy to postpone thinking about July and August, when the promise you're seeing now will turn into a rebuke. The weather by then might be stifling, and the ground will more than likely be parched. Of the plants growing before you, what can you count on for midsummer? You can't sustain the promise you're seeing now by relaxing. You have to propel yourself into July and imagine how it feels.

Hot and dry, or hot and humid, is probably how it feels—to both you and your garden.

For a long time I was lazy about watering, and it showed in the garden. Horticultural tough love—withholding water until your plants do what you want—isn't the answer; it's cruel. Midway into my tenure in my first garden we installed an underground sprinkler system, which was heaven: In the middle of every night, automatically, unless there had been a rainfall, there'd be this gearing-up, grinding noise, then the soothing sound of spraying. The lawn plants would sequentially be drizzled, misted or sprayed while we slept.

This time, I've had to "design" a sprinkling system of my own, but it doesn't really matter. My garden is smaller, for one thing. The other thing is that I've discovered soaker hoses.

Soaker hoses are extraordinary. They're black, porous and flexible. What you're paying for are the leaks; water seeps out all along their length, and you can screw several of them together to snake around an entire garden. The object is to set up your own irrigation system by winding them through the garden and leaving them in place, so that every time you turn them on, they'll soak it. If you leave them running for an hour, they'll soak an area three feet on either side of the hose. Since virtually all plants like being watered from below, directly into their roots, they'll be happy. You'll be happy, too, not having to drag conventional hoses around ten times a day.

I have only one outdoor spigot, so I also bought an attachment that screws on to the spigot to turn it into two spigots, with on/off switches. Then I began snaking my soaker hoses into the beds around the periphery of the yard. I figured that I could water the grass in the middle with the old sprinkler when I needed to, and use the regular hose, which isn't supposed to have any leaks, for spot jobs, and use just the soaker hose as necessary to water the beds everywhere else.

Spring is the best time to install soaker hoses, because the plants are just coming in, and you'll be able to tell at a glance how to wind the hoses around them. You'll also have the system in place come summer, when the rainfall slackens off. You can bury the hoses below the soil if you want, but it's not really necessary; the black virtually disappears as the garden grows up around it. Besides, if you bury the hose and decide to switch the garden around later, you might have to rebury it, which seems like a lot of needless effort. If, on the other hand, you want the hose to cut across a path or stretch of lawn, you can just bury it in a trench in that one place.

If you're watering the old way, with an overhead sprinkler, the best time to water is in the morning, when it's cool. That way, the leaves will have a chance to dry before the hot sun burns the water off. The evening is often recommended for watering, too, but the water, which won't have a chance to burn off, can leave the plants to get soggy overnight, without the sun to dry them off. Late afternoon is a better choice. With soaker hoses, you have a little more flexibility, since the leaves don't get wet. Late afternoon is okay, early morning is still better. High noon is to be avoided, because even soaking into the ground, the water will evaporate faster in the hot sun and be wasted. To make sure the garden has enough water throughout the summer, plan on watering about an inch per week; after several days with temperatures approaching the three-digit mark, by instinct you'll know your plants are as thirsty as you are, and give them something more to drink. If rainfall does the watering for you, so much the better. There are sophisticated computer timers for calculating the watering needs of plants, and there is also a simpler system: Put out a cup in a shady, out-of-the-way corner, and when it's empty of rainfall, it's time to water.

Beginning in mid-April, hardiest plants first, the garden is ready for planting. With the perennials all coming up now, you can see where the holes are in the garden; you'll want to fill them in now. If you've taken notes, or if you can remember from last year, you'll want to fill those holes with plants that bloom later or earlier than most of the plants you already have. Remember, it's not just a question of filling up the garden; it's also a matter of filling up the season, with something in bloom all summer.

Self-restraint will be necessary on your early visits to the nurseries. When you shop, avoid buying only perennials already in bloom—yes, they're pretty *now*, but they won't be so pretty in a couple of weeks. Choose instead new arrivals to the nursery that promise to bloom much later. They'll fill the hole now with green, and you won't notice them much now, but you'll be planning your own flowering surprise party for later. And don't buy all your plants at one time. The nurseries get new shipments in every week, and by waiting, you'll be able to come across plants in June that are meant to bloom in August. To save yourself a little extra time and trouble, forget about planting by the moon, an old wives' tale that may or may not be true— scientists are divided. Plant instead by the weather. Plant either just after a rain, when the soil is wet and easiest to dig, or just before, so you won't have to water afterward. After a rainfall is also the best time to pull weeds (more, unfortunately, on this in the next chapter) for the same reason; the ground is soft.

Much of May is taken up with the outdoor spring cleaning, generally readying the garden for summer. May is also the time to plant annuals, another good way to fill in holes in the perennial garden, and to start annual cutting beds and container plantings. They're sold first come, first served, so it's best to call the nurseries every couple of days to see if what you want has arrived. Or ask the nursery if they'll reserve the plants you want. In mid- to late May, I bring out the houseplants, giving them a good pruning of oldish-looking leaves and scraggly stems, knowing that the sun will fill them out again in no time. The places they took up indoors are filled with lilacs and mock orange from the garden, and tulips: Last year, for the first time, I finally planted enough tulips so that I could actually bear to cut some for indoors. Toward the end of the month, I scatter seeds in the border and tamp them for sweet alyssum and gypsophila, which will be up in a month. In what is by now an annual ritual, Michael spray-paints our wrought-iron table and chairs, giving, in the process, white tails to the dogs. And one of these days, I always think, there might actually be time to sit down in those chairs and enjoy the longer days, before June 21, when they begin, almost imperceptibly at first, getting shorter.

$\mathcal{S}ummer$

It's easier for me to picture spring or fall in the garden than it is to picture summer, because spring and fall have active rhythms and chores that define them. In those seasons I'm actually inside the garden, putting things in, pulling things out.

The tableaux for summer, the garden's high season, are different.

You can't get in or out of the garden so easily in summer, because the plants are at their fullest, but if you've done your spring tasks well, you won't have to: The lion's share of work won't be so much on your hands and knees, which is a relief, but at a more human height, deadheading and trimming and clipping the flowers. The gardener circles the garden in summer, enjoying, studying, admiring, redesigning it, and hovering around its edges. There's a pleasing sameness to spring and fall, preparing the garden for summer, preparing it for winter, things coming up, things going down. Every summer, on the other hand, the garden is different, because every summer different things take place in it.

In a funny way, the summer garden scenes that pass through my mind evoke people and places as much as they do plants, because, for me, gardens are only memorable if people congregate there, with the plants as a backdrop, however dramatic, to the even more resonant human drama. Or if they help me to freeze a moment in time.

I can remember summer gardens by recalling, for instance, lunches that took place in various ones, particularly lunches when a morning rainfall made everything preternaturally clean and sparkling. The taste of summer food—lobster rolls, tomato and basil salads, cold grilled chicken, fresh peach ice cream—is vivid in my mind, the garden always an impressionistic and fragrant haze in the background. At such lunches, someone invariably sighs and says the scene is so beautiful it feels like England or France or Italy, and I always wonder if, in England and France and Italy, it's ever so beautiful it reminds someone else of America.

I also recall, in a memory that came to me only this summer, being driven, as a child, past shady roadside beds of what I now know were the common daylilies that line the old Route 6 on Cape Cod, where my grandmother, aunt and cousins lived.

Along the turnpikes of western Pennsylvania, where it's mountainous, the sloping median strips of the highways are planted with crown vetch (*Coronilla*), which blooms in August and has small flowers that look like those of clover. Crown vetch is a scraggly disaster in formal or cottage-size gardens, but along the highway it ripples like waves, really pretty. In vacant fields in New Jersey and the Midwest, I've seen *Lythrum* blooming wild in July, purple and rampant. No wonder it's so sturdy in cultivation. I went to a wedding once in Connecticut, in May, and mostly what I remember were lilacs everywhere, white ones, but the bride carried peonies. Last summer, Michael and I went to the Pacific Northwest—to Seattle and up into the San Juan Islands. I was surprised on that trip to drive through some of the neighborhoods just outside Seattle and see how Oriental in feeling the gardens were, at least in front of the houses. Layers of arborvitae, juniper, and cypress, all green, all different but compatible, sloping down the hilly front lawns. It felt quiet. We once went, too, to western Texas, but I was disconcerted by that summer landscape, even though the desert does bloom richly in its way. But it was still desert, and for all its majesty, it seemed ravaged. I'm more at home in landscapes that are full and cushiony and that impart softness.

All of this sounds idyllic, I know, and the summer garden is, after all, why people take up gardening in the first place. But you can relax in the summer only up to a point. Behind the scenes, there remains a lot of upkeep to be done.

SUMMER RITUALS

The first chore of summer is putting spring to rest. For all their cheeriness in spring, for example, the daffodils are terrible early-summer insomniacs, nearly impossible to cajole into sleep.

The good news about them is that they naturalize readily, which is to say that, with help, the bulbs will multiply, embed themselves into the garden and come back every year, like reliable perennials. To facilitate the process, cut the stems back after the flowers begin to wither, so as to divert the plant's energy from the bloom, and then let the leaves, which will begin to splay, turn yellow and look totally unappetizing for the next six weeks or so. (Much like the marsh marigolds.) Somehow, the daffodil replenishes itself this way, through these pathetic looking leaves—bad design, maybe, but it works. This will go against all your tidying-up instincts, but you have to do it this way: otherwise the bulbs won't naturalize.

My guess is that this necessary messiness is why so many gardeners plant daffodils away from the house, or clean up the daffodil bed prematurely, thereby ruining their chances to have their bulbs naturalize. To counteract the messiness, other gardeners braid the daffodils' leaves, giving the bed a dreadlocks look. Still others object to the braiding, arguing that braids don't allow enough air to circulate among the leaves; these gardeners fold over the leaves and tie them in bundles, like sheaves of wheat.

Even easier, if you don't like tying your plants into bows, is to "comb" the leaves with your fingers and twist them into a topknot, tucking the ends under the knot. That way the remains of the daffodils resemble those button candies you buy glued to strips of paper, but at least the bed is neat. If you've planted perennials to take their place, they'll start coming up among the topknots, helping to obliterate the daffodils' weird look; if you're planning to plant annuals, the bed will at least look expectant and cared for until it's time, finally, to cut the stems all the way back to the ground. The rest of the garden is growing higher, but for the moment, this will be the "low" garden, until it fills in again. A few deep blue pansies or Johnny-jump-ups among the topknots will also reinforce the scale, suggesting that this is a bed growing low, but on its own terms.

MULCHING

The bed will look even better designed if you mulch it.

I love everything about mulch—the way it looks, feels, and smells, and the way you just know it's doing good things for the garden. I think of applying it as a summer chore, because summer is when plants need the most protection from heat and droughts. An application of mulch will help prevent weeds, retain moisture and, as it slowly decomposes, help fertilize the soil. But you can apply it, or reapply it, anytime.

Particularly when the garden is new, and therefore sparser than it will one day be, mulch will give the garden a finished, smooth, cool look. A generously carved, well-edged bed, covered in a thick (up to two inches) layer of mulch, looks gardeny and inviting, even if there's just one dormant shrub in it. Bare soil by itself will look parched and depleted; mulch looks fertile. Sure, one day you might get around to underplanting everything in the garden, with small bulbs like *Scilla* or groundcovers like the flat-growing ajuga. But mulch in the meantime can cover most sins of omission.

There are several kinds of mulch, but my preference is for ground cedar mulch, which looks rich, spreads well, stays in place and, when it starts sinking into the soil, fades like a sinking blanket, without leaving clumps behind.

Pine chips, or pine nuggets, almost the size of eggs, are popular mulches, but too coarse, in my view, for beds of flowers or flowering shrubs; they're great, though, for woodland-type paths or obscuring weed-prone dark areas out of the direct line of sight of the garden. Peat moss, too, is popular as a mulch, but, ecological issues aside, as it depletes over the course of a season, it breaks apart into unsightly fist-size clumps.

I became enamored earlier this season of the designer mulches, made of cocoa husks or buckwheat hulls, but that infatuation lasted just a short time. I think that their selling point is that they're pretty to look at but, to my mind, mulch isn't something you want to call special attention to. Bags of each, more costly than cedar mulch but relatively inexpensive all the same (a big bag of mulch, as much as you can carry, is usually under $5) turned out to smell earthy, like the sources from which they came. The cocoa in particular smells exactly like what it is, chocolate, and after I'd put it down in my daffodil bed, I'd get hungry for sweets every time I walked by, which I didn't find amusing. The smell grows stronger with the first rain, then fades.

There's a chance that both cocoa and buckwheat mulches can grow fungus, and some gardeners suggest spraying them with a fungicide before laying them down. I was uncomfortable with the idea of spraying them, but my problem with them turned out to be much different. Our dogs (which is why I didn't spray them; I'd worry, too, that any visiting children or stray cats might like to taste the chocolate) tend to tear around the garden, turning as if on a dime to tear around the other way, which keeps them busy most of the day but, needless to say, doesn't do much for the garden. As they tore around the newly mulched beds, the cocoa husks and buckwheat hulls would scatter, finally dispersing completely before I had the chance to see whether they would have grown fungus or not. With my cedar mulch, on the other hand, I can just plump it back into place after the dogs have momentarily turned their attention elsewhere.

I have gathered, over the years, that it's a violation of horticultural etiquette to apply mulch over the perennial border and other flower beds, on the theory that these beds will be a bounty of perfect soil and profuse blooms and not need a mulch. (Rose beds are the exception, and Bob mulches his with cocoa husks, figuring that there's so much fungicide being sprayed into the roses anyway that a little more, sprayed directly on the mulch, won't hurt.) My border, however, is new enough not to be replete, exactly, and I still have a fair number of weeds. Nor is my soil perfect yet. So I finally broke down and applied cedar mulch anyway, all through the perennial border, figuring that for now it would be a good thing. It was. The border looks much better and, as the flowers grow lusher, the mulch is less and less apparent. In a year or two, I hope to dispense with it, while keeping it as an edging to the shrubs elsewhere in the garden.

By the time the daffodils' topknots are fading away and the mulch has been spread, the petals will have fallen off the tulips, leaving the stem and leaves behind. The sight of clusters of these topless stems is very odd, and the next chore in the sequence—never a dull moment—is to get rid of them.

Many gardeners will tell you that some tulips—those known as wild, species or botanical tulips (they go by different names, like con men with aliases)—will naturalize as readily as daffodils (which, come to think of it, also go by other names, narcissuses and jonquils) and by following the same directions: Cut off the stem, leave the leaves to wither and self-replenish on their own. I have tried this many times. Occasionally, the leaves rose again the second year, but never did I get a second bloom, much less a whole lovely cluster of naturalized tulips. Try it, certainly, but don't get your hopes up. These days, I treat my tulips like annuals: when they're done, they're done. And when I get rid of them, I find it's easier than cutting them back to pull the tulips, bulbs and all, out of the ground, so they won't rot or otherwise get in the way when I go to plant something else in their place.

ENOUGH IS ENOUGH: WHEN TO STOP PLANTING

Another point of contention among gardeners is when it's best to stop planting, and the technical answer is never: As long as you water well, plants can become established all spring, summer and fall. That's too easy an answer for me. Planting too late in the season—my own personal cutoff date is the end of June—is starting plants at a handicap. I can handle the requisite inch of water a week all through the garden all through the summer, but I can't promise myself I'd give new transplants extra water every day for the first couple of weeks, particularly if it gets very hot and dry. Unless someone gives me a plant as a present after my cutoff date, I don't plant again until late in August or the first week in September.

This restraint is hard, because as spring recedes and summer comes unmistakably into focus, the garden is entirely new, and I can see clearly where the flaws will be.

Early bloomers refer to gardens that, like some people, peak on the early side. Spring gardens, that is. As far as gardens go, late bloomers peak from mid-August on—autumn gardens. Mid-bloomers? Perhaps there's no phrase for them, because the midsummer blooming season is so hard to get right. Spring is easy, with all its soft, billowy things. A few spectacular things in fall, when the garden is slowing down, also make an impression. Every year I get a little closer to getting midsummer right: more phlox, foxgloves, roses, *Platycodon*, coreopsis, rudbekia and so on. Even so, every year I still have a few disappointing midsummer holes.

The end of June is my last-chance deadline for anticipating and trouble-shooting such holes in advance. A second sprinkling of general-purpose fertilizer around the garden after the peonies are over will help, as will a reseeding of sweet alyssum and annual gypsophila (if it's destined to be a brutally hot summer, the first seeding might wilt too early). A few lilies planted on the late side will guarantee a few lilies that bloom later than the first round. Annuals, or container plantings, take up the rest of the slack. When the last impulse buy goes in rain or shine at the end of June, apart from watering, I take a two-week hiatus, until Bastille Day.

I once read that a final summer application of general-purpose fertilizer in mid-July would stimulate growth just enough to last the rest of the season, before the plants began to prepare for dormancy, which makes sense; I remember the rule by thinking of Bastille Day and Marie Antoinette, who doubtless had cake-eating minions who performed the task for her at Versailles.

The sprinkling of fertilizer—if possible just before a good summer rainstorm—is easy. Another task which I postpone until mid-July is more precise and time-consuming.

MORE MAINTENANCE: SECURING THE VINES

By now, after the spring and early summer spurt of growth, the vines and other climbing things will have outgrown last year's restraints, and need to be reanchored again. If you only want to anchor them once per season, this is the time to do so.

Use whatever is at hand. I fill a basket with my essentials: a hammer, cellophane tape, biodegradable gardeners' hemp, green pushpins and some handy curved arcs of plastic with a small nail at each end that I found at the hardware store (they're used to hold electric wires in place for hanging lamps), plus a few curved gardeners' nails, which are made specifically for the purpose.

Cellophane tape, I find, will hold narrow-stemmed vines (clematis paniculata, and climbing honeysuckle, for example) in place until they find a way to stay in place themselves. Just tape them to the trellis, fence or wall. If it rains, some of the tape will fall off, but it's easily replaced.

Pushpins, never pushed through a stem but holding it in place firmly, not strangling it, from the side, will hold smaller new stems of just about anything (pyracantha, climbing holly or euonymus) that's sticking out. As the stems grow, the pushpins in turn can be replaced by the electrical wire holders, which will also pull out easily enough when the stems grow even bigger, big enough that is to need the permanent gardeners' nails. As for the string, anything that's still sticking out can be tied to whatever's at hand; you'll probably have to gently hammer a few small tacks here and there into a wall or fence, on which to tie the errant stems. Rubber bands will also hold a stem to a tack or nail.

MORE MAINTENANCE STILL: WATERING, WEEDING AND DEADHEADING

While securing vines is a one-time chore, except for touchups, the ongoing work of summer—watering, weeding and deadheading—can be as unrelenting as a hot, humid spell unbroken by a cooling rain. Still, if you ever want to have one of those memorable lunches in your own garden or to pause in pleasure at what you have created, you have to keep on top of summer.

If you've installed a system of soaker hoses, the watering will be as easy as it is satisfying. One turn of the nozzle and you're spreading thirst-quenching benevolence all over your empire. It truly is gratifying to see your plants perk up as they soak up the water you've fed them.

Weeding, however, has to be your own private quest. No one will notice all the weeds you removed, only those you left behind. High summer is the time many weeds are setting their seed; this presents you with a choice: remove one now, or remove twenty next year. Or have your strongest weeds literally choke your more delicate plants to death.

There is no need to learn the names of weeds; it's hard enough as it is to remember the names of the plants you're *trying* to grow. For practical purposes, however, a weed is anything you're trying *not* to grow. There are occasional exceptions to this. Early this fall, I visited a friend who had a long row of pretty purplish flowers—the blooms were similar to those of sedum spectabile 'Autumn Joy'—growing along the woodland side of her driveway, which I asked her about. "Those are 'Joe-pye,'" she said. "Weeds." That same week, our local paper devoted its garden column to cultivating joe-pye weed, actually a kind of *Eupatorium,* in the autumn border. And then there are my marsh marigolds. If you like a weed, it's your call.

How will you recognize a weed? Early in the spring, as your plants and weeds are rising through the soil, competing for space and light, it might in fact be hard to tell them apart; if you're not sure, wait before you pull out what may turn out to be your boltonia.

The weeds will make themselves known soon enough, no problem about that. Even the worst gardeners I know soon learn to recognize the weeds most treacherous to their own gardens. First of all, if they like your garden, they usually grow here and there all over, not just where you may or may not have planted something. (Makes you wonder—probably not for the first time—why you didn't put those plant labels in, after all!) If you see matching plants among your shrubs, and in your border, herb garden and annual bed, they're weeds.

Often, weeds—the fun ones to pull, anyway—are shallow rooted. If you give it a firmish tug and the plant loosens immediately, the odds are good it's a weed. Most perennials grow roots before making an appearance; in general, weeds would rather cause their trouble in full view.

At the other end of the scale, some weeds—the more destructive ones—are nearly impossible to pull out. I have several kinds of these, but I couldn't begin to guess at their names. Just keep at it. Try to do your weeding after a good rain or watering, when they'll be easiest to remove. Use a trowel or a shovel. If you simply can't get the entire root this time, cut the weed at ground level. That way, at least, it won't set seed. There are a few inconveniently placed weeds in my border that I can't manage to dig out without digging up the whole garden and probably the house, so I just keep cutting them back every time I see a new leaf. Maybe it's my imagination, but they seem to be getting weaker, more spindly, each time they start to grow back, losing their will, perhaps.

Along with watering and weeding, deadheading, nothing more than removing the dead heads of the flowers or cutting back wilted blooms, is a summer chore necessary to keep your garden growing and pretty.

The cutting of annuals is particularly rewarding, because the aim is to cut them not when they're dead but when they're almost at their peak, to have cut flowers for indoors all summer long and, at the same time, prevent the plants from going to seed. Like Hybrid Teas, many annuals will keep producing blooms until you stop picking them, or until a sharp frost. Some annuals, not considered cutting flowers—*Brachycome* and browallia, both low little blue plants most often seen in container plantings, for instance—also benefit from a midsummer cutback if they've begun to wilt. Cut them back halfway down, fertilize them with a houseplant fertilizer, and the chances are sixty-forty that they'll grow back again, good as new.

Perennials need deadheading, too, which isn't nearly as pleasurable as cutting annuals, because in many cases they won't come back again. Part of the reason for cutting them back is aesthetic: The garden will look terrible if it's full of brown, wilted flowers. Part of the reason, though, is to divert the plant's energy from the now-spent blooms. With some biennials and perennials, however—foxgloves, delphinium (if you got them to grow the first time round) and nepeta—deadheading will encourage a second bloom. With others, among them coreopsis, gaillardia, aster, rudbekia, and mums, rigorous deadheading will increase the length of the blooming season.

Flower and stem come off in the deadheading process, either with clippers or with your fingernails. And when the whole perennial has had it, cut the stems back to just an inch or two above the ground. Usually new growth will start again from the ground up. This is not growth to get excited about, because it won't really go anywhere and will die back again in the fall. But it marks the plants' spaces and invigoration and offsets in green those plants that remain in colorful bloom.

Bloom you can enjoy over lunch, wearing summer whites; bloom that, however ephemeral in the garden, lasts forever in one's memory.

Afterword

The course of two years is a very short time in the life of a garden, and there's still a long way to go until the garden I have in my mind matches the one outside the door. Even so, as the second summer (not counting the first one, with the Mustang shell and all the car parts) draws to its close, the transformation of this small plot of land takes my breath away. Shrubs envelop the space, with something or other in bloom from March through October. The buddleia anchoring my border seems to have been the right choice. The shrubs are more than eight feet high now—eight feet!—and white butterflies flutter around them all day long. Fewer plastic roses find their way to the surface of the soil, now that the peonies have filled in and entrenched their roots. At the back of the border, the rudbekia maxima, which was shoulder height last year, is now well over six feet high; I have to look up to it.

Butterflies also seem to like the nepeta at one edge of the bed of herbs; the bees favor it, too. Plus it's already time to divide the rampant tansy, which is sprawling a little too close to the santolina and chives. For once, *I'll* be the one with a clump of something to pass on to a friend. As I'd imagined, it's wonderfully satisfying to be able to snip fresh, fragrant herbs for cooking all summer.

I wish I'd put a notch on the side wall of the neighbors' (large) house, marking the height of the bamboo when we first planted it. I forget now how high it was—but it's well on its way to doing its job: screening with a vengeance. As for my 'Nikko Blue' hydrangeas, they're twice the size they were last year, and this year produced many more of the deep blue snowballs. This time, I did the spacing exactly right, and in another couple of years, they'll lightly touch each other and look, as I'd hoped, like dramatic waves breaking into the garden.

So much work went into this small garden, but all those days of sweaty, unpleasant digging grow fainter in memory as the rewards of the garden become greater. There's still plenty of digging, planning and planting to be done, of course, not to mention the wish list—ornamental ponds, that rose garden, finding room for all those plants I'd like to have but haven't yet gotten around to (a silvery-leaved elaeagnus still heads the list). And one still tends (*I* tend) to fall behind in the weeding and other maintenance chores. I'm still no perfectionist.

But just as the garden has begun to settle in, so have I begun to settle into the routines of gardening. The chores have a pleasant—well, not entirely unpleasant—rhythm to them, and I like knowing that some things about next season and the one after that are predictable. I like measuring and watching time in my small, pretty retreat. Two years ago, I couldn't have imagined how much pleasure and comfort my garden would give me, and so soon. I wish you the same joy in yours.

5

Glossary

❧

THE PLANTS AT A GLANCE

Following is a review of all the plants mentioned in this book, including genus, species and common names (when different from the genus name); pronunciation; color, shape and size; sensibility; ball park blooming period; application; and special planting or maintenance notes—quick basics for planting and growing them. Unless specified otherwise, the plants can be planted and divided in either spring or fall. All-around basic care (fertilizing, etc.) for plants and shrubs is covered in the text itself.

When possible, I've tried to tell you everything you need to know to grow the plants. For the genera that are vast and varied and have different requirements for each species, I've at least tried to demystify all this overwhelming information, to tell you what you'll need to find out when you scout the plants at a local nursery.

In the interest of brevity, an asterisk after the Latin name indicates a plant that has been discussed extensively in the text; see the Index for page numbers. When possible, I've tried to indicate how far apart plants should be planted, but this too can vary, depending on how big the plants are to start with; the nursery tags will usually tell you how to space them. In general, consider their ultimate height and spread, especially when planning where to plant shrubs or trees, and plant them far enough apart to grow to full size unobstructed. If they're plants that spread fast and well, they can be planted even farther apart than plants that don't, to give them ample room to roam.

The information is presented in this order:

Genus and species names (and sometimes variety)

Pronunciation

Common name (if it's different from the genus)

What kind of plant it is and where to plant it or how to use it in the garden

Sun/shade requirements

I've tried to be truthful, offering the disadvantages of the plant as well as its virtues.

When you like a plant, it's easy to take a gamble with it, because the investment is relatively small. If you like it, maybe it will work well for you and maybe it won't, but there's not all that much you can do beyond following the instructions for sun, soil, water, and general upkeep. When it comes to investing in more costly trees and shrubs, however, I'd recommend first discussing how you want to use them with a knowledgeable plant person, someone who works at a nursery you trust.

In addition to the plants mentioned here, there are plenty of others that are worthy and reliable, even as starters; this Glossary is not meant to be an encyclopedic guide, only a review of the plants discussed in the text. Depending on where you live and what you like, you'll find many other things you'll want to try—and that's the idea. You've got to start somewhere (and stop somewhere), and this is one gardener's starting point.

ABELIA*, *ah-BEEL-ee-ah*, Flowering evergreen (or pretty much evergreen) shrub; use in groups or plant one among other shrubs; Sun or part shade; no special needs. This understated, usually late-flowering shrub grows and spreads to about four or five feet. The green leaves look as if they've been sponge-painted lightly in red. The trumpet-shaped flowers are particularly delicate. They look best planted in groups. Prune only as necessary to shape after the blooms fade. Generally, nurseries carry only one species in this small genus, so it's only necessary to make sure you're buying a late-flowering shrub, if that's what you want.

ACER PALMATUM, *AY-sir pall-MAY-tum*, Japanese maple; Deciduous tree; use to anchor a large border, center a bed of herbs, or as a specimen; Sun in the north, part shade in the south. Occasionally you might also find Japanese maple that answers to the species name *A. japonicum* (jah-PON-ih-kum). There are numerous subcategories here, so you have to decide by looking whether you want etched leaves in greens or crimson, some of which provide wonderful autumn color. These are often listed under the variety 'Dissectum', presumably because the leaves are dissected. These decorative maples grow like hoop skirts, eventually reaching all the way to the ground. Ultimately, they can reach fifteen feet, but they grow *very* slowly; they'll never seem to overtake anything. They only need pruning here and there to shape wayward branches. The crimson-leaved ones are particularly lovely with silvery things planted around them.

ACHILLEA, *ah-KILL-ee-ah*, Yarrow; Perennial; use for an informal touch in the border and in wildflower gardens and meadows; Full sun. Homespun in feeling, these perennials, usually about two feet high (but check—there are many varieties, some dwarf, some higher), bloom for a long time in midsummer, smell musky like summer and have a kind of wildflower feel, at least the reds, oranges and yellows do; in white the plant, which looks rather like Queen Anne's lace, seems more formal. The foliage is often described as fernlike, but it's really too sparse for that. Excellent cut flowers, fresh or dried. They do best and will spread where it's hot and dry, drainage is good and the soil is decent; plant them about a foot apart.

ACONITUM, *ah-kun-ITE-um*, Monkshood; Perennial; use in the back of the border and in woodland settings; Sun in the north, part shade in the south. Tall and stately, monkshood has a sensibility not unlike that of the delphinium. The individual blossoms, many of which line every stalk, do look like little hoods; they're purple or blue, they bloom mid- to late summer, depending on variety, and the taller ones often need staking. Good gardeners will tell you they're a cinch to grow planted about two feet apart in good soil and full sun (or part shade where summers are very hot), but they haven't been for me; a friend of mine, on the other hand, has them growing and spreading perfectly well in dappled shade through a woodland part of his garden. You can dig the clumps up and divide them if they grow too thick and cramped—you'll need a sharp knife to divide the clumps—but do so carefully; they don't much like to be moved. It makes me nervous, too, that if ingested, every inch of it is deadly poisonous to human beings and animals, but that might not have made me so nervous if I'd had better luck with it, or if deer or rabbits were thwarting all my efforts to garden.

AEGOPODIUM PODAGRARIA 'Variegatum'*, *ay-gah-PO-dee-um poh-da-GRAR-ee-ah veh-ree-GOT-um*, Gout weed or Bishop's weed; Perennial; use as a groundcover, to edge single shrubs or beds of shrubs, or along the front of the border; Sun or part shade. A pretty groundcover, with light green-and-white variegated leaves, that spreads anywhere in sun or shade and like crazy. But it's easy to get rid of where you don't want it. Aegopodium produces nice enough and long-lasting flowers in early summer, but it's grown mainly for the pretty foliage and excellent, fast coverage. Looks especially good in dark corners, and under trees, ferns, hosta or shrubs, because the considerable white in the leaves seems to illuminate the dark. To divide, dig up a clump in spring or fall and pull apart gently, then replant.

AGROSTEMMA, *ah-grow-STEM-ah*, Annual; use for early spring coverage in the midborder; Light shade. This tiny genus of annuals, only about three varieties, all told, produces subtle pink blooms on narrow stems, up to three feet high, quite pretty in its simplicity in the spring garden at the back of the border. Unfortunately, these can't stand the heat and usually vanish by midsummer—but by then, you'll probably have more things in flower as the back of the border fills in. Because their season is short, it's better to avoid fooling around with growing them from seed; you'll get off to a better start by installing plantlettes from a nursery.

AJUGA, *ah-JOO-ga*, Bugleweed (common name rarely used); Perennial; use to edge paths or between stones; Light to fairly deep shade. A groundcover in the truest sense: The leaves, either variegated or not, flatten out and spread around to cover up the ground wherever you plant them. (If you plant them along a path or between stones, however, don't apply salt to melt the snow, or you'll kill them.) They grow fast; you'll notice a good spread in just one season. In the spring, fun flowers, bluish purple or pink, that look like bottle brushes rise straight from the leaves. When the *Ajuga* patch gets big enough, dig up and pull apart gently to divide. Pretty close to foolproof.

ALCHEMILLA MOLLIS*, *ahl-kha-MIL-ah MOL-lis*, Lady's-mantle; Perennial; use in the front of the border, as edging or in the herb garden; you can dress it up or down; Sun or very light shade. If all the perennials were to hold a contest to see which had the prettiest leaves, lady's-mantle would be a close contender. Its leaves are pleated at first, then open up like a fan but remain cupped to capture drops of rain or dew. The midsummer yellow-green flowers, rising to about a foot and a half, are tiny and sweet. Plant about a foot apart in sun or light shade; they should look massed. If you're lucky, they'll self-seed, and you'll have enough for some in the border, a few in the herb garden, under shrubs or just about anywhere else that seems to need a flowering carpet.

ALLIUM SCHOENOPRASUM*, *AL-ee-um sho-en-ah-PRAIS-um*, Chives; Perennial herb; use in the herb garden; Sun. The *Allium* genus comprises all kinds of oniony plants, many with lollipop-like blooms rising straight up from the foliage; there's nothing more cheerful, and some are elegant enough for a flower garden. Chives (just ask for chives; don't bother with the proper name) grow nearly a foot high in dense green clumps in full sun and can be clipped for a thousand culinary uses all summer. In the spring, they produce small, round blossoms, usually lavender, that are fully edible and pretty to toss on a salad or to decorate a platter. If you don't want your chives to spread, these blossoms are best cut off, and vice versa. If you start with a modest six-pack and plant each "plug" six inches apart, in a couple of years you'll have a satisfying hedge of chives to admire (and eat).

ALTHAEA*, *al-THEE-ah*, Hollyhock; Includes annuals, biennials, and perennials; use in the back of the border or against a wall or fence; Sun. That hollyhocks can be annuals, biennials or perennials may seem confusing, but try the perennials first, because if they work for you, you won't have to try the others. Even with the perennials, however, it's worth adding a few every year, as their life expectancy isn't very long, although I know some that are flourishing in their eighth year. They produce beautiful puffy (or sometimes single) blossoms on stems up to six feet tall, and belong in the back of the full-sun border or lining a wall or fence. The blooms come out in late midsummer, at a moment when little else is happening in the garden, so they seem to have a season all their own; and they're happy in the spotlight. They may need staking, but no need to do so until they start to tilt precariously. They might also develop a kind of rust on the leaves, but it doesn't spread; it's just one of those things. They may sound like a lot of trouble, but they're really not—and, for their grandeur, they're certainly worth a try.

Alyssum, see *Lobularia.*

ANEMONE × HYBRIDA*, *ah-NEM-ah-nee HIB-rid-ah,* Japanese anemone; Perennial; use in the front of the border or in woodland settings; Sun or, in the south, light shade. While some anemones are bulbs (to be planted in the fall), these are sturdy perennials, which, as their common name suggests, do show off the wind. They begin blooming in late summer, with pink or white blossoms rising up to eighteen inches high and lasting into autumn. Give them a couple of years to settle in, and chances are good that they'll spread nicely. They like a year-round mulch to protect them and help keep them moist.

ANETHUM GRAVEOLENS, *ah-NAY-thum grah-VAY-oh-lens,* Dill; Annual herb; use in the herb garden; Sun. Dill grows as high in the ground as it does in the store. If you're buying the little six-packs, plant them about six inches apart, and plant more than just one six-pack. For dill to make an impression, either in the kitchen or in the garden, the crop needs to be profuse. If you let it go to seed, then you'll be able to gather dill seeds for cooking—plus it may reseed itself.

ANTHRISCUS CEREFOLIUM, *an-THRIS-kris kare-ee-FOH-lee-um,* Chervil; Annual herb; use in the herb garden or as an underplanting; Part shade. With delicate, lacy foliage, chervil is delicately unassuming and, unlike most herbs, can be tucked into a partly shaded corner. For cooking, you can snip it over chicken or fish without having any particular recipe in mind. It grows only about eight or ten inches high and remains compact and self-contained.

ANTIRRHINUM, *an-tee-REE-num*, Snapdragon; Annual; use for the cutting garden, or as filler (used sparingly) in the border; Sun. Usually blooming in mixed pastels, but occasionally available in all white, snapdragons might be the quintessential annual of summer—upright, optimistic and always bouquet-ready. New cultivars—some lower than the ten-inch average, some higher—are increasingly available. Grow profusely for cutting, and sparingly for ornamental use; otherwise, they'll seem like a cliché.

AQUILEGIA*, *ah-kwa-LEE-jia*, Columbine; Biennial; use in the front of the midborder; Part sun, part light shade. Columbines have beautiful foliage, which looks more fragile than it is and stays in place all season and into the fall, and exquisite blossoms from late spring into early summer. This biennial usually reseeds itself dependably enough so that it will come back for at least several years, although it doesn't hurt to add a plant or two each season to keep supplying new seeds. If the leaves on top turn yellow or brown and look as if they've had it, cut them back to expose the fresh new ones underneath.

ARTEMISIA*, *ar-teh-MEEZH-ee-ah*, Perennial; use depends on species; Sun. The artemisias, valuable in the garden for their foliage, not their flowers, are a divergent lot, not always easily recognized as being related. For the sunny front of the border, *A. ludoviciana* (loo-doh-vik-i-AH-nah) 'Silver Queen' or (the slightly higher) 'Silver King' will shimmer all season in a silvery green with the sensibility of a small shrub and is a better bet than the easily found *A. schmidtiana* (schmit-ee-AN-ah) 'Silver Mound', which flattens by the second or third year. Plant them as you would a small hedge. *A. bachonia* (bak-OH-nee-ah), a sunny midborder selection, grows taller (to two and a half feet) and isn't shrubby at all, but produces upright, silvery foliage with odd beadlike "blooms," not unlike small clusters of grapes, in midsummer. These should be planted only a few inches apart and won't make much of an impact unless you have several, although they will spread well if they're happy. *A. dracunculus* (drah-KUNK-you-lus) is the herb tarragon—same root for both words as dragon—but you don't really need to remember that; asking for tarragon is enough. Tarragon belongs in the herb garden; it grows low, rarely more than ten inches. The plants are not very exciting to look at, but they have a licorice-like flavor, much revered in summer cooking.

ARUNCUS*, *ah-RUN-kus*, Goatsbeard; Perennial; use in the back of the border or in a woodland setting; Part shade. This is a whimsical perennial, big enough (about five feet, a little higher in bloom) to serve almost as a shrub, best spaced two feet apart to impart a massed effect. The midsummer blooms, soft-looking creamy spires that seem to point in every direction, aren't delicate, to say the least, but certainly noticeable and ebullient.

ASTER × FRIKARTII, *AH-ster frih-KART-ee*, Hardy aster; Perennial; use in the front of the midborder; Sun. Blooming in white, pink or lavender from late summer well into fall, varieties of this species usually grow about twenty inches tall—front-of-the-midborder height—but some cultivars are said to grow much higher, five feet or more (I've never seen these)! Ideally, plant them in spring (late fall, after they bloom, is another option). Cut the whole plant back a couple of times during the late spring/early summer, to encourage thicker blooming. Once they do bloom, deadheading makes their long blooming season last even longer; they're also good cut flowers. They should be divided every three years or so; the stems and roots in the middle will be the weakest, as the vigorous new growth is always on the outside. Pull apart the clumps, replant the strong new bits, and put the rest in the compost.

ASTILBE*, *ah-STILL-bee*, Garden spirea; Perennial; use in the front of the midborder, massed or in woodland settings; A good deal of sun to fairly deep shade. These are unkillable classics—a little sun, a little shade, they'll do fine. The midsummer bloom spires, which can be cut fresh or used in arrangements dried, are pretty as well, in cream, pink, peach and salmon. The blooms of the so-called plumed astilbe varieties spew higher than the usual two feet or so and are particularly graceful. Plant about a foot and a half apart.

*   *   *

Autumn crocus, see *Colchicum.*
Azalea, see *Rhododendron.*
Bamboo, see *Pseudosasa.*
Basil, see *Ocimum.*
Bay Laurel, see *Laurus.*
Bee balm, see *Monarda.*
Bishop's weed, see *Aegopodium.*
Black-eyed Susan, see *Rudbekia.*
Blanketflower, see *Gaillardia.*
Bleeding heart, see *Dicentra.*
Blueberry, see *Vaccinium.*
Blue cornflower, see *Centaurea.*

BOLTONIA ASTEROIDES 'Snowbank'*, *ball-TONE-ee-ah as-ter-OI-dees,* Perennial; use in the back of the border; Sun. Growing and spreading about four or five feet high and wide, this boltonia is covered with countless tiny, daisylike blossoms in early autumn and beyond. 'Snowbank' is a cultivar blooming in white, and it's also easy to find 'Pink Beauty,' which blooms in aqua (only kidding, it really blooms in very light pink). The foliage isn't particularly showy while it's growing, but in bloom it does a wonderful job of seeing the summer out. It isn't very exciting its first or second year, but fills out dramatically by the third, so be patient.

Boxwood, see *Buxus.*

Brachycome, *brah-key-KOH-me,* Swan River daisy; Annual; use for container plantings or at the front of a shaded border; Light shade. A sweet little daisylike annual, too small to be used for cutting, flowering in masses of pink, white, or blue blossoms, formal enough for a border setting and best planted in dappled shade (it likes to be cool, but not in the dark). If you buy a bigger plant to start with, as opposed to planting several smaller ones together, for some reason it will stay moundier through the season. If it falters midseason, cut it back and fertilize, and it will grow in again just fine.

BROWALLIA SPECIOSA, *broh-WALL-ee-ah spee-see-OH-sa,* Annual; use for container plantings, at the front of a shaded border, or in a woodland area; Sun or, if summers are very hot, light shade. Flowering continually in blue or purple, browallia is low-growing (to about ten inches). They attract more attention grown in pots or the way I saw them once, tucked in front of hostas and ferns, where you wouldn't expect to see much color. If they stop blooming, they're probably getting too much heat. Cut them back and fertilize, and they may revive. (Or move them to a cooler place.) Supposedly, you can dig them up and bring them inside for the winter, but I can't vouch for that.

BUDDLEIA*, *BUD-lee-ah*, Butterfly bush or summer lilac; Deciduous flowering shrub; use to anchor a border, massed or grouped among other shrubs. This shrub is fast growing and long blooming (from midsummer on in various shades of purple or white, or rarely, red or yellow), does indeed attract butterflies and is thoroughly useful and even pretty, from its first year on. When you're buying them, pay attention not only to bloom color but to the color and texture of the leaves; some are more silvery and delicate. As discussed in the text, *B. davidii* (dah-VID-ee-ee) 'Nanho Blue' is a good selection for a smaller garden, with delicate leaves and a smaller size than some, about eight feet high and wide. Plant in sun, fertilize only lightly and prune each year early in the spring, to about ten inches from the ground.

Bugbane, see *Cimicifuga*.
Bugleweed, see *Ajuga*.
Burning bush, see *Euonymus*.
Butterfly bush, see *Buddleia*.

BUXUS, *BUKS-is*, Boxwood or box; Evergreen shrub; use to anchor a border or bed, to create a low (or eventually higher) hedge, in a grouping of mixed shrubs; Sun or light shade. Rounded in form, with bright shiny leaves, elegant and formal enough for a border and versatile enough to be used just about anywhere else. *B. sempervirens* (sem-per-VY-rens) is the species thought of as the common box, is utterly reliable and rarely needs pruning, except a snip here or there to shape. (Unless you want to sculpt them ornamentally into whimsical shapes, in which case, sculpt away.) Spacing depends on the size of the plants you start with, but remember, they do grow slowly so don't plant them too far apart. If the leaves ever look rusty, the shrubs probably have contracted what's cleverly called rust, and your nursery will give you an insecticide/fungicide to treat it; otherwise the shrubs shouldn't cause you any trouble.

CALTHA PALUSTRIS*, *KAL-tha pal-US-tris*, Marsh marigold; Perennial bulb or tuber; plant in a lawn or in a woodland setting where it can spread freely. Subject of very modest horticultural debate: weed or not? I think not, and you wouldn't either, if you could see the foot-high burst of buttercup yellow every spring. If you ever come across any, they're a novelty item definitely worth a try.

CAMELLIA, *kum-EEL-ee-ah**, Evergreen flowering shrubs; use as a specimen, in the border or mixed among other shrubs; Sun in the north, a little shade farther south; they like shelter, so a good spot near the house or against a wall is ideal. With their shiny green leaves and blossoms resembling graceful tropical plants, camellias are actually much sturdier than they look. They bloom early in the spring, usually in white, pink or red. Because they bloom so early, planting them near the house will shelter them well and also enable you to enjoy them most readily. They prefer acid soils, but have been known to thrive elsewhere; even so, fertilize in the spring with an acid fertilizer. As for pruning, remove flowers after they've bloomed, along with any wood that looks weak or spent.

CAMPANULA, *kam-PAN-you-lah*, Bellflower or Canterbury bells; Includes annuals and perennials; use depends on species; Sun or light shade. *Campana* means "bell" in Latin, and here's the first clue to breaking the code of the bellflower, a genus encompassing about two hundred and fifty varieties of mostly perennials and a few annuals: the flowers look like bells. Not much help. The blooms are blue, white, or occasionally pink, in heights ranging from ground-hugging to three feet or so. In general, the higher the variety, the shorter the blooming season, and because the high ones also often need staking, it might be best to start with the shorter varieties. They belong in the border, a rock garden or nestled under shrubs, which will provide them a bit of shade. They like sun or dappled shade, good soil and a situation that is moisture retentive (a summer mulch will help). A rigorous cutting back of spent blooms will encourage a second spurt of bloom; sometimes they bloom again in early autumn. *C. medium*, grown as an annual where I live, likes it cool and only blooms early in the season (but magnificently), six months after germination indoors, for several weeks. You can take a chance and plant the seeds outside in midautumn, covering them when the ground freezes with something protective (like the boughs from your Christmas tree), and if the winter isn't too cold, they'll come up in the late spring. The catalogs offer varied selections of perennial *Campanula*, and ordering a few to try out is a good place to start to understand this wide-ranging genus.

CAMPSIS, *KAMP-sis*, Trumpet vine; Perennial vine; use against fences, walls, and so on; Sun. This vine grows like a tidal wave over one friend's fence, and another friend's porch balustrade, and both swear that the vine grew that way without their having to affix it in any way. Full hot sun, the most ordinary soil, and an energetic early spring pruning are all it needs to climb just about anything, bloom brightly, in mid- to late summer, for a long time, attracting hummingbirds, if there are any nearby. I've seen them grow and drape up to about thirty feet, so plant sparingly. Usually you see it in reds or oranges, but the yellow (*C. radicans* 'Flava') is much softer.

Candytuft, see *Iberis*.
Canterbury bells, see *Campanula*.

CATALPA, *kah-TAL-pah*, Indian bean tree; Deciduous; use as a shade tree; Sun. Catalpas are especially welcoming as shade trees because their leaves are unusually large and of a light, translucent green that remains so even after the leaves of shade trees nearby are beginning to coarsen as summer deepens. In the spring they flower in pale pink (or white or purple, depending on the species). The flowers are followed by long, curious pods, which accounts for the common name. (The "Indians" in question are Native Americans; the tree is native to the Midwest.) They'll grow to some sixty feet, or a little higher or lower, depending on the species.

Catmint, see *Nepeta*.

CENTAUREA CYANUS, *ken-TAU-ree-ah see-an-us*, Blue cornflower; Perennial; use in the front of the midborder; Sun or very light shade. The cornflower at first registers more in the back of your mind than in your full consciousness, and then you come to like it more. Of a moundy habit about two feet high in bloom, with dark leaves, criss-crossed buds and fuzzy blue flowers with traces of black, it blooms in early summer and, with vigilant deadheading, keeps blooming for a fairly long time.

CENTRANTHUS RUBER, *ken-TRAN-this ROO-ber*, Valerian or keys of heaven; Perennial; use in the back of the midborder; Sun or very light shade. This easily grown perennial comes in white ('Alba'), or a curious, cotton-candy pink, and blooms in midsummer. It'll spread well if it's happy, which is good, because it looks best massed. Particularly good, too, if you have rabbits, who hate it. The key won't necessarily gain you admittance to heaven, but there you are.

CERASTIUM TOMENTOSUM, *sir-AS-tee-um toe-men-TOE-sum*, Snow-in-summer; Perennial; use in the front of the border; Sun. Starry white blossoms (about a foot high) in late spring precede the silvery foliage of this perennial for the sunny front of the border. Each plant may creep three feet in any direction (except up), so give them plenty of room at the start, and be patient; they may take two or three years to look as if they belong. Once they do, you may want to dig up and pull apart the clumps, so as to have more for elsewhere, but do so only just after they've finished blooming or in the fall.

CERATOSTIGMA PLUMBAGINOIDES*, *KAH-rah-toe-STIG-mah plum-bag-in-OI-des*, Plumbago; Perennial; use in the front of the border, to underplant around shrubs or as an ornamental groundcover; Sun in the north, part shade in the south. These perennials grow eight inches tall, with a one-foot spread; they're a groundcover all season, then they bloom nicely in a striking vivid blue early in the fall as the foliage deepens to crimson—a nice combination.

CHAENOMELES SPECIOSA*, *kah-NOM-ah-lees spe-see-OS-ah*, Flowering quince; Deciduous flowering shrub; use in groupings of mixed shrubs or as a specimen; Sun. These bloom beautifully in the spring, in shades ranging from whitish to pink to deep red, and produce podlike fruits (quince) in the fall. They take a couple of seasons really to get going, but once they do, they bloom enthusiastically. They can grow ten or fifteen feet high, kept shorter by pruning, or they can be trained by clipping and nailing the branches to grow against a wall or trellis. You can force the branches indoors, too, and given a choice, I'd plant them over forsythia any day.

Prune to shape after they flower in the spring. Quinces used to fall into the *Cydonia* (sid-OH-nee-ah) genus, and sometimes they're still labeled *Cydonia* (or even *Pseudocydonia!*)—another murky area in gardening. When you're shopping for them, it might be worthwhile to ask for both, just in case.

Chervil, see *Anthriscus.*

CHRYSANTHEMUM, *kris-AN-the-mum,* Mum or daisy; Includes annuals and perennials; use depends on species; Sun. "A service-able flower," thought Miss Jean Brodie of chrysanthemums—but that doesn't begin to explain it. There are perennial and annual versions; early-, late- and all-season blooming versions; and some daisies are considered mums and some are not: Most confusing! The way through the puzzle would fill a book in itself, so with daisies, the best way is around the puzzle. Daisylike flowers can be found in a number of different genera, among them *Chrysanthemum, Boltonia, Heliopsis, Echinacea, Rudbekia, Aster* and *Anthemis.* They can come in oranges, yellows, pinks, whites and blues; these latter (in some cases!) are known as painted daisies. So, with the exception of the floppy shasta daisies (easily—too easily—grown from seed, planted in the autumn for bloom the following season), the thing to do is to erase the notion of daisies from one's mind entirely, and choose dai-sylike flowers by sight, blooming time, height, color and so on. Walking the nurseries or perusing the catalogs will begin to help sort the problem out; there'll be daisylike flowers over here, and more over *here,* different botanically but easily grouped together in the garden. (Compare the situation to choices in cars: Any number of car companies offer jeeplike vehicles, not Jeeps, strictly speak-ing, but they'll still get you there. So it is with daisies.) As for the autumn-blooming chrysanthemums, the mums that go with cider and football games, you can find annual or perennial versions. These are planted in summer when they become available at the nurseries, and the buds should be pinched back from time to time until mid-August, at which time you apply a dose of fertilizer and let them rampage into autumn, deadheading to lengthen the season of bloom. My objection to the perennials is that they take up too much room in the garden all summer: Why waste prime garden real estate on bushy perennials that need pinching all season and don't flower till so late? The annuals look so good in pots, and they're dirt cheap in the fall when they're in bloom, that a few in containers (replacing summer annuals), or dug into the earth at the last minute, or set out in their pots on the porch, suggest autumn just enough.

CIMICIFUGA RACEMOSA*, *key-mih-kif-FEW-gah ras-ah-MOS-ah*, Bugbane; Perennial; use in the back of the border or in a woodland setting; Shady, moist area. The bugbane's white candlelike flowers, which come in midsummer, shoot out in every direction and are very noticeable, because these shrubby plants can reach six feet in height. A single plant looks rather as if you'd made a mistake. It takes at least three to show you knew what you were doing.

CLEMATIS, *KLEM-ah-tis*, Perennial vine; use to drape over gates, fences, posts, trellises, and walls, and to trail over other plants and vines; Sun. There are more than three hundred varieties of clematis, flowering sequentially throughout the season in reds, pinks, whites, purples, blues and yellows. They're expensive; they're slow to take off (they usually pay more attention to their roots for a few years before they flower well); they're slightly fussy (they like moist, fertile soil, twice-a-year applications of compost, cool roots and sun on their crests; stones around the base, or a thick layer of mulch, will cool the roots). They're also worth every bit of trouble, because the first season they take hold, you'll have a cascade of solid blooms prettier than you could have imagined. Some species require pruning every spring; some never require pruning at all. When buying clematis, whether from a catalog or nursery, check the requirements for the specific species you've chosen. Plant it, and wait.

CLEOME*, *klee-OH-me*, Spider flower; Annual; use in the cutting garden or interspersed among back-of-the-midborder perennials; Sun. This spiny thing is a totally ridiculous-looking annual (reseeds itself almost every time), which grows nearly five feet high with several thick shoots per plant (which makes it seem bushy) and keeps on flowering from May through October. Usually comes in pinks, occasionally in creamy white as well. Give it a sunny place with plenty of room in which to grow effusively, and cut it as much as you want. It may take some getting used to as a cut flower, but if you're growing it, you *will* get used to it.

*   *   *

COLCHICUM*, *KOHL-kih-kum*, Autumn crocus; Perennial, bulb; use for naturalizing in meadows or in woodland settings; Sun or light shade. There are a number of *Colchicum* species, but *C. autumnale,* a bulb known as the autumn crocus, is the one I've maligned so thoroughly in the first pages of this book. To grow it anyway, plant bulbs in early August, four inches apart and four inches deep, keeping in mind that the flowers grow only as high as crocuses. (Hard to do: the bulbs are big.) You'll have sparse lavender blooms early the first autumn, huge leaves the following spring (which you have to leave alone, and they're not very pretty as they're disappearing) and an effusive bloom the second autumn. Sometimes they naturalize and form colonies. And take care with them around children and animals, as the bulbs are poisonous, not deadly (except if ingested in great quantities), but poisonous enough to be extremely careful with.

Columbine, see *Aquilegia.*
Coneflower, see *Rudbekia.*

CONSOLIDA AMBIGUA, *kon-SAHL-ee-da am-BIG-you-ah*, Rocket larkspur; Annual; use in the cutting garden or as an annual filler in the back of the midborder; Sun. A kind of poor man's delphinium, this annual grows almost three feet high and blooms in dusky blue, lavender or cream—great for cutting, and looks most effective grown in profusion, particularly if you plan to cut a lot of it for indoors. Set each plant just three inches from the next to ensure a look of abundance.

COREOPSIS GRANDIFLORA, *kor-ee-OP-sis grand-ih-FLOR-ah*, Tickseed; Perennial; use in the border (height varies with species) or in a meadow or wildflower setting; Sun or very light shade. There are coreopsis with fernlike foliage and coreopsis with leafy foliage; don't let this throw you off. There are also dwarf cultivars and those growing higher (but not more than two feet); some coreopsis are available in lavender, too, though most are bright yellow, like the 'Early Sunrise' cultivar that I planted. And some sport a single row of blooms, others double rows, which look fluffier. The '*grandiflora*' is a bit exaggerated, however. The flowers aren't exactly grand, but on their thin stems, they move nicely in the wind and last through and slightly beyond midsummer if you deadhead.

*   *   *

CORNUS ALBA 'Elegantissima'*, *KOR-nis AL-ba el-a-gan-TIS-ee-ma*, Dogwood; Deciduous flowering tree; use massed, as a single specimen or to anchor a border; Sun or very light shade. The dogwoods are trees, shrubs or trees that can be pruned to act like shrubs, some with beautiful blooms, some with leaves more handsome than others, some with neat-looking berrylike fruits in the fall. Many, too, are rightly touted for winter interest in the form of interesting bark or bright red stems. The trees, which sooner or later (depending on what size you start with) become proper tree-size ornamental specimens in perfect scale with a cottage-size garden, can stand in the garden alone or, grouped, help define a certain area of it. The dogwoods are easy to grow and care for, although they vary in their requirements—some require a little pruning, others like to be left alone, a few are fussy about soil, that kind of thing. In general, decent soil and a mulch to conserve moisture will start them off just fine. *C. a.* 'Elegantissima' can grow up to fifteen feet high, or be kept pruned to any size you want. Pruning, which in this case should be done in the spring, will also encourage lush growth.

CORONILLA, *koh-roe-NIL-ah*, Crown vetch; Perennial; use in meadows, to cover banks and to prevent erosion; Sun or light shade. This sprawling groundcover, with nice little midsummer flowers that look like those of clover or chives, doesn't actually cover the ground so much as "wash" over it in foliage "waves" growing to three feet high. In any kind of structured or formal setting, it looks wrong. It needs a far-off perspective and a space big enough to require worry-free, all-over coverage.

COSMOS*, *KOS-mos*, Annual; use in the cutting garden or in a small jumble of its own against a gate or fencepost; Sun. An annual that often reseeds itself, cosmos is one of the comforting and familiar sights of summer, growing as it usually does in full sun in a high tangle of pinks and white—that species is *C. bipinnatus* (bye-PIN-ah-tus), but will usually answer to just cosmos. Increasingly, too, you can find pure white, or dwarf varieties, nice variations on the theme. More interesting are the *C. sulphureus* (sul-FEAR-ee-us) varieties, fluffier versions in yellow and orange, such as 'Bright Lights' and 'Sunset', which are commonly known as the Klondyke varieties.

*   *   *

COTONEASTER, *kah-TAWN-ee-as-ter*, Includes deciduous and evergreen shrubs; use to cover a bank or berm or as an edging for a bed of mixed shrubs; Sun in the north, a little shade in the south. Actually in the rose family, cotoneaster works as an elegant, undulating groundcover, about two feet high, with so-so flowers in late spring and prettier berries in the fall. It's much more interesting covering a bank than, say, pachysandra and also good juxtaposed to rocks. Plant to allow for ultimate spread, which for most species is about three or four feet, and prune only as necessary to shape in late winter or early spring. There's a sweet dwarf version called 'Tom Thumb', which does the same thing only it's smaller.

Cranesbill, see *Geranium.*

CROCOSMIA, *krow-COS-me-ah*, Perennial bulb; use in a meadow or woodland setting or near water; Sun. These are members of the iris family, with pretty foliage to prove it; most have curious mid- to late-summer blooms that look like a delicate tropical bird in red, yellow or orange. Easy to grow, they like moisture and if you give them room, they'll spread as a groundcover. They're unusual enough, too, to attract queries and attention, so you'll get extra credit for having them. Don't divide the corms as you would irises; these will spread on their own. Plant each corm about three inches deep and three inches apart, which will give them the room they need to spread.

CROCUS, *KROH-kis*, Perennial bulb; use anywhere—in the lawn, in the front of the border, or to edge shrubs; Sun or part shade. One of the first signs of spring, the crocus blooms warily: There's scarcely a stem to topple over, just those ground-hugging petals of color. It takes very little to coax a crocus into bloom. Plant the bulbs in the fall, in the pattern in which you want them to grow (never let the bulbs touch), having first sprinkled a little peat or compost (like sugar over cereal) into the hole. They'll come up just fine. Then leave them alone for three years or so. If they have come back in the ensuing years, dig them up, pull off the new little "bulblets" and replant them: you will have grown a colony of crocuses.

Cupflower, see *Nierembergia.*
Cydonia, see *Chaenomeles.*
Daffodil, see *Narcissus.*

* * *

DAHLIA*, *DAHL-ee-ah*, Annual, bulb; use in the cutting garden; Sun. Dahlias, of which there are more than three thousand varieties, grow from bulbs called tubers, and will flower in most any color from midsummer till frost if you are diligent about pinching off extra buds, so that the stems will not have to bear so many blooms—you can figure this out, though, as you go along. Plant in early summer, after the soil is well warmed up, two feet apart and six inches deep in sun. They grow from one to five feet high or even higher, depending on variety, and all but the dwarf ones require major staking—sturdy structural beams for plants. They also like to be fertilized a couple of times during their blooming season. After the first frost, dig up the bulbs and store in a cool place over the winter. For optimum results, you can do special things to the tubers while they're being stored (what? I don't know), and if you're going to go to all the trouble of digging up and storing the tubers, you might want to check into this.

Daisy, see *Chrysanthemum*.
Dead nettle, see *Lamium*.

DELPHINIUM, *del-FIN-ee-um*, Perennial; use in the back of the midborder; Sun. These outstandingly beautiful perennials almost always need staking and refuse to look quite lush enough, unless you live in England or Maine, or a few other lucky places in New England and the Pacific Northwest, in which case plant them with impunity. They bloom in midsummer, in shades of ice blue to deeper blue and lavender; if you cut off spent blossoms, they may bloom a second time later in the season. Otherwise, have someone send you some from a florist.

DIANTHUS, *dee-AHN-this*, Pinks; Includes annuals, biennials and perennials; use in the front of the border, to edge a path, or in a rock garden; Sun. This genus comprises more than two hundred varieties, including the florists' carnation. Catalogs and all nurseries have a good collection of perennials and a good choice of color—salmons, pink, reds and whites. These perennials are beloved, and you'll never have trouble finding them. Most are fragrant and grow densely on blue-green stems, about ten inches high. They bloom for a long time, but repeat blooming requires vigilant deadheading. *D. barbatus* is the species known as sweet william, with pretty blooms on stocky stems; I've never seen sweet william take off in a big way. (If you cut them for indoors, you have to remember to change the water every day or two, or it gets slimy and begins to smell, not very sweetly.)

DICENTRA EXEMIA; D. SPECTABILIS*, *die-KEN-trah ex-IM-ee-ah; spec-TAB-ih-lis*, Bleeding heart; Perennial; use in the front of the midborder; Dappled shade. I've usually heard the genus name pronounced die-SEN-trah, but it comes from the Greek *di*, meaning "two," and *kentron*, meaning "a spur," because the spring-blooming flowers have two spurs, whatever they are. So it must be die-KEN-trah, after all, although you may be "corrected" for your pronounciation. They bloom in pink or white and have either etched, fernlike foliage (*D. exemia*) or three-pronged leaves (*D. spectabilis*) and a slightly bushier form. Bleeding hearts can take a good deal of shade. The foliage of *D. spectabilis* goes dormant in midsummer. Carefree and reliable, it's a classic.

DIGITALIS, *dij-ih-TAHL-is*, Foxglove; Biennial; use in the back of the midborder; Sun or very light shade. The name comes from the Latin for digit, or finger, and this biennial has blooms you do want to stick your finger into, as if they were gloves. Truly aristocratic in bloom, they should be planted only about a foot apart; they show to best effect when massed. Usually they're available in mixed colors, which is fine, and if you cut the blooms back after they're spent, there's a good chance you'll have a second bloom that same season. Plants reseed themselves fairly readily. Or try planting seeds in the fall for bloom the following spring—may work, may not.

Dogwood, see *Cornus*.

ELAEAGNUS, *eel-ee-AHG-nus*, Silver berry, silverberry, or oleaster; Evergreen and deciduous trees and shrubs; use depends on species; Sun. The members of this genus are notable for their glinting silvery leaves and are particularly useful near the shore, because they don't mind the salt air. Varieties of *E. augustifolia* are grown as small (twenty to thirty feet) trees; other species—see what's available in your zone and nurseries—are grown strictly as shrubs, pretty when massed together or just try one in a grouping of mixed shrubs.

EUONYMUS*, *you-WAN-a-mus*, Evergreen and deciduous shrubs; use depends on species; Sun or light shade. This wide-ranging genus comprises a good number of totally durable and handsome shrubs, some that climb, and some with not terribly exciting flowers or berries—the foliage is the thing. While they'll never be regarded as centerpieces of the garden, used here and there as small hedges, in mixed groupings, or climbing a fence or wall they'll give a garden texture and complexity and a finished look. The glossy-leaved evergreen 'Manhattan' (ask for *Euonymus* 'Manhattan') is a variety of *E. kiautschovicus* (ke-out-SHOW-vi-cus) and can sometimes be found preaffixed to a trellis, if you want it to climb. *E. alatus* (ah-LAH-tus) has the common name of burning bush, because of the way the leaves burst into scarlet in the fall before dropping. There are smallish shrubs, those known as 'Variegatus', with leaves variegated in green and white or green and yellow; these will climb by themselves, if you plant them against a wall. These are mix-and-match shrubs of great value, aesthetically and otherwise.

EUPHORBIA, *you-FOR-bee-ah*, Perennial; use in the front of the border or grow as a low hedge; Sun or light shade. The main attraction of the *Euphorbia* species are the truly pretty, narrow leaves, which seem to grow almost like petals reaching up, that stay in place all season. Sometimes you can find variegated foliage, which is loveliest of all. Depending on the species, the flowers are greenish yellow, greenish green or reddish and bloom anywhere from spring to late summer. Sometimes the stalks are reddish, too, in the autumn when the leaves fall off. (To be honest, the flowers are strange looking, and you'd never grow euphorbia if it weren't for the foliage.) One caution, though, is to wear gloves when you cut it; the stalks secrete a toxic juice that can cause a rash. Worth growing anyway.

EUSTOMA GRANDIFLORUM; LISIANTHUS, *you-STOH-mah grand-ih-FLOH-rum; leez-ee-AN-thus*, Annual; use in the cutting garden or to bring indoors; Sun. In lavender, pink or white, these annuals are delicate, fragile stemmed and supremely fussy (I've found them so, anyway). But they're graceful enough to keep trying. A wooden box of them growing inside gives you a feeling similar to a pot of orchids. I've seen them grown successfully outdoors for cutting, but for me they work better grown indoors in a sunny spot and left right in their pots—a minigarden of their own. In this setting, you can gently push the stems around to keep them balanced, and they'll last longer than an indoor bouquet, which seems fair enough.

Everlasting, see *Xeranthemum*.

FELICIA AMELLIODES, *feh-LEASH-ee-ah ahm-el-OI-des*, Blue marguerite; Annual; use in the cutting garden or in the front of the midborder; Sun or very light shade. These daisylike annuals bloom in light blue with yellow centers on stems about two feet high. They like it cool, so you'd have to start the seeds indoors or else buy the fledgling plants at a nursery. Plant somewhere where the heat won't be relentless. If the summer becomes very hot, they'll flag. Cut them back if they do, fertilize and water, and they'll usually reappear when it gets cool again.

Fennel, see *Foeniculum*.

Ferns; Most are perennials; Use ferns in a woodland setting; among shrubs to "finish" a bed; near water; or to edge a shaded fence, wall or post; Part to fairly deep shade. The plants known collectively as ferns fall into several genera, but all have the same requirements: more shade than sun, fairly consistent moisture, and a mulch to keep them cool and full all season, and fuller each year. When planting, the crown—which is a "hub" from which the fronds emerge—should be planted at or just below the soil level. Ostrich ferns (*Matteuccia struthiopteris*—mah-TEW-key-ah strew-the-OP-ter-is) hopscotch around most readily, reproducing themselves many times over the course of several years, if they're happy where they are. Lady fern (*Athyrium filix-femina*—ath-EER-ee-um FEEL-ix-FAX-min-ah) seems to float in layers held up by air; the silver-dappled Japanese painted fern (*Athyrium nipponicum*) reflects light most dramatically. . . . There are literally dozens of ferns to choose from, in different heights and shades of green; as good a place as any to start seeking them out is one of the good gardening catalogs.

FICUS BENJAMINA, *FEE-kus ben-ja-MEAN-ah*, Weeping fig; Tender deciduous tree; use as container plantings to anchor a bed of herbs or to adorn a terrace; Sun (but not relentless). Not hardy enough to withstand the colder of North American winters, the figs, weeping or otherwise, are nonetheless ornamental additions to the garden, so long as they stay in their pots and go back inside when the gardener does, before the frost, that is. They need some sun, but not beating, relentless sun; in heat waves, they should be moved to a lightly shaded place for the duration. Fertilizing once a month during the spring-summer season is recommended. You can count on graceful foliage and a lovely form, but not necessarily enough delicious figs to do justice to prosciutto. If you have a sunny, cool place for them inside, they can grow rather large, making it difficult to move them around too easily (the common fig, *F. carica,* accent on car, for example, can grow to fifteen feet)—but this takes a long time and is something you can worry about later.

Fig, see *Ficus.*

FILIPENDULA RUBRA 'Venusta'*, *fil-ih-PEN-dew-lah RUE-brah,* Perennial; use in the back of the border; Sun or, farther south, light shade. The species in the *Filipendula* genus vary widely, particularly in the leaves. Nevertheless, the blooms, in red, purple, pink or white—some of them like plumes—are dramatic and manage to look windswept and proud at the same time. The foliage has a nice way of growing, seeming to buoy the blooms, and looks fine even when the early summer blooms have gone. *F. r.* 'Venusta' grows to six feet and spreads to about three feet, blooms in pink, and doesn't need staking.

FOENICULUM*, *feh-NIK-you-lum,* Fennel; Perennial herb; use in the herb garden; Sun. Growing fennel, whether or not you like to eat it, is a pleasure. The stems, which can reach three feet high or more when they're in bloom, rise up like a geyser and look fluffy and sort of hairy, kind of like dill. It flowers late in the summer in yellow, and sprinkles its seeds around afterward, so if you don't want it to spread, cut the small flowers off as they fade. (Or let nature take its course and see what happens.) It's widely available with stems in bronze or lime green and should be planted in the sun and any kind of soil. It's usually thought of as belonging among herbs, but the foliage is a nice way to "garnish" flowers as well.

*　　*　　*

Forget-me-not, see *Myosotis*.

FORSYTHIA, *for-SITH-ee-ah*, Deciduous flowering shrub; use mixed among other shrubs or as a specimen; Sun or light shade. It is such a signal of spring and so good for forcing indoors that it seems a pity not to have a forsythia. On the other hand, it's not very exciting after the bloom and takes up space—they can grow ten feet high and wide—all year. For my taste, anyway, it's best to avoid planting hedges of these (too garish) or clipping them into tight forms (too constricted). I think it's best to have one or two, allowed to spew. Prune a little if it needs shaping just after the blooms are finished.

Foxglove, see *Digitalis*.

GAILLARDIA, *gul-ARD-ee-ah*, Blanketflower; Perennial; use in a wildflower garden, in a meadow, or in the border; Sun. This is a nicely patterned, reliable perennial, flowering with the coreopsis in midsummer, which you can dress up or down. In a wildflower setting, it looks like a wildflower; in a setting slightly more formal, toward the front of a border, it will rise to the occasion. They grow a foot high or less, depending on the variety you choose.

GERANIUM*, *jur-AYN-ee-um*, Cranesbill; Perennial; use in the front of the border; Sun. The main thing to remember here is that this perennial has nothing to do with the annual geraniums you see everywhere, all summer, in pots. Those are, in fact, members of the *Pelargonium* genus, but are always called geraniums; I don't know why. Nor do I know why *these* geraniums, the perennial ones, are also called cranesbill, but they are. There are a good number of cultivars to choose from, some larger, some slightly smaller; they bloom for a long time in the spring in pink, blue, white or purple, with a tidy self-contained form. They need full sun and decent soil. As for the musky, familiar, red-or-white annual geraniums, the *Pelargonium*, plant them in full sun. If you keep trimming off the stems and blooms as the blooms begin to turn brown, you'll have blooms all season. Increasingly, new cultivars of geraniums are available with smaller, denser leaves and more delicate blooms sometimes in pink as well as red and white. These will trail over their pots, and they're a welcome change from the ubiquitous upright geraniums.

*   *   *

GLADIOLUS*, *glah-DEE-oh-lis*, Gladiolus; Annual bulb; use in the cutting garden; Sun. Members of the iris family, these are, of course, excellent for funerals. Choose the color (or colors) you want, and plant the corms or bulbs closer together by half than the directions say. If you're going to plant them at all, plant in abundance. If you want, you can dig up the corms, store them over the winter in a cool place, and replant them late the following spring; you might want to try leaving them in place, as they sometimes come back on their own and colonize.

Gooseneck loosestrife, see *Lysimachia.*
Gout weed, see *Aegopodium.*

GYPSOPHILA*, *jyp-SOFF-ih-lah*, Baby's breath; Includes annuals and perennials; use in the midborder (height varies with species) or in the cutting garden; Sun. Here the experts differ on everything from pronunciation (one plant dictionary I use says it should be pronounced with a hard *g*) to soil requirements (high lime content is necessary or it's not). The name translates from the Greek *gypso philos,* or "gypsum loving," and there are about five dozen varieties, some perennials, some annuals. Following a friend's advice, I abandoned the perennial baby's breath, which toppled over, refused to flower lavishly or in a bright white, never returned for the promised second bloom and didn't come back the second year. Instead, I started sprinkling seeds of annual *Gypsophila* wherever I wanted it, tamping them down lightly. Ever since, I've had prettier blossoms and much better luck with it. Planting several times a season, two weeks apart, ensures annual baby's breath from early summer on.

Hakonechloa macra 'Aureola', ho-kohn-eh-KLOE-ah MAK-ra, see Ornamental grasses.

HEDERA, *HEAD-er-ah*, Ivy; Perennial, evergreen; use to cover walls, banks, and trellises; to edge lawns or groupings of shrubs, and to trail over window boxes and containers; Very light shade. The ivy league schools are those old enough to have their brick facades covered by ivy: a sign that such an institution is established. The *H. helix*, or English ivy (new cultivars include those with smaller or variegated leaves, in addition to the conventional leaf size), will indeed climb a facade up to about one hundred feet, giving the impression that the garden is settled, that it *belongs*.

Ivy is amazingly tenacious, and needs no support to climb; it has little suction cups, called holdfasts, to affix it to whatever wall is in its way. Plant the ivy two feet apart, and expect them to grow about a foot a year. It is best not to plant them near foundations, because they can make their way through concrete or stone. Prune any time, to keep ivy away from where you don't want it.

HELIANTHUS*, *heel-ee-AN-thus*, Sunflower; Includes annuals and perennials; use depends on species; Sun. Because this genus is native to North America, you'd think that all the sunflowers would be considered perennials. Not so. Most are billed as annuals, although some do reseed themselves fairly reliably. Planting these directly into the soil after there's no more danger of frost will yield you a good number of daisylike "flower-flowers" from midsummer through early fall, depending on where you live and when you plant. There are many varieties to choose from, all bright, and in yellow, orange, bronze, or cream. The huge annual sunflower, *H. annus* (ANN-us), looks best if you have a whole field to give over to it from midsummer through early fall, depending on when you've planted. More delicate choices include the hybrid *H. annus* 'Italian White', formal enough for the back of the border; it can grow to ten feet, but with several stalks instead of one and many smaller blooms per stalk. *H. annus* 'Autumn Beauty' blooms like a sunflower but is smaller, only three or four feet in height, and is great for cutting. As the common name suggests, this blooms late, in late summer/early autumn, along with its bigger relative.

HELIOTROPIUM ARBORESCENS 'Marine', *hay-lee-oh-TROHP-ee-um ar-bor-ES-enz*, Heliotrope; Annual; use in container plantings or in the front of the border. This is a really exotic-looking annual, musky and aromatic, with lovely purple blooms all summer. It's best set off in a special place on its own, in an ornamental pot, say, adorning a terrace. (It's also best bought at a store, not grown from seed.) Full sun is ideal, except where summers get very hot, in which case it likes to be shaded part of the day (all the more reason to display it in a pot, so you can move it); be sure, too, not to let it dry out. It can mix well with perennials, and looks particularly good next to silvery things.

*　　*　　*

HEMEROCALLIS*, *ha-me-roe-KAL-is*, Daylily; Perennial bulb; use in the border, in a bed of their own, or as an edging plant; Sun or light shade. These go-anywhere, move-anywhere perennials are best grown in herds, stampeding across the garden from bed to bed, wherever their mass is needed. You never grow just one. A well-chosen mixture will yield you some that bloom early, some in mid-season and some late—yet their leaves will match, flow in the wind and fill in in no time. Planting in too much shade (i.e., full shade) will yield fewer blooms; if you're planting big clumps, plant them about two feet apart, smaller clumps closer together. Cut back the stems after the blooms have finished, and cut back the leaves then, too, if you want; they'll grow in refreshed for the rest of the season. Divide every few years by digging up the bulbs, pulling them apart with your hands, and replanting, or the blooms will be less profuse.

Honeysuckle, see *Lonicera.*

HOSTA, *HAH-stah*, Perennial; use as a groundcover, as an edging for shrubs, in a woodland area, or near water; Light to fairly deep shade. For once, all the species in this genus are recognizable as hostas, whether the leaves are green, bluish green, greenish blue, green with yellow or yellow with green, white with yellow or yellow with white—you get the idea. There are also dwarf and larger-growing varieties as well as a few that are sun tolerant. With hostas, the leaves count most; the midsummer flower spires are more of a distraction. Decisive and handsome, hostas require no special care beyond a mulch to help them keep moist. As they get overcrowded (after five years or so), they can be dug up and cut in half with a knife, then replanted; do this in spring or autumn.

HYDRANGEA*, *hy-DRAIN-jah*, Deciduous or, rarely, evergreen flowering shrub; use depends on species; Sun or very light shade. Several of the hydrangeas are discussed at length in the text, and there are many others as well. Most are deciduous but there are some evergreens; there are some climbing varieties. Some are distinguished by different kinds of leaves (rough, smooth or hairy) and different kinds of flower heads (the big fat ones are known as mophead, the flat ones as lacecap). As a rule, they are mid- to late summer bloomers, and the exact blooming schedule depends on the species you choose. All do well by the seashore, though many are available in most other areas as well; a little checking at the nurseries will tell you your choices. In the border, anchoring a bed, as specimens, in groups of mixed shrubs, they're classic, beautiful in bloom, and well rounded the rest of the season. They like their roots to be cool and not too dry. A mulch will help here. Any spent flower heads you haven't cut for indoors should be left in place till early the following spring, then pruned; this helps protect the plants over the winter. As for pruning the stems, each of the species likes to be pruned a little differently, which is the only confusing part. For those mentioned in the text: For *H. macrophylla* (mak-roe-FIL-ah) 'Nikko Blue', prune old shoots (they'll look old) to ground level every couple of years early in the spring to encourage new growth. For *H. paniculata* (pah-nik-you-LAH-ta), *H. p.* 'Grandiflora' (grand-ih-FLOR-ah), and *H. arborescens* (ar-boh-RES-enz) 'Annabelle', cut the branches that flowered the year before back by half. These won't flower this year, but the pruning will encourage better growth next year. With any of the hydrangeas, if you miss a year or two of pruning, don't worry about it.

IBERIS SEMPERVIRENS, *eye-BEHR-is sem-per-VIH-rens*, Candytuft; Perennial; use in the front of the border; Sun. The genus *Iberis* can be confusing, because there are annual, biennial and perennial varieties. This one grows under a foot tall and should be planted as if you were planting a carpet; there should be only a little space between plants to allow them to fill in. The small white blossoms first appear in high spring and will probably come back in the fall if you cut them back after they're spent.

ILEX*, *EYE-lex*, Holly; (Mostly) evergreen trees and shrubs; use depends on species; Sun or light shade. A vast genus—nearly four hundred varieties in all—of mostly evergreen trees and shrubs, the hollies are used every which way—for hedging, as specimens, in mixed shrub screens and to anchor a bed. Some have rounded or weeping forms, not pyramidal, and some look nothing like Christmas. The ultimate height and shape will dictate what you'll do with each variety. Plant in acid soil or use an acid fertilizer, and try to plant them where you're sure you want them to remain, because they hate to be moved. (If you must move them, do so in mid-spring or very late summer, digging up as much soil around the rootball as you can.) Any pruning, mostly to shape, should be done late in the summer. Hollies are polygamous (in the plant kingdom, dioecious is the word for this), which means that if you want berries, you have to plant at least one male, non-berry-producing holly to pollinate several female, berry-producing ones.

IMPATIENS, *im-PAY-shuns*, Annual; use in container plantings, under trees or as an edging; Light to deep shade. The great less-is-more shade annual, available in white, reds, pinks and salmons. Massed plantings of them induce horticultural boredom, while a couple of six-packs of them spread discreetly (a foot or a foot and a half apart) can look surprising and fresh. The white ones look great tucked into woodland settings. Some people prefer the New Guinea impatiens, which produce more yellow-dappled leaves than flowers. Not me.

IPOMOEA, *ip-OH-mee-ah*, Morning glory; Annual vine; use to climb a post, fence, or mailbox or in the cutting garden. Blooming in white, red, pink, blue or purple, the morning glory is—when it's happy—one of summer's triumphs, like having a clematis that sticks around all season long. Seeds should be sown at least three weeks after the last frost date (later than most seedlings; morning glories don't like the cold), after having been soaked first for eight hours in lukewarm water. Plant them where they'll have a ready support to which they can attach their tendrils. When the seeds germinate and stems, leaves and buds begin to grow, pinch new buds back at first by half, so as not to diffuse the plant's energies too much. After they begin to bloom profusely, forget about the pinching and enjoy them the rest of the season.

IRIS*, *EYE-ris*, Perennial bulb; use in beds of their own, in the front of the midborder and near water (the Japanese and Siberian ones, anyway); Sun or light shade. The spring-blooming irises— lower or taller, with different kinds of leaves, in practically any color you can think of—encompass two hundred species in all, and many more cultivars. Many like to be planted in the fall, some can tolerate being planted either in the spring or fall, and a few prefer to be planted only in the spring, all of which is to say that, easy as irises are to cultivate, you have to pay attention to the needs of each cultivar. If you're buying plants from a nursery or catalog, this won't matter much, because they'll be available only when they're meant to be planted. But if you're helping a friend divide his or her irises, check a catalog to see when they should be divided. If you're still uncertain, you'll be fairly safe dividing after the plant has bloomed. Planting and dividing, which should be done every three or four years, are covered fully in the text.

Ivy, see *Hedera.*
Japanese anemone, see *Anemone.*
Japanese maple, see *Acer.*
Johnny-jump-up, see *Viola.*
Juniper, see *Juniperus.*

JUNIPERUS, *joo-NIP-er-us*, Juniper; Evergreen shrubs; use depends on species; Sun. There are as many different uses for junipers as there are species and varieties. They can be green, silvery, bluish or yellowish; they can spread high enough for screening or low enough for rock gardens or groundcover; some are even columnar. They are among the genera known as conifers, which means they produce their seeds in cones—that is, pinecones. Their habit is sort of prickly, not unattractively so but enough to suggest that the only place they don't belong is near soft-colored, soft-textured perennials. Otherwise, in rock gardens, lining driveways, marking entrances or grouped together to set off a specific area, they're terrific. One requirement is a moisture-preserving layer of mulch year-round. And prune only to trim off wayward little bits that get out of line or branches that have definitely turned brown.

KALMIA, *KAL-mee-ah*, Mountain laurel; Evergreen shrubs; use in a woodland setting; Part shade (especially in the south). Application is found in the common name: these evergreen shrubs, most of which grow (slowly) to about six feet, belong in woodland settings, where in bloom—pale pink to red—they're awesome. A cool damp setting will suit them best, and they like acid soil, so you'll have to fertilize accordingly. Their roots are at the surface of the soil, so they can't "reach" down very far for water; a good mulching will help keep them damp. Usually you'll find varieties of the species *K. latifolia* (accent on FOL), and the variations have to do with ultimate size and color of bloom. Prune only minimally to shape any wayward branches, once the blooming season is over. And plant the biggest shrubs you can find, because mountain laurel grows slowly.

KERRIA JAPONICA 'Pleniflora'*, *ka-REE-ah ja-PON-ah-ka*, Deciduous flowering shrub; use in groupings of mixed shrubs; Sun or shade. Whereas most deciduous flowering shrubs require a good deal of sun, the kerrias can be happy and flower well in a fair amount of shade. The single or double blooms, which seem to have a couple of extra layers of petals, come out in midspring usually in neon yellow or occasionally orange; the stems stay bright green all winter. They grow only five feet tall, with a slightly greater spread. Pruning is easy; just cut back any branches that look noticeably worn out, which will reinvigorate the shrubs. *K. j.* 'Pleniflora' is an extremely vigorous choice.

Keys of heaven, see *Centranthus.*
Lady's-mantle, see *Alchemilla.*
Lamb's ears, see *Stachys.*

LAMIUM*, *LAY-mee-um*, Dead nettle; Perennial; use as a groundcover, under shrubs. or in the front of the border; Sun or shade. This spread-like-crazy, low-growing (six inches) groundcover will work in sun or shade, but spreads more in sun. Many are variegated, and will light up dark areas effectively. The flowers seem to me not to suit the leaves somehow, as if someone had toyed with the plant's genes, but *Lamium* is grown for the foliage primarily, so maybe it doesn't matter much.

LATHYRUS ODORATUS, *LAY-thrus oh-doh-RAH-tus*, Sweet pea; Includes annuals and perennials; use to climb low trellises or posts or in the herb garden; Sun. Thoughts of the sweet pea evoke the beloved annual, easily grown from seed, which climbs up low trellises or gates by means of little tendrils. (There are also some perennial sweet peas, sometimes thought of as wildflowers, farther south than Long Island.) Plant seeds, spacing according to directions, as soon as the danger of frost has past, and provide something for them to climb—even a post. They'll grow about four or five feet high. The tiny, fragrant blossoms, usually in mixed colors, and little peapods, wonderfully edible (raw, in salads or very lightly sautéed), won't last the summer, because they like the weather cool, but they'll stay around longer if you mulch them after they begin to produce their leaves and start climbing.

LAURUS, *LAUR-us*, Bay laurel; Tender tree; use in containers on a terrace or to anchor a bed of herbs; Sun. If you lived around the Mediterranean, you could have huge trees of bay laurel and pluck your own leaves to cook with or for making garlands whenever you wanted. If you live in most of North America, you're better advised to grow these trees in pots, bring them outside in summer and back into a sunny place to spend the winter. The leaves are exactly like those you usually see in jars, except not dried, you can keep them clipped into a rounded-on-top form and use them to set off a bed of herbs. One day, they'll grow too large for you to move them around easily—but this will take a long, long time.

LAVANDULA*, *lah-VAN-dew-lah*, Lavender; Perennial; use as a low hedge on its own, in the front of the border, or in the herb garden; Sun. A low lavender hedge—they're usually under two feet— with silvery leaves and midsummer flower spikes in lavender or sometimes white, is a timeless garden touch, erect and formal in demeanor. The leaves are also used in making potpourri and flavoring desserts. Plant them about two and a half feet apart. They're not hard to grow by any means, but lavender is the kind of plant that will either do well where you put it or it won't. If it doesn't, try planting *Santolina* in its place next time.

Lavender, see *Lavandula*.
Lavender mist, see *Thalictrum*.

LIGUSTRUM VULGARE*, *lee-GUS-trum vul-GAHR-ee*, Privet; Deciduous shrub; use for hedging; Sun or very light shade. Excellent for screening, and sometimes used very creatively—perfect windows and doorways can be carved out of the middle of a privet hedge, for example. They can grow to fifteen feet or higher, they flower in high summer and should be planted eighteen inches apart to ensure proper screening. To encourage thicker branches, prune to six inches after you plant them, and prune severely for the same reason every spring for the first several years, plus anytime you want, to shape. They're so reliable one tends to forget about them, but if they're off somewhere by themselves, don't forget they need watering during periods of drought.

LILIUM, *LIL-ee-um*, Lily; Perennial bulb; use in the front or back of the midborder, depending on height; Sun. The hardest thing about growing lilies is figuring out which to grow; make sure you get those that are fragrant and tall enough to make a statement. Keep their "feet" cool (an underplanting of annual *Gypsophila* is one way; just sprinkle the seeds), and they're otherwise surprisingly agreeable about following orders. Spacing will depend on their ultimate height, but when you plant them, plant five inches deep, sprinkle a little bonemeal (like sugar on cereal) into the planting hole. and never let the bulbs touch. To replenish the bulbs, cut the flowers just after they peak, before they set their seeds.

LIMONIUM, *lih-MOAN-ee-um*, Statice; Includes annuals, biennials, and perennials; use in the cutting garden; Sun. Though there are perennial and biennial versions, the statice most of us know—upright, thick stalks with small, unmoving purple or white flowers, most often seen dried—are annuals. I've grown them from seed, sown right in the soil in spring, with so-so luck, but that's because I planted them in too much shade, I think; they need sun. In sun, I see rows of them growing all over the place, doing just fine. Mostly they're grown to be dried, which is done by placing them in water while they're in full bloom (and even full bloom isn't all that exciting), then letting the water evaporate.

Lisianthus, see *Eustoma.*

LOBULARIA MARITIMA*, *lob-ew-LAH-ree-a ma-ri-TEE-ma*, Sweet alyssum; Annual; use in the front of the border, as an edging for container plantings or in window boxes; Sun or very light shade. Best and easily grown from seed, this annual, with its masses of tiny blossoms, will trail in white or yellow over just about anything low. It's probably overdone, but that's because it's dainty and useful and reliable. If you live in a place prone to very hot summers, you're advised to plant a new batch of sweet alyssum seeds every week over the course of several weeks, so that even if the heat causes the first batch to fade, you'll have more coming in. They often reseed themselves as well, so generous plantings at first might also yield a greater permanent bounty later.

LONICERA, *low-nih-SER-ah*, Honeysuckle; Deciduous (occasionally evergreen) flowering shrubs and vines; use in groupings of mixed shrubs, as a hedge.or to climb a wall or trellis; Amount of sun depends on species. There are full-sun cultivars and some that can take a little shade, some are good for hedges, some are wonderfully fragrant, some flower more vigorously than others, some flower in the spring and others flower from midsummer through midautumn: a honeysuckle for every need. There are also varying sizes, although honeysuckles average about six feet at their maximum height. Pruning requirements vary, too; some prefer spring prunings, others after the blooming season, and still others in the autumn. Once you figure out what you want, though, they're the easiest plants you can imagine, growing surprisingly fast in perfectly ordinary soil.

Love-in-a-mist, see *Nigella*.
Lupine, see *Lupinus*.

LUPINUS*, *lou-PIN-is*, Lupine; Perennial; use in a meadow or in a wildflower setting; Sun. A bane of my horticultural life, lupine is one of the prettiest perennials you'll ever see, flowering early in the summer on spires a yard high, in red, pink, yellow and purple. Often you find the colors mixed together, so if you want all of a single color, you may have to seek it out specially. Part of the reason they're hard to grow is that they like poor soil, and diligent gardeners do everything they can to make their soil rich. Thus the border, where the soil is good, is not the place to plant them. Try them, if you're so inclined, in full sun or very light shade, planted a foot apart, and in a place where it's not too moist. Cut back the blooms after they're spent.

LYSIMACHIA CLETHROIDES; L. PUNCTATA,* *leez-ee-MOK-ee-ah kleth-ROY-des, poonk-TAH-tah*; Perennial; use depends on species; Sun or light shade. The former, sometimes known as gooseneck loosestrife, is a sun or light shade perennial that belongs in the back of the midborder or, better, in a meadow setting: It spreads like crazy. The midsummer blooms do look like white goose's necks (or the soft ice cream that comes from a machine, upside down), and massed, they're very pretty—but invasive and hard to dig up. Installing metal edging a foot wide and deep is the best way to contain them. *L. punctata* is less bold and has green spires with mid-summer blooms in yellow; the blooms are subtle and make the eye seek them out, in a nice way; they're an acquired taste. These do well in a bed of informal flowers, or in the sunny herb garden, as a kind of blooming filler between and among herbs.

LYTHRUM*, *LITH-rum*, Purple loosestrife; Perennial; use in the back of the midborder; Sun. In ideal conditions (which here means on the moist side), *Lythrum* will spread well—too well, in some areas, where the worry is that they'll choke out less hardy plants in places they grow wild. They're easily kept in check in more genteel settings, where in sun 'Morden's Pink' and most other varieties will grow about a yard high, blooming in midsummer on spires lined with tiny blooms.

MACLEAYA MICROCARPA, *mak-LAY-ah mi-kro-KAR-pah*, Plume poppy; Perennial; use in a wildflower setting or near a pond; Sun. The plume poppy is sensational, with fuzzy silvery leaves that are darker underneath, rising up to six feet or more. It produces plumes in midsummer, in ivory or peach, and the leaves themselves, which seem to refract the light in the wind, are enough of a show the rest of the season. These would be considered invasive, if they weren't relatively easy to get rid of where you don't want them. Plant them almost a yard apart (they take up a fair amount of room), and in full sun.

MALVA SYLVESTRIS*, *MAHL-vah sill-VES-tris*, Mallow; Perennial; use in the back of the midborder; Sun or light shade. There are annuals, biennials and perennials in the *Malva* genus, some of them carrying the common name mallow. *M. sylvestris* is a perennial, which looks fragile but is hardy as can be—the best combination. Wonderful pink blossoms in midsummer about a yard high, for the back of the midborder, in full sun and with no special requirements at all. You'll see the little seedlings in the spring on the undersides of the plants: Scatter them around, tamp them down lightly, and there's a good chance you'll have a mass of them next year and from there on, which is how they show themselves to best advantage.

*   *   *

MANDEVILLA*, *man-deh-VIL-ah*, Annual vine; use as a container plant, attached to a trellis or something else it can climb; Very light shade. The great impulse buy among annuals, the mandevilla is a tropical vine that flowers beautifully in white or pink all summer, the blooms set off by big shiny green leaves. Even in the far south, this is considered a container planting, one that can climb, if given a trellis on which to affix itself (it may need some help in doing so—string will hold it). Very light shade will suit it best. If you can manage to keep it alive inside (in a sunny place) over the winter, prune it decisively in the spring before it starts a new spurt of growth, then fertilize it and bring it outside after there's no longer any danger of frost.

> *Malus*, see Ornamental fruit trees.
> Marigold, see *Tagetes*.
> Marjoram, see *Origanum*.
> Marsh marigold, see *Calthus*.
> Meadow rue, see *Thalictrum*.

MENTHA*, *MEN-thah*, mint; Perennial herb; use in the herb garden; Sun. There are many different varieties of mint, lemony mint, peppermint, spearmint—and all are easier to grow than not to grow: Spreading like mint is as apt a phrase as spreading like wildfire. So the important thing in growing it, aside from giving it sun, is containing it, either by planting it in the soil right in its container with the bottom cut out, in a ceramic pipe, or by planting it in a pot *not* installed in the ground. It looks bright and clean growing in, but inevitably becomes scraggly and leggy by the end of the season—about the time you're ready to trade in fresh iced tea with mint for a cup of steaming hot soup.

> Mint, see *Mentha*.
> *Miscanthus sinensis* 'Morning Light', mis-CAN-this sih-NEN-sis, see Ornamental grasses.
> Mock orange, see *Philadelphus*.

MONARDA*, *moe-NAR-dah*, Bee balm; Perennial; use depends on species; Sun. Blooming in pink, red or white, these perennials are easily grown, so easily, in fact that they may become invasive, but they're not very hard to get rid of where you don't want them.

They bloom in midsummer, attracting hummingbirds and butter-flies as much as bees, and they'll bloom a long time if you pluck off the spent heads the way you're supposed to. They're often thought of as right for a wildflower setting, but many cultivars—*M. didyma* 'Croftway Pink' is one—are softly colored and surely formal enough for the border. Dig up and pull or cut apart the clumps when they seem overcrowded, every three or four years.

Monkshood, see *Aconitum.*
Mountain laurel, see *Kalmia.*

MYOSOTIS SAPPHIRE*, *mee-oh-SO-tis*, Forget-me-not; Perennial; use in the front of the border; Sun-tolerant, they prefer light shade. An easily grown perennial (sun or light shade; ordinary soil) that blooms beautifully in a blue haze for a long time—from midspring through early summer. It's also easily grown from seed (sprinkle seeds in the fall, tamping down lightly, for bloom the next spring). Once the plants finish blooming, they'll get disreputably leggy. Leave them alone for a while, and they'll scatter more of their seeds. Then cut them back. Their only downside is that the foliage after the bloom, what little there is of it, isn't much to look at, so be sure to plant other things close by to fill in the space over the rest of the summer.

Nasturtium, see *Tropaeolum.*

NARCISSUS*, *nar-KIS-us*, Daffodil or jonquil; Perennial bulb; use anywhere—in the lawn, in front of the border, or to edge shrubs; Sun or part shade. Although technically, daffodils, narcis-sus and jonquils are all grouped under the *Narcissus* umbrella, that's just a quibble: Where I come from, it's good enough to call a daffodil a daffodil. There are hundreds to choose from, and some (those sold as paperwhites) work particularly well for forcing indoors. I choose by price and the picture. Plant them in the autumn in "bouquets," the way you want them to come up in the spring, about five inches deep and close together but not touching. Sprinkle a little bonemeal into the planting hole (like sugar over cereal) before you plant them. Cutting off the stems and permitting the leaves to wither for longer than you'd like will encourage them to naturalize.

*   *   *

NEPETA*, *NEH-pet-ah*, Catmint or catnip; Perennial; use in the border, as a low hedge, or in the herb garden; Sun. A low, shrubby genus with a number of species and cultivars, all fine on their own or mingled, most about two feet high. They bloom first in the spring, on muted lavender spikes that last a long time, and will bloom again in the fall if you cut the blooms back when they fade to gray. The wonderfully etched leaves, however, remain lush all season. These require little in the way of care, just full sun and a soil that's not overly fertile. It's best if you don't cut them back in the fall, but wait and cut the old stems the following spring, but if you forget and cut them back when you're cutting back everything else in autumn, they won't mind too much.

NIEREMBERGIA, *near-em-BERG-ee-ah*, Cupflower; Annual; use in hanging baskets or in the front of the border; Sun or light shade. Of a mounded habit, about a foot high with dense, cup-shaped flowers all summer, this plant is, oddly enough, a member of the potato family. Therefore, you'd *think* the seeds would grow pretty readily. I've only tried it once, and never got a purple flower, much less a potato. Best to buy the plants at a nursery, and potatoes at a farm stand.

NIGELLA HISPANICA; N. DAMASCENA 'Miss Jekyll'*, *nih-JEL-ah his-PAN-IK-ah; dam-as-KAY-nah*, Love-in-a-mist; Annual; use in the cutting garden or in the front of the border; Sun or light shade. The name comes from the Latin *niger*, or "black," and refers to the small black seeds, which shake themselves onto the ground and multiply the plants so readily from little pods that this quiet annual can almost be thought of as a perennial. They're about a foot high with foliage like that of dill but looser, neater and upright. The blooms are small and pretty in clear blue or slightly musky lavender. They need sun or very light shade, and they don't much like to be transplanted. Plant seeds in the autumn for bloom the following spring.

OCIMUM, *OH-kih-mum*, Basil; Annual herb; use in the herb garden; Sun. Fragrant on its own, basil is the traditional herb to accompany tomatoes and is useful in the kitchen in dozens of other ways as well. Buy it by sight, because there are new varieties in addition to the standard green, ten-inch high variety: purple-leaved basil, the tiny-leaved mounded kind (pretty and delicious) and other new cultivars, it seems, every year. Be sure to keep cutting basil, so it won't be allowed to flower. When it does, it'll be too late to use in the kitchen, and it will go leggy in the garden besides.

Oleaster, see *Elaeagnus.*
Oregano, see *Origanum.*

ORIGANUM*, *oh-ree-GONE-um*, Oregano; Perennial herb; use in the herb garden; Sun. One great, big (well, relatively big; they only grow two feet high at their peak) healthy oregano plant will see you through many summers, and many Italian meals. *Origanum vulgare* (vul-GAHR-ee) is the species you'll usually find, and it grows like a small shrub, with aromatic foliage in a muted green and handsome lavender and white blooms in midseason—these are nice to arrange in the kitchen in a teacup. Cut the blooms back after they fade. These belong in the herb garden, but if you don't have one, they're subtle enough to set off showier flowers, used as you'd use, say, lavender. Sweet marjoram is a variation on the theme of oregano, *O. marjorana* (mahr-johr-AHN-ah), and is grown the same way but doesn't grow as vigorously as the common oregano and may not work as a perennial in your area. It's useful for cooking anyway, even chopped over a fresh salad.

ORNAMENTAL FRUIT TREES
MALUS; *MAL-is;* Flowering crabapple;
PRUNUS; *PRUNE-is;* Flowering peach, almond, cherry, and plum;
PYRUS; *PIE-ris;* Flowering pear; Deciduous flowering trees; use as specimens, in groves, or to shelter an outdoor dining table; Sun.

These ornamental fruit trees are often grouped together because their cottage-garden size is ideal for the smallish scale on which most of us garden today. Except for the flowering crabapple, which produces perfectly fine crabapples, these are grown more for their ornamental value than for their fruits, which are best left for the birds (who will get to them first anyway). There are literally dozens of varieties of ornamental fruit trees: some dwarf and larger (usually no more than thirty feet high), some weeping, some with noteworthy bark; they bloom in various shades of pink and white. They're all easy to grow and care for and require little pruning (only to shape or to get rid of branches that are growing too close together; the trees need air flow among the branches), which should be done in midwinter, when the tree is dormant. All like summer mulches to help them conserve water. Weekly trips to the nurseries in the spring, when the trees are in bloom, will help you decide which ones you want. The catalogs are also a good source.

ORNAMENTAL GRASSES*

As a group, the ornamental grasses (bamboo is often considered in this category, but has a separate listing here) can be used in any number of ways: for hedging, for screening, as dramatic accents, for contrasting textures and as a big gesture in the backs of some borders; some can be used almost as shrubs. There are big high grasses and low delicate ones, like groundcovers. Usually, they provide winter interest, too, if you leave the plumes they produce late in the season in place over the winter. There are grayish, yellow and green variegated, red, green, and bluish varieties; when full grown (it takes about three years for most of them), all add a texture to the garden that's both wild and refined. In general, they like sun or lightly dappled shade, and good soil, which can even be a little on the dry side, since they're drought tolerant. They also like to be cut back severely in spring. In recent years, catalogs have begun giving more and more space to the grasses. Reading those entries is a good starting place.

PAEONIA*, *py-OHN-ee-ah*, Peony; Perennial; use in the border; Sun or light shade. The triumphant peony is as regal a perennial as you'll find, its late spring blossoms big enough to hold in both hands and its restrained, stay-in-place foliage reliable all season. Check carefully—there are many cultivars, in pinks, reds, whites, creams—to make sure the peonies you've chosen are fragrant, since that's half the beauty. Fertilize once in early spring when you fertilize everything else, then again after the (short) blooming season is finished, for better blooms next year; foliage should be cut to the ground in the fall. And try not to move them unless you absolutely have to, as they hate to be moved.

Pansy, see *Viola.*
Parsley, see *Petroselinum.*

*　*　*

PAPAVER*, *pah-PAH-ver*, Poppy; Includes annuals, biennials and perennials; use depends on species; Sun. The ruffly garden poppies won't put you to sleep the way they did Dorothy in that field in Oz: they're too lovely—and also, much more vigorous than their delicate beauty would lead you to believe. The perennials, like the many Oriental poppies, can bloom (early summer) in any height from one foot to four, and in red, pink, salmon, orange or white. Because they're plants you'll want to view singly, they belong closer to the front of the border than their height suggests. Each blossom, like every snowflake, is worthy of study. The foliage is insignificant, disappearing after the short but breathtaking blooming season. They're deep-rooted, and don't much like to be moved, but when they spread, which is what you'll hope for, they often need to be thinned out, so a tough-love approach will often have to work, where you dig out those that seem to be crowding the others. The annuals, like corn poppies or Shirley poppies, are surprisingly easy to grow. Just sprinkle the seeds around the front of the border, cover over lightly with your fingers and wait: They'll come up when they're ready. They like to germinate in the cold, so plant the first batch as soon as you can work the soil, in late winter or early spring. If you keep planting them every week for a while, they'll keep coming up every week till it gets too hot for them. To avoid the need to thin them out when they start coming up, mix seeds with a little sand, so they'll grow a little farther apart.

Pelargonium, see *Geranium.*
Peony, see *Paeonia.*

PEROVSKIA*, *per-OHV-skee-ah*, Russian sage; Perennial; use in the back of the midborder, in the herb garden or as a low hedge; Sun. A plant that fairly shouts Good Taste, it grows in a V shape, about three feet high, with silver leaves and spires of long-lasting purple blooms in mid- to late summer. Plant about three feet apart. It costs about as much as a bottle of good Russian vodka but will serve you far longer.

PETUNIA, *peh-TOON-ee-ah*; Annual; use in window boxes or container plantings; Sun to very light shade. Blooming in white, pinks, purples or blues, the trumpet-shaped petunias signal summer loud and clear. They're a high-maintenance annual, since the slightly sticky blooms need to be plucked when ever they collapse, and particularly after heavy rains, to keep them looking their best. They're especially pretty when they trail—but be sure to get a trailing variety if that's what you are after; some just grow upright and floppy. And mulch them. They like it damp and cool.

PETROSELINUM*, *pet-roh-sell-EEN-um*, Parsley; Annual herb; use in the herb garden; Sun. All you need to know is that it's called parsley and that (so far at least, and thankfully) it only comes in two kinds—curly and flat-leaved Italian. Both are pretty, clean and green, and both, of course, are valuable in the kitchen, snipped on just about anything except possibly breakfast cereal. It grows to the height you find it in the store. It needs full sun, and the little "plugs" of it shouldn't be planted more than a few inches apart, so that it will grow lush, like a big bouquet. Technically a biennial, it may reseed itself in fairly warm climates; it's also easily grown from seed.

PHILADELPHUS × 'Beauclerk'*, *fil-ah-DEL-phus*, Mock orange; Deciduous shrub; use in groupings of mixed shrubs, to anchor a border or as a specimen. This genus of deciduous shrubs is always lovely and mostly fragrant in bloom; the trick is finding those varieties that are also graceful when the shrub is not in bloom. 'Beauclerk' has an arching form and is sublimely fragrant, but there are other selections that will also fit the bill. The mock oranges bloom profusely in white, sometimes with a flush in the center of the blooms, and mostly in early summer. Ordinary good soil, not overly moist, and as much sun as possible (for maximum flowering) are all they need to start. After quite a few years, you may notice that the plant is blooming less than usual. This means that the wood has started to get old, and the shrub should be cut way back, down to a couple of feet off the ground, after the shrubs' bloom. You might miss a blooming season the following year, but after that the plants come back good as new. Insist on a fragrant one, and cut plenty of blossoms to bring indoors.

PHLOX PANICULATA; P. SUBULATA*, *Flocks pan-ick-you-LAH-tah; sub-ew-LAH-tah*, Perennial; use depends on species; Amount of sun depends on species. *P. subulata,* low growing and early blooming in whites and pinks, belongs in the front of the border or in the rock garden, in full sun. The spreading, deep-green foliage is ever-green, and when the plant's in bloom, the blooms blanket the foliage—really pretty. Much as I like it, I've never been able to get it to come back a second year; it's worth a try, however, and it might be perfectly happy in your garden. The classic *P. paniculata,* on the other hand, is totally sturdy, *can* take a little shade, and grows in thicker every season. (Divide by digging up and, using a shovel, cutting the clumps apart hard, in spring or fall, about every four years.) The long-lasting blooms arrive in early late summer—a yard high and wonderful for cutting—in white, pink, red, or violet, though if you mix the colors in the garden and fail to cut them back when they produce their seed, nature may later give you a weird mongrel version in a color you hadn't planned on. Plant these in the back of the midborder.

PHOTINIA BENTHAMIANA*, *foh-TIN-ee-ah ben-thom-ee-AH-na,* Evergreen shrub; use to make a hedge, planted among other shrubs or as a specimen; Sun. This genus comprises generous-size ever-green shrubs (or sometimes trees) once believed to be too tender for our climates, but increasingly available, owing to stronger new cul-tivars and our warmer winters. The leaves are sort of coppery, nicely so, and the plant moves well in the slightest breeze, seeming to move somehow even when it isn't breezy, if you can imagine that. Plant them in a sheltered spot—not in the middle of a field, in other words. Prune only to shape. *P. benthamiana* grows to about fifteen feet.

PLATYCODON, *plah-tee-KOH-dun,* Balloonflower; Perennial; use in the front of the midborder; Sun or very light shade. Blooming in pink, blue or white, the balloonflower is most compelling for the *way* it blooms: the buds actually do puff up like balloons before they open; each two-foot stem produces many such balloons, which open sequentially. Plant them about a foot apart for a showy effect, as they are rather restrained in their demeanor. One warning: they're extremely reliable, but they're slow to come up every spring. Don't forget where they're planted and accidentally plant something else to take their place.

Plumbago, see *Ceratostigma.*
Plume poppy, see *Macleaya.*

Poppy, see *Papaver.*

POTENTILLA, *poh-ten-TILL-ah,* Cinquefoil; Perennial; use as a low hedge, in a rock garden, at the front of the border or to edge a row of shrubs; Sun. A distant member of the rose family, *Potentilla*—there are three hundred varieties—takes its name from the same Latin root as *potent,* for its reputed medicinal uses. The common name refers to the flowers' five petals. These are low-growing (some are dwarf; the rest rarely reach two feet high) and bloom in early summer in white, yellow, pink or red. Some species are shrubby in their form, others are more like standard flowers. They should be pruned only of dead wood early in the spring. These haven't been the easiest perennials for me to grow, but having seen how pretty a low hedge of them can look, I know I'll keep trying.

Primrose, see *Primula.*

PRIMULA*, *PRIM-you-lah,* Primrose; Perennial; use in the front of the border, as edging or to bring early spring color to a woodland setting. Laid plant to plant in dappled shade, these are lovely, low, early spring flowers—*primus* means "first" in Latin. There are zillions of colors available, and they look fine mixed. Often the leaves disappear sometime over the summer, but if they're kept cool, they'll stick around a long time.

PSEUDOSASA JAPONICA*, *soo-doh-SAH-sa ja-PON-ik-ah,* Bamboo; Perennial grass; use as a hedge or screen; Light shade. This, the most common of the bamboos, grows high (to fifteen feet or more), fast, and cool and can save a garden or destroy it. Once it takes hold, it spreads with kamikaze force and is best kept in line by acquiring panda bears to eat it; otherwise, metal barriers must also be "planted" a foot or more deep to prevent its spreading where you don't want it to. They like to be planted in sheltered spots where it's not too sunny or dry, and they prefer to be planted in the spring, not the fall. Once they really kick in, which can take several years, they must be thinned, which means whacking stems overly grown together, to let in air and keep them from strangling each other. (It's best to have a professional show you how the first time.) Bamboo is a slightly confusing subject, because in addition to pseudosasa, there are a number of other genera that are considered to be bamboo, and naturally, there are other species within these genera: It's a big subject. Unless you want this all-purpose screening bamboo, it might be worth exploring what else is available in your area. Increasingly, you can find less invasive varieties, lower-growing varieties, and varieties with unusually variegated leaves.

Prunus, see Ornamental fruit tress.
Purple loosestrife, see *Lythrum.*

PYRACANTHA, *pie-roh-CAN-thah*, Firethorn; Evergreen tree; used as a standard tree or espaliered against a wall or fence; Sun or light shade. This evergreen is one of the easiest plants to espalier, which means to train a plant to grow flat against a wall or trellis. Everyone always says the white spring blossoms are "insignificant," but I have two espaliered firethorns against a fence way in the back, and I happen to like the blossoms, even if you have to get up close to study them. It's true, though, that the autumn berries make a better show. I also see it growing as a standard tree all over New York, where it thrives, and if it can grow there, it can probably grow anywhere. Keep it trimmed to a nice shape, however, and do the pruning after the blooming season; too often, reaching for the sun, they get scraggly. Run-of-the-mill care is about all they need.

Pyrus, see Ornamental fruit trees.

RHODODENDRON*, *roe-doe-DEN-drun*, Includes evergreen and deciduous flowering shrubs; use it mixed among other shrubs or as a specimen; Light shade. The evergreen rhododendrons inspire garden-variety garden writers the same way roses inspire poets. Writes one, in his chapter on shrubs: "Congratulations! You have discovered rhododendrons!"[1] If you're suffering from rhododendron fever, first see if it's contagious: Are there rhododendrons planted nearby? Doing well? If not, find out why, by discussing local pH conditions with a knowledgeable plant person. If so, to plant them, you have to consider how they'll fare in both summer and winter. Relentless sun at any time of the year, along with strong winter winds, can kill them, so choose a location sheltered

1. Jerry Baker, *The Impatient Gardener* (New York: Ballantine Books, 1983), 117.

by a north or east wall, or by a few trees, which would leave the rhododendrons in bright shade. When you're planting, dig in some peat, compost, or rotted grass clippings. Their roots are shallow, so don't plant deeply; plant at the same level they're planted in their pots. Water well after planting, then sparingly (only when the leaves droop and don't recover overnight); they prefer rain water, thank you very much. Mulch them with a two- or three-inch layer of coarse mulch (cedar is fine). Don't fertilize them when you plant them, but do so every spring thereafter with an acid fertilizer. Removing spent flower heads will help, too. And prune only as necessary to shape, after the blooming season. Azaleas (ah-ZALE-ee-ah) are members of this genus, too, and are deciduous; they should be planted and cared for in the same way.

Rocket larkspur, see *Consolida.*
Rose, see *Rosa.*

ROSMARINUS*, *roz-mahr-EYE-nus*, Rosemary; Tender perennial herb; use in the herb garden or in ornamental pots; Sun. Rosemary grows like a shrub, or can be pruned to a single stalk and grown as a tiny tree. The leaves, pungent and aromatic, are like little needles, and grow dense in full sun, producing small, pale lavender or blue blossoms in summer. And if you've ever used fresh rosemary to cook with, you'd never bother using dried rosemary again. There's a groundcovering variation that spreads flat instead of growing upright, but to me that's missing the point. Rosemary is proud and classic, it should be allowed to reach for the sun. If you have enough sun indoors to keep it alive over the winter, plant it in the ground directly in its pot in the summer, then dig the pot up and bring inside over the winter. Otherwise, in northern zones, you'll have to treat it as an annual. A light pruning after it finishes blooming will encourage bushier foliage growth. Rosemary is extremely difficult to grow from seed, so don't try.

ROSA*, *ROHZ-ah*, Rose; Deciduous flowering shrub; use depends on species; Sun. In their infinite variety and beauty, the roses already have an entire chapter in this book devoted just to them. For the Hybrid Teas, there are no shortcuts; you'll have to read the whole chapter. The low-growing 'The Fairy' roses are in a different category. They're shrub roses, easier to care for than the

Hybrid Teas. They belong in a sunny place in the front of the border and will bloom pretty much on their own from June till the frost. The fragrant 'Sea Foam' roses are similarly long blooming and easy to care for; they will also climb an arch or a trellis if you give them one to climb on.

Russian sage, see *Perovskia.*
Rosemary, see *Rosmarinus.*

RUDBEKIA*, *rude-BEK-ee-ah*, Coneflower or black-eyed Susan; Includes annuals, biennials and perennials; use depends on species; Sun. Daisy-shaped blooms, usually centered in fuzzy black or mahogany, in some shade of yellow or another make up this genus; most bloom late in the summer and into the fall. All the *Rudbekia* are native to North America, and they're sometimes called coneflower, although the petals remind me more of a badminton shuttlecock, the way the petals slope down from the center into a cone shape. Several species (and many more cultivars) also fall under the common name black-eyed Susan—these are the two- or three-foot high varieties one sees in the border and wildflower displays. *R. maxima* (MAX-ih-ma) is a sturdy choice for the back of the border. It grows up to six feet, with bright yellow blooms usually lasting into the early autumn. All prefer full sun, are great for cutting, and many reseed themselves nicely into colonies.

Rue, see *Ruta.*

RUMEX, *ROO-mex*, Sorrel; Perennial herb; use in the herb garden; Sun. The floppy, coarse-leaved sorrel isn't very pretty and so is grown primarily for culinary use—sorrel soup or to accompany shad and shad roe (sorrel comes up early in the spring, when the shad are running). It grows and spreads about a foot high and wide, so plant a foot apart, and because it's a heavy looking herb, put it next to something lighter, for balance.

RUTA GRAVEOLENS*, *ROO-tah grah-VEE-oh-lens*, Rue; Perennial; use in the herb garden, in the border or as a low hedge; Sun or very light shade. This immensely satisfying shrublike perennial, known simply as rue, seems always to grow in perfect form, about two feet high, with etched silvery leaves and midsummer flowers that are nice enough; still, with rue the foliage is always the show. They look terrific planted near *Santolina*. They require no special care, except at least half a day of full sun. There's almost never a need to prune them during the season and cutting them back in the fall is optional.

Sage, see *Salvia*.

SALVIA*, *SAL-vee-ah*, Includes annuals, biennials and perennial; use depends on species; Sun. This genus is a truly confusing jumble of annuals, biennials and perennials (including the herb sage) in all colors, shapes and sizes and requires great alertness on the part of the gardener, or you'll end up with the feathery red annual salvia, to my mind the ugliest plant in cultivation (but maybe that's because it's overcultivated to the point of overkill). What the species have in common is that they all take their name from the root word for *salve*, for their reputed healing properties, and that they need sun or very light shade. As for the herbs, the shrubby sage grows a foot or two tall and is available in its natural grayish green, mottled purple, green and white variegated and tricolor (yellow, green and red); there is also a pineapple sage, scarcely reminiscent of pineapple as far as I can tell. Choosing the herbs is a matter of taste, but if anyone put any of them except the traditional grayish green one on my plate, I'd flee the table. *S. farinacea* (fair-ih-NOTCH-ee-ah), or mealycup sage, is an annual that will start to get you excited about this genus: three-foot high purple spires that keep appearing throughout the summer and into the fall, great for cutting and a distinguished plant for the back of the midborder. The perennials available vary widely from catalog to catalog and from nursery to nursery even in the same area, so it's well worth a round of comparison shopping before you settle on something permanent for the garden. There are many perennial selections, most flowering in pinks and blues, for the front of border.

SANTOLINA*, *san-tah-LEEN-ah*, Perennial; use in the border, in the herb garden, or as a low hedge; Sun. You can tell by looking whether you're getting the pure green foliage (*S. virens*, VIH-rens) or the silvery (*S. chamaecyparissus*, kah-mee-cue-pah-RIS-us); nurseries usually carry only one or two varieties of this small genus of low, shrubby plants. Technically considered herbs, they're aromatic and thus can be used anywhere you'd use, say, lavender. The foliage is dense, thick and lacy. They produce funny yellow flowers, like fists, in midsummer; some people don't like these and, to avoid them, prune the plants hard in the spring. (Don't do this, though, till you've seen them. Some people like the flowers just fine.)

SAPONARIA OCYMOIDES 'Splendens'*, *sap-oh-NAHR-ee-ah ah-kah-MOI-des*, Soapwort; Perennial; use in the front of the border, in the rock garden or anywhere you need a low plant that trails; Sun or very light shade. With masses of tiny pink flowers late in the spring, saponaria blooms just after the forget-me-nots. You won't forget these either.

SEDUM SPECTABILE 'Autumn Joy'*, *SAY-dum speck-tah-BIL-ee*, Perennial; use in the front of the border or in a rock garden; Sun. Although SAY-dum is technically correct, you can also get away with SEE-dum, which is all I've ever heard them called. 'Autumn Joy' is a presence all season, with thick stems and leaves that look like succulents rising from late spring on. It blooms late in the summer and into early fall, in a musky pink that deepens to brown; these blooms can be left in place to dry over the winter (winter interest!). They're easy as can be, as long as their situation isn't soggy and they get full sun. The other sedums available in your area are also worth exploring for use in herb or rock gardens or as groundcovers in full sun. In general, they have a succulent texture, they feel like delicate desert plants and look best when they're massed. Most have pretty blooms as well.

Silverberry or silver berry, see *Elaeagnus.*
Snapdragon, see *Antirrhinum.*
Snow-in-summer, see *Cerastium.*
Soapwort, see *Saponaria.*
Sorrel, see *Rumex.*
Spider flower, see *Cleome.*
Spiderwort, see *Tradescantia.*

SPIRAEA TRILOBATA 'Swan Lake', *spee-REE-ah tri-low-BAH-tah*, Bridal wreath; Deciduous flowering shrub; use in the back of the border, planted among other shrubs, or as a specimen; Sun. This genus name has nothing to do with spires but comes from the Greek for a word describing plants used in garlands—hence the common name.

S. t. 'Swan Lake' grows low, to just four feet, and blooms in white in May and June. (It can hold a back-of-the-border position because it blooms so early, before other things have grown up too high. The foliage marks the space over the rest of the season.) All the *Spiraea* varieties are lovely, with most offering lush arching clusters of blooms in white, pink, cream, or occasionally, yellow. But it's a big genus, with shrubs of various heights (even dwarf ones), and those that bloom anytime from early spring till late in the season, so you'll need to explore a little to see what you want and what's available nearby. In general, the early blooming varieties should be pruned of faded flowers just after they bloom, while those blooming later in the summer should be given an overall trim early in the spring.

STACHYS LANATA* or BYZANTINA, *STAH-kis lah-NAh-tah or biz-AHN-tih-nah,* Lamb's ears; Perennial; use in the front of the border; Sun. As soft and fuzzy as their common name suggests, these are silver-leaved perennials that will trail or flop willingly, dying at the center and spreading from year to year to the sides in the most natural way. Give them plenty of room at the outset, and just be a little patient; soon you'll have a colony. The eighteen-inch-high flowers are strange, though, and since many people cut them off because they don't like them, growers have obliged with *S. l.* 'Silver Carpet', a variety that doesn't produce blooms at all.

Statice, see *Limonium.*
Summer lilac, see *Buddleia.*
Sunflower, see *Helianthus.*
Swan River daisy, see *Brachycome.*
Sweet alyssum, see *Lobularia.*
Sweet pea, see *Lathyrus.*

SYRINGA, *sir-ING-ah,* Lilac; Deciduous flowering shrub or low tree; use among other shrubs, in a lilac grove or to anchor a border or bed; Sun. If you're a Walt Whitman fan, you might also plant one in the door yard to measure the passing of the years. There are more and more cultivars of lilacs available, most highly fragrant and blooming in spring in various shades of lavender, white and occasionally, yellow or pink; the tallest of the species can reach fifteen feet. Lilacs are truly easy to grow, but just a little finicky about pH, so if you don't see any in your neighborhood, have the people at the nursery tell you how to prepare the soil. Lilacs should be planted at least six feet apart, with some manure chopped into the planting hole, and then a summer mulch should be applied throughout at least their first few summers. Remove the flowers once they're spent to divert the plant's energy toward next year's blossoms.

TAGETES*, *tah-GAY-teez*, Marigold; Annual; use in the cutting garden; Sun. Place fledgling plants about four inches apart in the sun, and cut them all summer; they perch upright on their thick stalks and smell muskily fragrant. There are more than two dozen varieties—make sure you get the height, color and size of bloom you want. The blooms last a long time indoors if you change the water every (or every other) day.

TANACETUM*, *tah-nah-SET-im*, Tansy; Perennial; use in the herb garden, in a meadow or in a wildflower setting; Sun. These are usually just called tansy, because this is a relatively small genus and there aren't very many types to choose from in the nursery. In fact, the only one I've ever grown (or seen, so far as I know) is the common tansy, *T. vulgare* (vul-GAHR-ee), which grows a yard high and wide in a pleasantly rumpled way, producing charming little yellow flowers in midsummer. (A cautionary note: foliage is toxic if eaten.) It spreads readily. The preeminent horticulturist Graham Stuart Thomas recommends *T. herderi*—with dense, filigreed silvery leaves—as a front-of-the-border plant; if I could find one, I'd try it in a second.

Tansy, see *Tanacetum.*
Tarragon, see *Artemisia.*

TAXUS BACCATA, *TAX-us bah-KAH-tah*, Common yew; Evergreen shrub; use in groupings of mixed shrubs or as a hedge; Sun or very light shade. This berry-producing evergreen shrub comes in spreading and columnar forms as well as the common shrub you see in foundation plantings and to mark entryways—as familiar as it is lovely. William Robinson bemoans the fact that yews are too often clipped and shaped to within an inch of their lives; they're best kept shaggily clipped, but not overly shaped—too confining. Once they're planted, watch the plants around them to make sure they're not starving. Yews are heavy feeders, absorbing more than their share of water and nutrients. (They can also steal nutrients from nearby plants, so just make sure none of its neighbors are unusually droopy.) And if you've got them growing at full blast, be sure to shake off any snow that weighs heavily on them in the winter, or the branches will lose their form.

THALICTRUM ROCHEBRUNIANUM*, *thah-LIK-trum rosh-brin-ee-AH-num*, Meadow rue or lavender mist; Perennial; use in the back of the border; Sun or light shade. This graceful perennial will "hold" the back of the border in spring, when few other plants will reach their peak height. They'll grow to six feet, maximum, with a neat spread and the most delicate foliage, enough in itself. The spring blooms, however, are a haze of lavender rising above the top of the plant—and do look misty and fine. Occasionally this will need staking, but don't bother unless there's a need to (if it's tilted beyond the point where you can push it back in place). Other species of thalictrum can sometimes be found, but they're usually lower growing, sometimes with white or yellow blossoms and belong farther forward in the border, depending on height. If you're lucky, thalictrum may reseed itself. Otherwise, it rarely needs dividing or any special care, other than trimming back spent flowers. If the leaves turn yellow in the midsummer heat, cut back the yellow ones, and new growth will come in to replace them.

THUJA, *THOO-ya*, Arborvitae; Evergreen shrubs or trees; use to mark an entryway, as hedging, or in a grouping of shrubs; Sun. Arborvitaes are excellent conifers, column-shaped and distinguished. They grow well and—depending on species—in varying heights of lighter or darker green. Just be careful of planting them too closely together, or they'll look like too many people cramped into an elevator; find out their ultimate spread *before* you plant them. Trim only as necessary to shape. *Thuja occidentalis* 'Emerald' is a variety I found in a catalog, which ultimately grows to about six feet; those used for screening, readily available at nurseries, grow much higher.

Thyme, see *Thymus*.

THYMUS*, *TIE-mus*, Thyme; Perennial herb; use in the herb garden; Sun. These shrubby herbs are fragrant, handsome to look at and sweet in bloom; but they're grown mostly for their usefulness in the kitchen. Choose the ones you want by sight—green, or green variegated in white or yellow. Planted in full sun or grown from seed, they'll grow shrubby, and about a foot high, blooming in mid-summer (cut the blooms off when they fade). The one that spreads flat and has a matte look with gray-green leaves is, in my experience, harder to grow. The rest are easy.

Tickseed, see *Coreopsis.*

TITHONIA ROTUNDIFOLIA*, *tih-THOE-nee-ah,* Mexican sunflower; Annual; use in the cutting garden; Sun. Blooming in a musky orange or velvety yellow with daisylike flowers, tithonia grows up to six feet tall, producing several branching stems and blooms per plant. (Despite the height of the plant, the blooms remain daisy-size.) Tithonia likes hot, hot locations, is drought resistant and doesn't need staking.

TRADESCANTIA*, *tray-dis-KANT-ee-ah,* Spiderwort; Perennial; use in the front of the midborder; Sun or light shade. With blooms in white, pink, purple or red, these usually grow about two feet tall and belong where the soil is damp and cool; often they'll spread willingly. Supposedly there are varieties that bloom for an unusually long time, even into the fall, but I've never seen them. Most topple over after they bloom, leaving their thick stems behind, and making it hard to fill their space for the rest of the season. Plant them (about a foot apart) in the spring, which they prefer to the autumn; should you have to transplant them, the spring is the best time for that, too.

TRILLIUM, *TRILL-ee-um;* Perennial; use near water or in woodland settings; Light shade. Preferring cool woodland conditions, the trillium, spring blooming, less that a foot high with three leaves and three pink or white petals, take their name from the Latin "tri," for three. As appealing as the prospect is, don't cut them for indoors, or they very likely won't come back next year and colonize.

TROPAEOLUM*, *troh-PIE-ah-lum,* Nasturtium; Annual herb; use in the herb garden or trailing over the sides of pots; Sun. There is actually a genus called *Nasturtium,* of which watercress is a member, but the nasturtiums that are easy as can be to grow by seed aren't to be found in their namesake genus. Luckily, nasturtium seeds mean you'll get nasturtium, so that's all you really need to know. Both leaves and blossoms are pretty (and edible) and have a nice trailing habit, which I think is better suited to growing in a container; in the garden, the trailing can look unkempt. But that's a matter of taste. Soak the seeds for a couple of hours, stick them in soil about an inch deep with your finger, and voilà! A packet of seeds will yield you a summer's worth of salads and pretty blossoms for tiny arrangements indoors.

TSUGA, *SOO-gah*, Hemlock; Evergreen shrubs and trees; use as a hedge, as a specimen, or planted in groves; Sun or light shade. Rarely seen in Europe, hemlocks of one species or another can be found nearly everywhere in North America, as far north as Alaska. (The hemlock with which Socrates supposedly committed suicide was a weed that grows at the edge of water.) Hemlocks, which are conifers, are best sought out at local nurseries, as the sizes and shapes available vary profoundly from region to region. In general, the elegant weeping hemlocks usually are the varieties known as 'Sargent's' or the species *canadensis*. These are soft-needled and grow to an almost perfect form. A year-round mulch is recommended, at least until the hemlocks are well established.

Tulip, see *Tulipa*.

TULIPA, *TOO-lip-ah*, Tulip; Perennial bulb; in the border, depending on ultimate height; Sun or light shade. Available in short, medium and tall; early and late blooming; striped, striated and parrot-shaped; and in almost any color you can think of, tulips have had all the hype they need ever since the tulipomania craze in Holland in the seventeenth century, when price wars drove the cost of rare bulbs sky high, even by today's terms. Plant the bulbs in the fall, six or eight inches deep, into a hole that has been sprinkled with bonemeal. Space them the way you want them to grow—in bouquets, not lined up like soldiers—allowing an inch or two of soil between the bulbs. To try to get them to bloom again the second or third year, fertilize them as they're about to go into bloom for the first time, then cut off the stems after the flowers are spent, leaving the leaves to wither the way you would with daffodils, though they're not nearly as easy to naturalize as daffodils are.

*   *   *

VACCINIUM, *vah-KEE-nee-um*, Blueberry; Flower- and fruit-bearing deciduous shrub; use in the back of an herb garden or as a hedge; Sun. Not considered often enough for ornamental gardens, the blueberry can be a handsome (and edible) accent at the edge of an herb garden, at least in appropriate zones—many can't take climates too far north. There are many varieties, with different heights (up to ten feet high, and many growing lower) and habits as well as different colors of blossoms (pink to yellow to white), so see what's available nearby before you plan where to put them. In general, the foliage is dense, which makes it good for screening, the flowers are sweet, the berries are terrific and the foliage of many varieties turns crimson in the fall, as the rest of the herbs are winding down. To ensure berry production, you have to plant several shrubs, so check with a nursery before you buy the plants. Also, they like a highly acid soil, so fertilize in the spring with an acid fertilizer.

Valerian, see *Centranthus.*

VERBENA, *ver-BEAN-ah*, Includes annuals and perennials; use depends on species; Sun or very light shade. Of various heights and colors (many pinks and blues), this genus has over two hundred varieties; where I live, most verbenas are grown as annuals. Among these, some are subtle and some showy, and while they can be planted among formal plants, they also look right in casual settings—like the low-growing *V.* × *hybrida* 'Pink Bouquet', which looks great planted and trailing among herbs or in containers. *V. rigida*, which grows up to two feet, can be used in the front of the border, planted among perennials. The taller *V. bonariensis* (bone-ahr-ee-EN-sis) can reach nearly five feet and has graceful tufts of light purple flowers atop the skinniest stems; it's an excellent filler for toward the back of the border, particularly when planted en masse. Don't try growing verbena from seed, for even very good gardeners have a deplorable success rate.

VERONICA, *vah-RON-ih-KAH*, Speedwell; Perennials, although many are tender and grown as annuals; Sun or very light shade. Like the verbenas and salvias, among other genera, there are simply too many veronica varieties (about two hundred and fifty) to make easy generalizations about how to use them in the garden. Like daylilies, veronicas have a varied blooming season: some bloom early, some midseason and some late (usually in blue, but occasionally in pink or white). With careful planning, you might be able to keep veronica in bloom throughout most of the summer. In general, too, the foliage (deep green and silvery) is attractive when the plant isn't in bloom. With some, *V. prostrata* (proh-STRAH-tah) for one, the leaves grow flat like a carpet, with eight-inch flowers rising densely above in early summer: nice. At the other extreme, cultivars of *V. exaltata* (great name) bloom at the end of the summer, in four-foot spikes of blue that never need staking.

VIBURNUM CARLESII*, *Vye-BUR-num CARL-see-ee*, Korean spice viburnum; Deciduous flowering shrub; use to anchor a border, in groupings of mixed shrubs or as a specimen; Sun. The viburnums comprise an enormous genus of shrubs in various shapes and sizes, some with notable berries, unusually pretty foliage, or great fall color. Most bloom in shades of white or pink, and different varieties bloom anytime from late winter to early autumn. *V. carlesii* grows to about six feet maximum, has pink buds opening to white blossoms in late spring, and is especially noteworthy for its wonderful fragrance. Most viburnums require virtually no pruning. Because there are so many to choose from, it's a good idea first to explore all the options at your nurseries and in the catalogs, and try to see several in bloom before making your final choices. Some species are evergreen.

VIOLA*, *VEE-oh-lah*, Pansy, Johnny-jump-up; Includes annuals and perennials; use in the front of the border, to edge a path or in a woodland setting; Sun or light shade. With their extraordinary faces, pansies belong tucked right next to each other or clustered just about anywhere else in the garden that needs a spring-into-summer touch. Pinching off spent flowers encourages more blooms.

VISCARIA or LYCHNIS, *vis-CAR-ee-ah or LICK-nis,* Annual; use in the cutting garden or in the front of the border; Sun. Although this is an annual, it'll come in handy as "filler" when the forget-me-nots, for example, have given up and before whatever's coming in next takes hold. Just buy little plants at the nursery and stick them into the empty spaces. Pink blossomed, on thin, somewhat sticky stems, rising about ten inches high, these will last until the summer heat begins to make everyone else cranky, too. Deadheading will lengthen the season of bloom.

* * *

WISTERIA, *wis-TEHR-ee-ah*, Deciduous vine; use to climb over walls, pergolas, fences or trellises; Sun. This wonderfully fragrant vine blooms in lavender, pink or white, eventually offering spring flower clusters so thick they look as if you're viewing them through a Vaseline-covered lens. Plant at least six feet apart, enriching soil with, in addition to the usual organic matter, superphosphate at planting time (superphosphate should also be applied every autumn). These are labor-intensive plants, particularly the first few years. They need to be affixed to the structure against which they're to grow (use sturdy gardening twine or nails). They also need sophisticated pruning: in the winter, the branches should be cut back by half; in the summer, when you notice new shoots popping out everywhere, pinch them back so that each new shoot on the branch has only one or two leaves: You want the branches eventually to grow in the same direction, and pinching and pruning them this way from the start will guarantee they'll grow in the direction you want—and also that they'll flower well.

XERANTHEMUM, *zeh-RAN-the-mum*, Everlasting; Annual; use in the cutting garden; Sun. Everlasting grows about two feet high and sprouts papery blossoms in white, pink, and lavender—these are classics for drying. If you sow the seeds outdoors after the danger of frost is past, they'll bloom in the second half of summer. (In the northernmost climates, they have to be started first indoors, as those growing seasons are short, and everlastings take a while to get going.) Plant in full sun, and be diligent about watering them as they settle in. To dry them, stick them in a water-filled vase while they're at the height of their bloom, then let the water evaporate.

Yarrow, see *Achillea*.

ZINNIA*, *zin-ee-ah*, Annual; use in the cutting garden or to dress up a bed of herbs; Sun or very light shade. Zinnias bloom in just about every shade but blue, vary a little in shape of the blooms and come in dwarf varieties as well as the more familiar foot-high cultivars. Place fledgling plants about four inches apart. Great for cutting, but remove the foliage, which gets kind of rank, before placing flowers in water.

Acknowledgments

I'd like first to thank Ngaere Macray, in whose garden, fully and amazingly in bloom in October, the photograph for the back of this book jacket was taken. Over the years, she has taught me much about gardening (sometimes, not surprisingly, growing exasperated in the process), and about friendship. David Seeler, her husband, generously (and perhaps skeptically) offered me my apprenticeship at the Bayberry Nursery in Amagansett, New York, and often let me follow him around as he talked about trees and shrubs to his customers—a humbling education. Bob Scheider, Melody and Bob Strubel, Teresa, Ken, Gary, Chloe and the other members of the Bayberry staff were also welcoming, knowledgeable and a great help to me there.

Farther back, the first real gardeners I ever met were Pam Lord and Robert Dash, and their wisdom, patience and encouragement at the outset, and ever since, have been gifts to a beginner like me. I hasten to add that they never taught me to make mistakes and take shortcuts; the mistakes I've made and any dubious shortcuts I've taken in this book, and in the garden, are mine alone, not that I'm proud of them. For their knowledge about gardening, I'd also like to thank Robert and Martha Wilson and my neighbor, Marilyn Bethany, who has also supplied much in the way of horticultural sympathy. (Her husband, Edward Tivnan, is also a fine neighbor, but he doesn't seem to be of much use in the garden.) For reading parts of or all the manuscript, and for their careful comments or various other kinds of enthusiasm, I'm grateful to Maria Matthiessen, Jason Epstein, Judy Miller, Carolyn and Stephen Reidy, Karen Lerner and Victoria Hughes. For making it worthwhile to start a garden, or just about anything else, I'm grateful to my husband, Michael Shnayerson. The person who has done the most sitting in the garden (without ever once helping) is Susanna Porter.

My gratitude goes as well to Binky Urban, a friend long before our gardening days and the best agent anyone could hope for. Susan Moldow at HarperCollins hated gardening and thus envisioned this book long before it existed. She, along with her colleague Keonaona Peterson, did everything possible to encourage it, and me, editorially. My thanks, too, for editorial and production help from Nancy Peske, Wendy Silbert, Karen Malley and Candace Levy (who taught me a lot with her copyediting). For their invaluable help with the look of the book, I'd also like to thank Ken Robbins and Simon Dorrell. I am especially grateful to Joseph Montebello, HarperCollins's creative director, who took this book under his wing, and was wonderfully enthusiastic throughout.

Starter Sources

Reading about gardening is at least as much fun as actually doing it. There are countless picture books that *show* you gardening, always hypnotic to leaf through. Spending time with these is a fine way to become acquainted with the great public and private gardens of the world and to gather ideas. The most useful among these are those books with texts as worthy as the photographs. The ones I turn to again and again are Penelope Hobhouse's *The Country Gardener* (Boston: Little, Brown, 1989); Caroline Seebolm and Christopher Simon Sykes's *Private Landscapes: Creating Form, Vistas, and Mystery in the Garden* (New York: Clarkson N. Potter, 1989); and Rosemary Verey's *Classic Garden Design* (New York: Congdon & Weed, 1984). There are dozens more with pictures (and text) that will inspire you.

The leap from one's own backyard to these fully mature gardens can, however, be daunting, and the books that have been most helpful to me are actual reading books, which immerse you into other people's gardens and thoughts about gardens and which give you a feel for how gardeners approach their subject. Even if you don't know everything the writers are talking about at the start, the books make you think and enable you to see what even a small garden can mean in the larger context of life. The best writers are enthusiastic, skeptical, opinionated and contradictory, with a passion that's contagious.

Women first, for no particular reason. Katharine S. White's *Onward and Upward in the Garden* (New York: Farrar, Straus & Giroux, 1988) circles the pragmatics of designing, digging and planting but talks about the culture of gardening—catalogs and nurseries, flower arranging, roses and lilies, how to *think* about gardening—in a way that's both challenging and reassuring. First published in *The New Yorker* beginning in 1958, the essays remain as delightful and apt now as they were then; this is one of the classics and as good a place to start as any. Eleanor Perenyi's *Green Thoughts: A Writer in the Garden* (New York: Vintage Books, 1983) is another classic collection of essays (alphabetically organized chapters include "Asters," "Earthworms," "Failures," "Partly Cloudy" and "Tree Houses") that is whimsical, beautifully written and full of opinions so convincing you'll take them as fact. Celia Thaxter's *An Island Garden* (Boston: Houghton Mifflin, 1988), with stunning pictures and illuminations by Childe Hassam, describes the author's garden (on Appledore in the Isles of Shoals, off the coast of New Hampshire) so vividly that you'll remember it forever and want to incorporate something of hers into your own.

In the text here I've summed up the five "commonest bad mistakes" made by gardeners, found in Henry Mitchell's *One Man's Garden* (Boston: Houghton Mifflin, 1992). He writes from the trenches; as you read him (and read anything of his you can find), you feel as if you were having a chat with him as he putters in his admittedly plant-crowded plot. Allen Lacy is another read-anything-you-can-find writer who gets interested in one facet of gardening or another, and follows it wherever it goes, as if it were a rambling vine. One of his fairly recent collections of essays is *Farther Afield: A Gardener's Excursions* (New York: Farrar, Straus & Giroux, 1986). Michael Pollan's *Second Nature: A Gardener's Education* (New York: Atlantic Monthly Press, 1991) is just what the subtitle suggests, a meditation on man's relationship with nature, but grounded in the author's own garden in progress. Slightly more how-to in feeling, Lee Reich's *A Northeast Gardener's Year* (Reading, MA: Addison-Wesley, 1992) talks about what he's doing in the garden month by month, as he's really doing it; it's full of intelligently presented information.

One also needs practical guides to turn to quickly and if I had to choose one standard gardening encyclopedia (a hard choice!), I'd probably choose *Wyman's Gardening Encyclopedia* (New York: Macmillan, 1977), which covers everything from the plants themselves to the blights out to get them to the sequence in which they bloom. There is also the long-format paperback *Taylor's Guides*—drawn from Norman Taylor's *Taylor's Encyclopedia of Gardening* (Boston: Houghton Mifflin, 1961), which was revised by Gordon P. DeWolf, Jr.—they are encyclopedic in the information they carry, one subject—annuals, bulbs, perennials, garden design, roses and so on—to a volume.

Penelope Hobhouse's *Gardening Through the Ages: An Illustrated History of Plants and Their Influence on Garden Styles—from Ancient Egypt to the Present Day* (New York: Simon & Schuster, 1992) is one of the most lavishly illustrated and wonderfully readable among the excellent histories of gardening worldwide for thumbing through or reading cover to cover. Seeing the evolution of gardening presented so clearly is tantamount to dining at one of the world's finest restaurants before studying the art of cooking. A reverence for what can be done will surely enhance what it is you *are* doing.

When it comes to actually planting shrubs and perennials, Graham Stuart Thomas has written two comprehensive books that sort out the various species within the genera better than any others I have ever come across. His *Ornamental Shrubs, Climbers and Bamboos* (Portland, OR: Sagapress/Timber Press, 1992) and his *Perennial Garden Plants or The Modern Florilegium* (Portland, OR: Sagapress/Timber Press, 1990) are pretty much the final words on the plants they cover. And although the author is extremely learned, he's also accessible—plus he'll tell you honestly the advantages and disadvantages of the various species available.

There's nothing more exasperating than seeing a flower somewhere and being unable to find out what it's called. Stanley Schuler edited Guido Moggi and Luciano Guignolini's *Guide to Garden*

Flowers (New York: Simon & Schuster, 1983), which is an excellent antidote to this, with clear photographs and clear descriptions; you can just flip through the photographs till you find the one you want. (You can also skip over the parts where they tell you that leaves are, say, "tomentose, sessile, ovate-elliptical and reticulate," and just go for the more perfunctory descriptions.) I have also found myself turning many times to Nicola Ferguson's *Right Plant, Right Place: The Indispensable Guide to the Successful Garden* (New York: Summit Books, 1984), which isn't quite indispensable but is helpfully cross-referenced to within an inch of its life, and even has a category setting forth which plants are suitable for crevices in paving.

If you want to be absolutely correct about the pronunciation and derivation of plant names, Allen J. Coombes's *Dictionary of Plant Names* (Portland, OR: Sagapress/Timber Press, 1990) will give you the rundown.

It is, of course, possible that you don't live in Long Island, where I've grown the plants discussed in this book, in which case you may want to zero in on volumes that focus specifically on your area. Among those that will take you farther south and west: William L. Hunt's *Southern Gardening* (Durham, NC: Duke University Press, 1982), Scott Milland's *Gardening in Dry Climates* (San Ramon, CA: Ortho Books, 1989), Neil Sperry's *Complete Guide to Texas Gardening* (Houston, TX: Taylor Publishing, 1982), and Sunset Magazine's *Western Gardening* (Menlo Park, CA: Lane Publishing, 1988). Often, in addition, you can find books written and distributed locally through, for example, garden clubs. These will give you tips for gardening in your area (so will your local newspaper column); some will also tell you which gardens nearby are open to the public.

Other special-interest books that might be helpful include: Ken Druse's *The Natural Shade Garden* (New York: Clarkson N. Potter, Inc., 1992), Foster H. Lincoln's *Rock Gardening* (Portland, OR: Timber Press, 1982), A. Kowaldchik and W. H. Hylton's *Rodale's Illustrated Encyclopedia of Herbs* (Emmaus, PA: Rodale, 1987), *The Bulb Book: A Photographic Guide to Over 800 Hardy Bulbs* (London: Pan Books, 1981), Roger Phillips and Martyn Rix's *The Random House Guide to Roses* (New York: Random House, 1988), Jeff Cox's *Plant Marriages: What Plants Look Good Together. . .* (New York: HarperCollins, 1993); and *Sunset Garden Pools, Foun-*

tains & Waterfalls (Menlo Park, CA: Sunset, 1992), Scott Atkinson, editor.

Tag sales, remainder tables at bookstores, libraries and horti-cultural alliances (you probably have one closer than you think) are among the worthy places to unearth gardening books. Those listed here are to give you a start.

Index